Children and Youth
during the Civil War Era

CHILDREN AND YOUTH IN AMERICA
General Editor: James Marten

Children in Colonial America
Edited by James Marten

Children and Youth in a New Nation
Edited by James Marten

Children and Youth during the Civil War Era
Edited by James Marten

Children and Youth during the Civil War Era

EDITED BY

James Marten

NEW YORK UNIVERSITY PRESS
New York and London

NEW YORK UNIVERSITY PRESS
New York and London
www.nyupress.org

References to Internet websites (URLs) were accurate at the time of writing.
Neither the author nor New York University Press is responsible for URLs
that may have expired or changed since the manuscript was prepared.

Library of Congress Cataloging-in-Publication Data

Children and youth during the Civil War era / [edited by] James Marten.
p. cm.
ISBN 978-0-8147-9607-8 (hardback)
ISBN 978-0-8147-9608-5 (pb)
ISBN 978-0-8147-6339-1 (ebook)
1. United States—History—Civil War, 1861–1865—Children.
2. Children and war—United States—History—19th century.
3. Children and war—Confederate States of America.
I. Marten, James Alan.
E540.C47C45   2012
973.7083—dc23   2011028196

New York University Press books are printed on acid-free paper,
and their binding materials are chosen for strength and durability.
We strive to use environmentally responsible suppliers and materials
to the greatest extent possible in publishing our books.

Manufactured in the United States of America

c   10 9 8 7 6 5 4 3 2 1
p   10 9 8 7 6 5 4 3 2 1

Contents

Acknowledgments

My greatest thanks go to Steve Mintz for his kind foreword and to the authors for their timely responses to what must have seemed an endless string of demands, suggestions, and queries. The anonymous readers provided helpful comments that strengthened the individual essays as well as the editor's introductions. The Children and Youth in America series has found a friendly home at NYU Press, thanks to Eric Zinner and the rest of the staff, especially Ciara McLaughlin and Despina Papazoglou Gimbel, and Susan Ecklund, who copyedited the manuscript.

The authors and I also thank the following repositories for granting permission to publish texts and images from their collections: the American Antiquarian Society for "The Early Development of Southern Chivalry"; the Atlanta History Center for excerpts from the Carrie Berry Diary; the Dartmouth College Library for "A Few Words to the Trustees"; the Library Company of Philadelphia for "Maltreatment of Inmates of the Schools for Soldiers' Orphans"; the Library of Congress Prints and Photographs Division for "The Four Seasons of Life: Youth"; the Missouri History Museum for the ambrotype of "H. E. Hayward and Slave Nurse Louisa"; the New Jersey Historical Society for excerpts and images from the Newark High School *Atheneum*; and the State Archives of Florida for the photograph of "Magby Peterson and His Nanny."

Foreword

——— STEVEN MINTZ ———

Unlike other books on the Civil War era that focus on key events, epic political controversies, and great men—presidents, members of Congress, and generals—this volume places another cast of characters center stage: children and youth. At the time of the Civil War, fully half of the nation's population was under sixteen, and the young, like their elders, found themselves caught up in the major developments of the era: the growth of sectionalism, the moral debates over slavery, and the transformation of the sectional struggle into the first modern total war. More than mere bystanders or victims, a surprising number of young people participated directly in the era's upheavals and carried the impact of the Civil War into the succeeding decades. Viewing this era through children's ordinary eyes yields extraordinary insights.

Children and youth were anything but bit players in the period's dramas. Like their parents, young people fashioned their own opinions about slavery and the sectional conflict in the decades preceding the Civil War. Many became highly politicized before or during the war, arguing the issues of the day in debating societies, joining juvenile affiliates of antislavery organizations, and publishing their own newspapers. In an essay on New England college students, Kanisorn Wongsrichanalai shows the extent to which these young men developed an intense anti-Southern ideology, expressing profound contempt for white Southerners and Southern society.

Meanwhile, images of childhood colored the political debates preceding the Civil War. The abolitionists' single most devastating critique of slavery lay in its impact on children: how the institution separated families and undermined parents' ability to protect their children and stripped the young of a childhood—making the early years a time of harsh labor and cruel punishment rather than a time of play and wonder. Indeed, as Rebecca de Schweinitz demonstrates, the slavery controversy led many Northern adults to think about childhood in a new way, as a stage of life that should, ideally, be free of work responsibilities and devoted to schooling and play. In the

South, in contrast, as Elizabeth Kuebler-Wolf shows, apologists for slavery presented highly idealized portraits of the lives of children in bondage and of the supposedly close relations between black and white children in their defenses of the slave system.

During the Civil War, some young people found themselves on the front lines. A surprising number of young people participated in the war, as drummer boys and boy soldiers. Perhaps 5 percent of the soldiers were under the age of eighteen. Yet far from the battlefield, the war also made itself felt. It proved impossible to insulate children and youth from the war's impact. Boys played soldiers, and girls, nurses. The young also participated in relief work and in fund-raising "sanitary fairs." Schoolbooks, children's literature, parades, panoramas, and fairs made the war a part of everyday life. As Paul Ringel reveals, the popular children's magazine *Youth's Companion*, which had scrupulously avoided sectional tensions before the war, began to feature incidents from the war and included stories emphasizing the themes of patriotism, duty, and sacrifice.

Children were the Civil War's most vulnerable victims. Noncombatants saw horrific acts of violence. War disrupted food supplies, resulting in hunger and disease, and displaced and separated families. Many young people became refugees, including the thousands of slave children who made up the majority of the "contrabands" who fled plantations to find refuge behind Union lines. Many experienced anxiety, fear, family separation, and loss. Sean A. Scott's contribution to this volume explains how children coped with wartime death, finding consolation from a religion that emphasized the reunion of family members in heaven. Even courtship became politicized. As Victoria E. Ott demonstrates, during the Civil War many young white Southern women, eager to prove their loyalty to the Confederate cause, denounced men who failed to serve in the military and rebuffed advances from Union soldiers.

The war was also a time of excitement and growing autonomy for the young. Thomas Curran recounts the story of fifteen-year-old Tommy Cave, who joined the Confederate army against his father's wishes. As this episode suggests, the Civil War had a profound impact on family relations, sometimes reversing family roles. Fathers' absence meant that many young people had to grow up quickly and take on added responsibilities.

The war's reverberations echoed long after the conflict was over. As Mary Niall Mitchell and Troy Kickler reveal, immediately following the Civil War, the status of slave children became a cultural and economic battleground. While missionaries and educators sought to instill evangelical and free-labor values, some landowners sought to place African American children and youth into forms of apprenticeship resembling slavery.

The children who suffered the most were those who were orphaned, a topic examined by Catherine A. Jones and Judith Ann Geisberg. Thousands of children lost their fathers during the Civil War, and in many instances their mothers were no longer able to care for them. The result was the creation of a vastly expanded system of orphan homes, where some children suffered terribly from neglect, deprivation, and abuse.

The war left a lasting imprint on the young people who grew up during the conflict. For many whites in the former Confederacy, the war became a defining factor in their political lives and would color their adult attitudes and values. Lisa Tendrich Frank describes how Southern white girls who experienced William Tecumseh Sherman's march through Georgia firsthand would subsequently draw on their sufferings to construct the post–Civil War mythology of the Lost Cause: the view that the Confederacy had fought in a noble cause and had only been defeated by overwhelming force. Strikingly, a century after the war's conclusion, groups opposing the civil rights movement, like the Children of the Confederacy, continued to draw upon this mythology to convince Southern white children and youth to defend the so-called Southern way of life against racial integration.

Impressive in its sweep and its attention to individual experience, this gripping volume allows us to view the key topics of the era—slavery, the battlefront, and the Civil War's lasting legacy—from a fresh angle: through the eyes of the young. Too often, the lives of the "ordinary" are omitted from history, and too frequently history dwells on objective realities such as accounts of elections or battles without giving us an adequate sense of the subjective, individual experience of historical events. Drawing on letters, diaries, and other personal accounts, this book gives us a richer, more inclusive history that allows us to sense the fevered emotions, the anguish, the exhilaration, and the losses experienced by the young. The authors show how the war transformed the lives of children and youth—black and white, free and slave, Southern and Northern—irreversibly. For many young African Americans, the Civil War decades generated a sense of hope and possibility; in contrast, for many young white Southerners, those same years produced intense feelings of victimization that contributed to the postwar efforts to overturn Reconstruction and reimpose a system of white supremacy.

By documenting children's perceptions and involvement in the upheavals of the Civil War era, this volume underscores an essential but often neglected fact: warfare is not for adults only, and combatants are not war's only casualties. In our own day, we have grown increasingly aware of the fact that many wars involve the young, as eyewitnesses, victims, and underaged soldiers, and that while many young people demonstrate remarkable resilience in the face of war's horrors and dislocations, these traumas can also leave lasting scars. The history presented in this volume is of much more than antiquarian interest. The history of children and war remains unfinished, and anyone who would like to know about war's impact on the young would do well to look at this poignant and provocative anthology.

Introduction

JAMES MARTEN

Implicit in the competing visions of America that animated the Civil War era were competing visions of childhood reflected through prisms of race, class, and region. Although northerners and southerners hurtling toward open warfare may not have consciously known that their actions would influence not only the political and economic future of the country, but also their children's and grandchildren's lives, they instinctively used domestic and childhood metaphors to describe their quarrel. The political conflict resulted in a "house divided," northern commentators during the war frequently referred to the "fratricide" of the rebelling states, and soldiers were called "boys" and sang songs like "Just before the Battle, Mother."

Children and families provide the emotional centers of the two most famous novels written about the Civil War era. In *Uncle Tom's Cabin*, Harriet Beecher Stowe made the kindly title character's cabin the physical and moral foci of a narrative that eventually sprawls across the Ohio River and down the Mississippi. By its end, although the sad little dwelling is no longer Tom's home, it remains a powerful metaphor in the book's description of slavery's inevitable ruination of families. The book's extraordinary popularity—300,000 copies were sold within a year of its publication—suggests that Americans at least instinctively shared Stowe's fear that slavery and sectionalism threatened not only her fictional families but also real-life families.

The novel's assumptions about family and childhood transcend the image of the cabin. The presence and, of course, absence of families provide powerful reminders of Stowe's deeply held belief that the peculiar institution of slavery and the sacred institution of the family were tragically intertwined. Many of the sentimental set pieces—Tom's departure from Aunt Chloe, Mrs. Bird's brave insistence that her husband help Eliza and Harry escape, Eva's famous deathbed scene, to mention just a few—take place in the bosom of family. Everywhere children observe, inspire, offer unconditional love, and require absolute faithfulness. Two of the featured characters—Eliza and St. Clare—are both presented as loving parents, treasuring smart, innocent

Harry and beautiful, kind Eva, respectively. Yet Eliza succeeds as a parent, braving terrible dangers to carry her son away from slavery, while St. Clare fails to save his own daughter, who succumbs to disease in much the same way that white and black families will, the novel implies, inevitably be weakened and corrupted by slavery. The peculiar love that knits families together also unites Stowe's sprawling plot. Indeed, much of the pathos of Tom's death comes from his utter isolation from home and family.

If *Uncle Tom's Cabin* provides one fictional bookend to the Civil War, focusing on the deepest well of contention between the North and South, *Little Women* provides the other. Rather than addressing the issues that started the war, Louisa May Alcott focuses on the ways in which the war could affect even those families living far from the battlefront. Lonely and strapped for cash, Meg, Jo, Beth, Amy, and Marmee March endure long days between letters from their army chaplain father and husband; each letter's arrival draws them into the tight family circle where Mrs. March reads it aloud. Aside from the enforced absence of Reverend March and his eventual return home because of illness, the war is, in a sense, only background. Indeed, the second half of the book begins three years after Mr. March finally returns home a few months before the war ends. But the emphasis on the love and support that characterize a true family, and on the ways in which a family can sustain individuals during times of crisis, even war, has rung true to modern Americans enduring crises and wars and provides an important link between the two books.[1]

Much as these fictional Americans can help us understand the emotional burdens imposed by the sectional conflict, so, too, can the lives of real Civil War children and youth and their parents help us understand the ways in which the issues raised and at least partly resolved by the sectional conflict, Civil War, and Reconstruction had a practical impact on Americans, white and black, North and South. As statesmen debated states' rights and government responsibility in terms of protective tariffs and the extension of slavery, a dimly parallel discourse began to take shape on the role of the state in the lives of children. As emerging models of free labor and the free market clashed with traditional notions of family-oriented farms, slave-based plantations, and small, independent workshops, children and youth were drawn into the equation: How could—or should—they contribute to the new economy? As Americans resigned themselves to armed conflict and sought desperately to deal with the unexpected scope and destructiveness of war, children were integrated and exposed to the conflict in previously unimaginable ways, contrary to developing notions of the nurturing and protection of children. And, perhaps most obviously, as the rights of a race of people enslaved for centuries were tested and explored, children were in the forefront of the debates over how best to facilitate freedpeople's transition to freedom. Uniting all these threads was the conviction by virtually all participants, rebels, Yankees, and African Americans alike, that these struggles for independence, for the Union, for freedom, would provide legacies for the futures of all children. As a freedwoman told a Freedmen's Bureau agent after the war, referring to her and to all former slaves' children, "It was on their account we desired to be free."[2]

Children and Youth during the Civil War Era appears more than twenty years after Maris A. Vinovskis's famous question: "Have social historians lost the Civil War?" Since then, historians have explored important issues related to the Union and Confederate home fronts, the roles of women, the effects of the war on African Americans, the inner lives of Civil War soldiers, and the long-term impact of the war on the men who fought it. The second edition of a popular textbook on the Civil War era lists scores of books published during the last generation on the social history of the war, ranging from the role of women to the social dynamics of southern dissent, from home front mobilization to the war's effect on religion, and from the racial implications of war and emancipation to the impact of the conflict on American nationalism.[3]

An equivalent question relevant to this volume is: Have historians of children and youth applied their special insights to the study of war? For twentieth-century wars, the answer is a fairly enthusiastic yes, as historians have offered provocative accounts of children in Nazi Germany, on the American home front, and during the evacuation of London during the Blitz, to name just a few popular topics.[4]

But for many years neither Civil War historians nor historians of children and youth paid much attention to Civil War–era youngsters. A number of anthologies featuring original essays on emerging topics have been published in both fields over the last decade or two. But none of these otherwise excellent collections, even the ones that focus on the social history of the Civil War, provide adequate coverage of the lives of children and youth. This includes a volume edited by Vinovskis, *Toward a Social History of the American Civil War: Exploratory Essays*, as well as two well-known anthologies edited by Catherine Clinton and Nina Silber, *Divided Houses: Gender and the Civil War*, and *Battle Scars: Gender and Sexuality in the American Civil War*, which, despite their almost exhaustive coverage of other elements of Civil War social history, barely touch on the experiences of children and youth. Anthologies on children during the period have also ignored the war, which is barely mentioned in two of the most respected anthologies on children's history: *Small Worlds: Children and Adolescents in America, 1850–1950*, edited by Elliott West and Paula Petrik, and *Growing Up in America: Children in Historical Perspective*, edited by N. Ray Hiner and Joseph M. Hawes.[5]

Despite the fact that a few historians have begun to explore the topic in recent years, the historiography of children during the Civil War is clearly very short. Emmy Werner chronicled the insights of Civil War children, especially combatants, in *Reluctant Witnesses*, and the editor of this volume explored the experiences of children on the home front in *The Children's Civil War*. More recently Victoria Ott and Edmund Drago have added books on Confederate girls and children in South Carolina, respectively, and Anya Jabour has explored the experiences of girls and young women throughout the region during the sectional conflict and Civil War.[6] Like most anthologies, this one does not claim to be comprehensive; a strict word count more or less forced authors to create case studies rather than an all-inclusive history of children and youth during the period. As a result, it does not address all the conditions faced by children during the era of the Civil War or all the issues raised by their historians. For instance, free African American and Native American children are largely absent. Yet from the essays emerge several useful contexts and fresh ways of looking at the impact of one of the most studied periods in American history. It may be obvious that we can better understand the histories of children and youth by placing them in the context of the sectional conflict. Less obvious, perhaps, as Steven Mintz points out in his foreword, is the fact that viewing the conflict through the lens of children and youth also helps us better understand the rift that threatened to destroy the United States.

The baker's dozen of contributors engage several historiographies relevant to these disparate fields, including educational reform, the emergence and evolution of literature for children, the rights of children and youth, Civil War causation, memory, and many others. But three major issues lie at the heart of the book.

The first is the rise of the middle-class family and the development of "modern" childhood, which built on the ideas of Enlightenment thinkers like John Locke and Jean-Jacques Rousseau. Rejecting both the traditional view of child depravity and the idea that a child's character was the product of certain innate traits, they helped pioneer the notion of "nurture," that a child could be shaped by creating an environment that instilled appropriate values and behaviors. Nineteenth-century educators and writers—including Louisa May Alcott's father, Bronson Alcott—celebrated childhood as a time of innocence and argued that children must be protected from growing up too fast. They believed that children should be allowed to explore the world on their own terms, to revel in their natural innocence, and to enjoy the nurturing and protection that they deserved simply because they were children.

A vital part of the reconceptualization of childhood was the emergence of a new form of family, shaped by affection, based on companionate marriage, and centered on the nurturing of children. Although it would never include most American families, the new model became a paradigm against which all other families would be compared. The family's economic role declined, and its emotional responsibilities increased. The modern family, argue Steven Mintz and Susan Kellogg, "ceased to be a largely autonomous, independent, self-contained, and self-sufficient unit" and turned inward to "the socialization of children and the provision of emotional support and affection."[7]

Another major literature in which these essays are located explores the lives of slave families and children before and after the war. American slave owners encouraged slaves to form families for both economic and religious reasons, but slaves also insisted on maintaining family ties. Although slave codes did not recognize slave marriages or kinship, masters and slaves alike assumed that bondspeople would, in fact, live in family units. Although a surprisingly large percentage of slave marriages remained intact, early death or the sale of family members sundered many slave families, and even if families were allowed to remain together, they were constantly haunted by the possibility of a future separation. Furthermore, slave wives and husbands often lived on separate plantations and were only allowed to see one another once or twice a month. But the presence of at least one parent and, frequently, of aunts, uncles, and other relatives, allowed members of the slave community to maintain at least a semblance of the responsibilities, assumptions, and privileges attached to a functioning family. Indeed, the use of the term "family" by many slave owners to describe their enslaved men, women, and children offers not only a tragic irony but evidence of the power of the family metaphor, even when applied to people whose families were not legally bound. A number of historians have examined the dynamics of slave families and the experiences of slave children. Wilma King led the way with *Stolen Childhood*, which provided the first comprehensive account of the specific experiences of slave children; a few years later Marie Jenkins Schwartz's *Born in Bondage* emphasized the agency of slave children as they negotiated the demands of slavery with the responsibilities of childhood.[8]

After the war, African American children shared the joys and traumas of liberation. Both black and white southerners struggled to create a new system of race relations mediated, sometimes, by northern missionaries, "carpetbagger" politicians, army officers, or federal agents. Legislatures in former Confederate states passed "Black Codes" to restrict the rights and movements of former slaves, and immediately after the war, the Bureau of Freedmen, Refugees, and Abandoned Lands—better known as the Freedmen's Bureau—provided some support for the transition to freedom. But, for the most part, the difficult path of emancipation and its aftermath had to be handled mainly by the people most directly involved: the former slaves and their former masters. A number of historians have explored that process, which offers both uplifting and tragic examples of the course of race relations in a postslavery world.[9]

Finally, several essays draw from and contribute to our understanding of the "Lost Cause," a movement that borrowed its name and its tone from the vain efforts of Scots to win their independence from England. The phrase was first applied to the Confederacy by Edward Pollard, the editor of the *Richmond Examiner*, in his history of the war published just a year after the war's end. Over the next few decades the Lost Cause grew to include a full range of pro-southern beliefs and values: the commemoration of the heroism of Confederate soldiers, an insistence that the war had been fought to preserve constitutional principles rather than slavery, and a nostalgic desire to return to the halcyon prewar plantation days. The movement was led by veterans and politicians who "redeemed" southern state governments in the 1870s and founded organizations and publications like the Southern Historical Society, the United Confederate Veterans, and *Confederate Veteran* magazine, and by southern women who helped raise money to build Confederate monuments, preserved Confederate cemeteries, and, mainly through the United Daughters of the Confederacy, sought to memorialize the sacrifices of the men and women of the Confederacy by celebrating Confederate memorial days, sponsoring educational events, and publishing memoirs that celebrated Confederate sacrifice and honor. The Lost Cause reached a crescendo between 1880 and 1910 but continued to exert a major influence on southern society and politics for years afterward—to the extent that, according to Charles Reagan Wilson, it became a "civil religion." The Lost Cause inevitably affected and was, in turn, influenced by Civil War–era children and youth. They witnessed the events that shaped the movement and were raised with certain expectations by the Confederate soldiers and women who had survived the war. But their own experiences and memories also helped fuel the Lost Cause, as they came of age in the 1870s and 1880s.[10]

The Civil War era slashed across a broad spectrum of childhoods, raising challenges and opening opportunities unique to the children and youth who were observers, actors, and victims of the conflict. *Children and Youth during the Civil War Era* transcends the war years to include both the antebellum and postbellum periods. The thirteen essays are divided into four parts. The first examines the ways in which children and youth formed their own political opinions and the ways in which adults used images of children to illustrate larger issues, while the second provides examples of the ways in which basic assumptions about life, death, courtship, and family dynamics were affected by the war. Part III explores the ways in which those children most affected by the war—former slaves and orphans—became the center of political, racial, and religious controversies. The single essay constituting the epilogue explores the use of children during the period of massive resistance to the civil rights movement in the South in the 1950s and 1960s. Finally, since circumstances dictated that the war would inspire the creation of countless documents produced by children or adults who were children during the Civil War—perhaps the first large outpouring of sources presenting history from the points of view of children and youth in American history—the final part offers the words of several young Americans that display the ways in which the war entered their play and schooling, affected family dynamics, altered their material lives, and led them to form deeply held political and personal beliefs. These primary documents are followed by a set of study questions that will help readers explore the themes presented by the essays, documents, and illustrations, and by a list of key secondary sources for the period.

NOTES

1. Harriet Beecher Stowe, *Uncle Tom's Cabin* (Boston: John P. Jewett and Company; Cleveland, Ohio: Jewett, Proctor and Worthington, 1852); Louisa May Alcott, *Little Women*, pts. 1 and 2 (Boston: Roberts Bros., 1868, 1869). Michelle Ann Abate provides an intriguing connection between the two novels in "Topsy and Topsy-Turvy Jo: Harriet Beecher Stowe's *Uncle Tom's Cabin* and/in Louisa May Alcott's *Little Women*," *Children's Literature* 34 (2006): 59–82.

2. Quoted in Mary Niall Mitchell, *Raising Freedom's Child: Black Children and Visions of the Future after Slavery* (New York: NYU Press, 2008), 154.

3. Maris A. Vinovskis, "Have Social Historians Lost the Civil War? Some Preliminary Demographic Speculations," *Journal of American History* 76 (June 1989): 34–58.; Michael Fellman, Lesley J. Gordon, and Daniel E. Sutherland, *This Terrible War: The Civil War and Its Aftermath*, 2nd ed. (New York: Pearson/Longman, 2008).

4. A sampling of some of the excellent work being done on children and war can be found in James Marten, *Children and War: A Historical Anthology* (New York: NYU Press, 2002). On the Second World War, see, for example, William M. Tuttle Jr., *Daddy's Gone to War: The Second World War in the Lives of America's Children* (New York: Oxford University Press, 1993); Deborah Dwork, *Children with a Star: Jewish Youth in Nazi Europe* (New Haven: Yale University Press, 1991); Susan Pedersen, *Family, Dependence, and the Origins of the Welfare State: Britain and France, 1914–1945* (New York: Cambridge University Press, 1993); and W. D. Halls, *The Youth of Vichy France* (London: Clarendon, 1981).

5. Maris Vinovskis, *Toward a Social History of the American Civil War: Exploratory Essays* (New York: Cambridge University Press, 1990); Catherine Clinton and Nina Silber, eds., *Divided Houses: Gender and the Civil War* (New York: Oxford University Press, 1992), and *Battle Scars: Gender and Sexuality in the American Civil War* (New York: Oxford University Press, 2006); Elliott West and Paula Petrik, eds., *Small Worlds: Children and Adolescents in America, 1850–1950* (Lawrence: University Press of Kansas, 1992); N. Ray Hiner and Joseph M. Hawes, eds., *Growing Up in America: Children in Historical Perspective* (Urbana: University of Illinois Press, 1985).

6. Emmy Werner, *Reluctant Witnesses: Children's Voices from the Civil War* (New York: Basic Books, 1998); James Marten, *The Children's Civil War* (Chapel Hill: University of North Carolina Press, 1998); Victoria Ott, *Confederate Daughters: Coming of Age during the Civil War* (Carbondale: Southern Illinois University Press, 2008); Edmund L. Drago, *Confederate Phoenix: Rebel Children and Their Families in South Carolina* (New York: Fordham University Press, 2008); Anya Jabour, *Scarlett's Sisters: Young Women in the Old South* (Chapel Hill: University of North Carolina Press, 2007), and *Topsy-Turvy: How the Civil War Turned the World Upside Down for Southern Children* (Chicago: Ivan R. Dee, 2010).

7. Steven Mintz and Susan Kellogg, *Domestic Revolutions: A Social History of American Family Life* (New York: Free Press, 1988), xiv–xv.

8. Wilma King, *Stolen Childhood: Slave Youth in Nineteenth-Century America* (Bloomington: Indiana University Press, 1995); Marie Jenkins Schwartz, *Born in Bondage: Growing Up Enslaved in the Antebellum South* (Cambridge: Harvard University Press, 2000).

9. Two classic studies are Leon Litwack, *Been in the Storm So Long: The Aftermath of Slavery* (New York: Knopf, 1979), and Joel Williamson, *The Crucible of Race: Black-White Relations in the American South since Emancipation* (New York: Oxford University Press, 1984). See also Jacqueline Jones, *Labor of Love, Labor of Sorrow: Black Women, Work, and the Family from Slavery to the Present* (New York: Basic Books, 1985). On the Freedmen's Bureau in general, see Paul A. Cimbala, *The Freedmen's Bureau: Reconstructing the American South after the Civil War* (Malabar, FL: Krieger, 2005). An early account of freedmen's education is Robert C. Morris, *Reading 'Riting, and Reconstruction: The Education of Freedmen in the South, 1861–1870* (Chicago: University of Chicago Press, 1982). A more recent exploration of the issues raised by the emancipation of slave children is Mitchell, *Raising Freedom's Child*.

10. The two most important studies of the Lost Cause were published in the 1980s by Gaines M. Foster and Charles Reagan Wilson. The latter held that the Lost Cause became a "civil religion" to Southerners. Gaines M. Foster, *Ghosts of the Confederacy: Defeat, the Lost Cause, and the Emergence of the New South* (New York: Oxford University Press, 1987); Charles Reagan Wilson, *Baptized in Blood: The Religion of the Lost Cause, 1865–1920* (Athens: University of Georgia Press, 1980). For southern women, the Civil War, and the Lost

Cause, see Catherine Clinton, *Tara Revisited: Women, War and the Plantation Legend* (New York: Abbeville Press, 1995); LeeAnn Whites, *The Civil War as a Crisis in Gender, Augusta, Georgia, 1860–1890* (Athens: University of Georgia Press, 1995); Karen Cox, *Dixie's Daughters: The United Daughters of the Confederacy and the Preservation of Confederate Culture* (Gainesville: University Press of Florida, 2003); and Caroline E. Janney, *Burying the Dead but Not the Past: Ladies' Memorial Associations and the Lost Cause* (Chapel Hill: University of North Carolina Press, 2008).

PART I

Children and the Sectional Conflict

> You know that, if you break a small wheel in a cotton-mill, the entire machinery will stop; and if the moon—one of the smallest lumps of matter in the universe—shall fall from its orbit, the whole planetary system might go reeling and tumbling about like a drunken man. So you see the great importance of little things,—and little *folks* are of much greater importance than little *things*.
>
> —Edmund Kirke, "The Boy of Chancellorsville"[1]

As indicated in this passage from a supposedly true story, told by Edmund Kirke, of a brave drummer boy who survives the Battle of Chancellorsville and a stint in Libby Prison, Civil War–era writers for children stressed that even youngsters had a role to play in the great events of the day. The essays in this part show how children and youth became both exemplars and, at times, actors in the racial and political issues of the sectional conflict that led to war. The war and the decades preceding it were a pivotal moment not only in the nation's development but also in the ways in which children and youth were integrated into that development.

Slavery was a major battleground between the new and old conceptions of childhood. Indeed, it may have represented the most violent clash between developing notions of innocent children and protected childhood and political and economic reality. One of the greatest ironies of this particular time and place is the fact that, even as affluent white children in the South actually benefited from this new version of childhood, the plight of slave children mocked the idea that childhood should reflect a period of safety and simplicity. Although the rural nature of the South, along with somewhat different attitudes about gender, class, and hierarchy, continued to influence child-rearing practices, many southern families also sought to protect and nurture their children. But new ideas about children and child rearing were layered over older ones; for instance, just as slave children had to learn how to be slave adults, so, too, did white children living in a slave society have to learn how to navigate their status as racial superiors, whether or not they were slave owners. In a larger sense, the practice of enslaving children became a central component of both the abolitionist attack on slavery and the slave owners' defense of the institution. Rebecca de Schweinitz and Elizabeth Kuebler-Wolf articulate and creatively address the rich ironies in the rise of sentimental childhood even as the decidedly unsentimental rearing of slave children flourished.

The young men in Kanisorn Wongsrichanalai's essay were the scions of some of those New England families raising the first generation of children nurtured in "modern" child-centered families. Perhaps that gave them the confidence to engage the political issues of the day, to challenge the teachers—and, in one case, their college president—and even their parents as the nation whirled toward civil war. Like young southern men of their generation, they challenged the status quo even as they sought ways to take roles in the rising conflict.

The slave children who appear in these essays are less real people than useful symbols of the northern critique and the southern defense of slavery. Yet the issues they represented engaged actual northern college students, who wrote about and acted on the issues raised by the sectional conflict. Perhaps they perceived the disjunction between their own protected childhoods and those of the slave children they had not met. In any event, they saw themselves as political actors perfectly capable of taking part in the great debates of the day. In their own ways, young slaves in the South and privileged young men in the North displayed, to paraphrase Edmund Kirke, the "great importance" of heretofore ignored segments of society.

NOTES

1. Edmund Kirke, "The Boy of Chancellorsville," *Our Young Folks* 1 (September 1865): 600.

"Waked Up to Feel"

Defining Childhood, Debating
Slavery in Antebellum America

REBECCA DE SCHWEINITZ

"A slaveholder never appears to me so completely an agent of hell, as when I think of and look upon my dear children," Frederick Douglass wrote in his 1845 autobiography. As a free man, Douglass could see to it that his children regularly attended school, slept in comfortable beds, and were trained "in the paths of wisdom and virtue." But it was precisely the blissful state of his current "domestic affairs" that made apparent the "grim horrors of slavery," horrors he himself had known as a child. Douglass's personal history juxtaposed the lives that America's rising middle class expected for its offspring with the precarious state of slave childhood. While northern middle-class children, including Douglass's, grew up with "holy lessons and precious endearments" from loving parents, the former slave, like most of the country's young blacks, grew up "haunted" by the image of an "inexorable *demigod*," his slave-master father, who regarded the boy as an economic asset, separated him from his mother as an infant, and "robbed" the terms brother and sister "of their true meaning." In Douglass's account, that slavery degraded childhood and made "strangers" out of families was its most damning characteristic.[1]

Other abolitionists, black and white, similarly described the "ghastly terrors" of slavery to the nineteenth-century American public through stories of children torn from their "frantic" mothers' arms, fathers selling their mulatto offspring "as marketable commodities" as if they were "brute beasts." Their writings imbued parental affections and evolving beliefs about the emotional value of children with political significance and urged white Americans to sympathize with slaves in their roles as parents. Put yourselves in the place of a slave parent, antislavery advocates urged, think of the "tender" slave child "robbed" of "parental care and attention . . . thrown upon the world without the benefit of its natural guardians . . . without hope, shelter, comfort, or instruction."[2]

Despite the impassioned arguments of Douglass and his fellow abolitionists, few scholars have examined the ways that both abolitionists and slaveholders used ideas about childhood in their efforts to challenge and preserve slavery. While other ideas and issues informed the creation, persistence, and eradication of American slavery, the repeated appearance of ideas about childhood in antebellum slave debates indicate important connections between slavery and the rise of sentimental notions of childhood. The prominence of ideas about childhood in arguments for and against slavery suggests that America's transition to modern domestic ideals helped to delegitimize the practice of human bondage. At the same time, slave debates themselves reveal America's transition to modern notions of childhood; indeed, they capture tensions between older, instrumental notions of childhood and newer emotional notions of childhood vying for cultural and political authority in nineteenth-century America.

In the 1780s shifting notions of families and children gave northern lawmakers a compelling reason to "extinguish" the condition of slavery. Decrying the "unnatural" practice of separating husbands and wives "from each other and from their children," legislators insisted that slavery "deprived [Negro and mulatto slaves] of the common blessings that they were by nature entitled to" and, in so doing, "cast them into the deepest afflictions." Although early emancipation statutes did not immediately end slavery, they generally provided that children remain with or near parents during infancy, and sometimes early childhood. As Rhode Island lawmakers asserted, "Humanity requires, that Children . . . remain with their mothers." It is suggestive of the expanding impact and political significance of sentimental notions of childhood that regardless of other reasons for ending slavery, northern legislatures reported that slavery's adverse effects on families are what motivated them to pass abolition statutes.[3]

Scholars have described the rising influence of sentimental domestic ideals among the emergent northern middle class and in the nation's print culture during the early decades of the nineteenth century. These trends coincided with the growth of the abolitionist movement and with its widespread use of images of children in the battle against slavery. Abolitionists recognized that "nothing can be done to abolish slavery unless we are waked up to feel." And, like the often fiery Frederick Douglass, many of them turned to sentimental images of children and families to realize that goal. In the antebellum North, with its growing middle class dedicated to sentimental ideals, such tactics seemed especially promising.[4]

Abolitionists repeatedly called on middle-class domestic sensibilities when they challenged their contemporaries to put themselves in the place of slave parents. In his famous exposé, *American Slavery as It Is*, Theodore Weld insisted that "every man knows that slavery is a curse." For if a white man were given "an hour to prepare his wife and children for a life of slavery," to "get ready their necks for the yoke, and their wrists for the coffle chains," then "*nature's* testimony against slavery" would be manifest in "his pale lips and trembling knees." The *Anti-Slavery Examiner* similarly encouraged readers to consider slaves' plight in the context of their own roles and sensibilities as parents by asking: "Am I willing to reduce my little child to slavery?" And, again drawing on the political potential of sentimental childhood, the *Non-Slaveholder* called "separating parents from their children, and children from their parents," a "merciless despotism" that "despoiled [families] of their rights, and deprived [them] of hope."[5]

The popularity of Harriet Beecher Stowe's *Uncle Tom's Cabin* confirmed that sentimental images of children and families were especially effective in helping antebellum America feel for the nation's slaves. Separated from their mothers, given no opportunity for education, suffering in ways that not even adults should have to endure, the slave children in Stowe's book and other antislavery literature pull on readers' heartstrings because they are not really children at all. Whether forced to grow up because their families were torn apart, because of hard physical labor, cruel punishments, or the loss of sexual innocence, these were not children according to the ideals of the emerging middle class.

Scholars have noted the ways that abolitionists used ideas about motherhood to capture public sympathy for slaves and encourage white women's political action.[6] But nineteenth-century notions of motherhood depended on particular notions of childhood. It was tragic for Stowe's Henry to be taken from Eliza, or Harriet Jacobs to be separated from her children, not just because Eliza and Harriet were mothers but because antebellum mothers were supposed to protect, nurture, and love their children and shield them from the public world of labor and licentiousness. The *Non-Slaveholder* explained some of the duties of mothers and the proper conditions of childhood with a poem telling "of the Captive's child; Whose tiny form is uncaressed, Whose lip in love is rarely pressed....With none to cherish, no one near / To hush the wail or wipe the tear." A century earlier, when Americans expected children to contribute directly to the family economy, when there was little distinction between home and work, and when high infant and child mortality rates affected most families, the relationship between mothers and their children did not carry the same social or political significance it did in the nineteenth century. Drawing on earlier notions of childhood, parenthood, and guardianship, nineteenth-century American slaveholders defended themselves by arguing that their slaves benefited from relatively low mortality rates and good health compared with other slave regimes. But as antislavery advocates understood, for antebellum middle-class mothers, raising children involved more than ensuring they survived to adulthood.[7]

Although most slave mothers did not consider murdering their own children, it is striking evidence of changes in notions of childhood and the ways that abolitionists employed childhood for political work that they described death as a preferable alternative to what historian Wilma King calls "stolen childhood." In *Uncle Tom's Cabin*, Eliza risks her family members' lives to save her son from being sold to slave traders, and Cassey poisons her child so he will not grow up in slavery. These mothers' suicidal and homicidal actions are portrayed as heroic. "O, that child!—how I loved it!" Cassey laments, but continues: "I am not sorry, to this day; he, at least, is out of pain." Harriet Jacobs suggested to readers in her autobiography that it is "mockery for a slave mother to pray back her dying child to life! Death is better than slavery." And Louisa J. Hall's poem "Birth in the Slave Hut" compared the "instinct of joy" that was supposed to accompany childbirth with the experience of a slave mother who wishes to "feel myself childless again / Or dare with my own hand to tear / The life from this creature of pain!" Abolitionists, especially women, repeatedly described death as a welcome "vision" that saves young people from repeated whippings by frenzied masters, reunites mothers with their children, and "unchains" spirits.[8]

Emotional evaluations of childhood shaped both abolitionists' personal lives and their political tactics. Like many antebellum mothers, Stowe lost a child. Her sixth, Charley, died in the summer of 1849, when barely a year old. With Charley's death the famous author became like other parents of the era who struggled to reconcile sentimental beliefs about childhood with improving but still formidable child mortality rates. Charley's early death made him what was commonly known as a "special child." Stowe captured the thinking behind the concept of the special child when she wrote to a friend: "Is there not something brighter & better around them than around those who live?" Scholars describe the emergence of such characters in nineteenth-century literature as a phenomenon best explained by the elevated status of the middle-class child juxtaposed to the continued threat of infant and child death. The idea that God sent particular children for a short time to their earthly families had "immense reconciling power in an era when many children did in fact die young."[9]

Reconciled or not, Stowe's personal tragedy made her well aware of what Joan Hedrick calls "the overwrought feelings of white, middle-class parents" toward their children. Images of sentimentalized childhood throughout antislavery literature indicate that many abolitionists shared Stowe's awareness and used it to forward their political agenda. In suggesting the possible advantages of death for child slaves, antislavery literature, like special-child literature, may have allowed middle-class whites to express anxiety about the ever-present possibility of child death. Free white children could be "creatures of pain" too, and white women might sometimes wish they had never given birth if their children died young. White mothers, like black slave parents, saw their children as "helpless human being[s] . . . tender and delicate" and could feel themselves similarly "robbed" of "heaven-ordained blessings" when their children died. In affirming that slave children would find happiness and freedom in the next life, and that there was a next life in which families would be reunited, antislavery literature offered comfort to worried or bereaved white parents.[10]

But abolitionist literature was not just cathartic and comforting; it was also intended to persuade an audience. While a range of contemporary authors employed sentimentalized views of childhood in literature for religious designs, antislavery advocates used those views for expressly political purposes. In *Uncle Tom's Cabin*, Eva, the most obvious special child in American literature, inspires others to strengthen their faith in God, like other special children who appeared in fiction and "true stories" of the era, *and* to become the kind of Christians who love and respect black slaves and worked for their improvement and freedom. Stowe suggested that children like Eva, imbued with a "deep spiritual light," had a divine mission to use that light and their "wiser than ordinary words" to turn the "wayward human heart upwards with them in their homeward flight." But Eva turned the wayward hearts of the white people around her outward as well as upward, to "all our people."[11]

Eva's ability to see people and life more clearly than others, especially the adults around her, made her stand out in Stowe's narrative. And Stowe intended the contrast between this special child and Marie St. Clare's decadence or Miss Ophelia's impatience to help readers reconsider their views on African Americans and slavery. In some ways, however, Eva was not that special; antislavery literature gave all children the natural ability to see a hotly contested (or completely avoided) political issue in the same human and humane terms in which Eva saw it. Abolitionist stories, poetry, and prose portrayed children as in the vanguard of antislavery sentiment. In "A True Tale of the South," despite the bad examples of adults around him and having "been placed amid sore temptation," a southern white boy helps some of his family's slaves escape and frees those he later inherits. Antislavery poetry suggested that God gave children "counsels" while "aged eyes" remained "sealed" to "the living words of liberty." And abolitionists who grew up in slaveholding families insisted that as children they had felt "grieved" witnessing slave whippings and tried to "intercede with tears in their behalf." Traditional theological conceptions of children, like those slaveholders used to defend slavery, portrayed children as sinful and in need of strict guidance from adults. But abolitionist literature rejected the idea of children's natural wickedness and suggested young Americans could become key actors in the nation's battle over slavery. While negative views about childhood remained tenable during the antebellum period, new understandings of children as naturally innocent, as "heralds of holiness," and adults as in need of guidance informed antislavery literature and tactics. In the words of Henry C. Wright, "children [were] born abolitionists." All abolitionists had to do was "keep them abolitionists."[12]

To this end, abolitionists created a literature specifically for children. Antislavery primers or stories in *The Child's Anti-Slavery Book*, the *Slave's Friend*, or Lydia Marie Child's mainstream *Juvenile Miscellany* encouraged what abolitionists portrayed as children's innate sympathy for slaves and aversion to the "sin" of slaveholding. In antislavery children's literature white children taught slaves to read and listened attentively and sympathetically to tragic tales of slave and free blacks. Such literature reflected abolitionists' desire to "impress and guide . . . the feelings of youth," their belief that children's natures made them "abler and better supporters" of antislavery principles than average adults, and their sense of the political power of childhood— both as a stage in human development and as an ideal.[13]

Abolitionists' attempts to encourage children's (and their parents') sympathies for and identification with slaves often resulted in paternalistic stories that perpetuated racial stereotypes, portraying prescient, privileged, and active white children who saved helpless blacks. Despite its limits, that literature also advanced sentimental notions of childhood and used them to shame whites of all ages into supporting the antislavery cause. The introduction to *The Child's Anti-Slavery Book* read like a nineteenth-century instructional manual: "Children, you are free and happy. Kind parents watch over you with loving eyes; patient teachers instruct you from the beautiful pages of the printed book; benign laws protect you from violence, and prevent the strong arms of wicked people from hurting you; the Blessed Bible is in your hands." The author contrasts this idealized image with the state of black childhood under slavery. Young whites learned about slave children who lost their families and who struggled not just to learn their letters or sit still in church but for the opportunity to learn to read or hear about God. The book asked readers to reflect on their comparatively fortunate circumstances and to define American childhood in color-blind terms. "Are all the children in America free like you? No, no! . . . Though born beneath the same sun and on the same soil, with the same natural right to freedom as yourselves . . . hundreds of thousands of American children are *slaves*."[14]

White children in antislavery literature, whether as implied readers or actual characters, became powerful symbolic counterpoints to other *American* children in that literature. While untroubled white children enjoyed the benefits of loving parents who encouraged their schooling and moral instruction, slave children (whom abolitionists described as equally deserving of the benefits of American childhood) only dreamed of their mothers, hid their efforts to learn to read, and developed into good Christians in spite of, not because of, the influences around them. While modern critics understandably focus on white writers' implicit racism in their treatment of black characters, the differences between the portrayal of white and black children in antislavery literature could help to underscore the "distance" between white and black childhood and encourage middle-class whites to take action against slavery. For instance, Stowe introduces Topsy, antislavery's most famous foil to the special child, as dark and wild, bad and evil. But, through Eva, readers discover that Topsy never knew her father or mother and since birth had been hated, exploited, and harshly punished because of her skin color and slave status. Stowe's book suggests that Topsy was not innately different from any other child. The girl's brutish looks and inappropriate behaviors, far from being indicative of any innate racial tendencies, simply resulted from her having been a victim of the same stolen childhood that (at least according to abolitionist writings) made slave children's death seem a reasonable wish. Indeed, as Miss Ophelia provides the requisite accouterments of sentimental childhood—protection, education, encouragement, even love—Topsy is transformed into a model child.

In creating the inverse image of Eva and Topsy and implying that the two characters might resemble one another through the correct conditions of middle-class childhood, Stowe revealed middle-class America's commitment to sentimental childhood. All children, not just those who died young, or even those with white skin, were special. In the nonfictional world northern judges reversed codes that upheld fathers' property rights in their children and claimed that "the custody of minors is given to their parents for their maintenance, protection, and education." Northern court rulings obligated judges to take children from fathers who "abused their paternal authority" and place them "under the care of persons proper to have control of them, and to superintend their education." Parents who treated their children with "cruelty," or neglected to fulfill their obligations, which included bringing children up "in the habits of industry, sobriety, and virtue," lost parental rights. Defenders of slavery, in real life and in antislavery literature, might liken slaves to children in order to highlight the supposed simplicity and dependence of blacks, but for northerners, childhood had become a sacred state with legal protections rather than a state of dependence. Drawing on sentimental constructions of childhood, abolitionists insisted that if slave owners wanted to call their slaves children, or if slaves actually were like children—as most whites in both regions believed—then they should actually be treated like children. In the case of *Uncle Tom's Cabin*, Stowe pointedly used expectations that childhood be protected by society at large, sympathetically describing Topsy's troubles and suggesting that a proper childhood, provided by an outside source if necessary (in this case a middle-class, Christian, northern, white woman), was the correct remedy for such children.[15]

The northern white middle class's own beliefs and anxieties about families and childhood allowed them to identify (to some degree) with slaves' plights. As Stowe wrote about Charley, "It was at *his* dying bed, and at *his* grave, that I learnt what a poor slave mother may feel when her child is torn away from her." Capitalizing on this point of empathy, abolitionists circulated an image of a slave mother jumping out of a window, "the cause of her doing such a frantic act" being the separation of her family. Antislavery publications repeatedly retold this story and others like it, explaining that reports of crazed slave women tearing at their hair, shrieking wildly, throwing themselves on the ground, even cutting their own throats or "heroically" cutting the throats of their children to "mortal effect," were perfectly understandable and "illustrative of the deep feeling of slave mothers for their children." Such accounts defied slaveholders' arguments that maternal bonds of affection did not "vex" black slave women and illustrated the deep feelings of white mothers for their children. At a time when sentimental family ideals encouraged women to focus all their energies and attention on raising children, the prospect of losing a child seemed devastating. White women who experienced or feared their own "cruel separations" could appreciate and, abolitionists hoped, want to help slave women who were "impelled . . . into a kind of madness" when their children were "torn from [their] maternal affection."[16]

Reports that legitimated slave women's seemingly insane reactions to family separations legitimated white women's own responses to child death and put those feelings to work politically. In "Little Lewis," Julie Colman explains both the suicidal actions of a slave mother separated from her children and her own feelings about such separations when she remarks, "Poor woman, she was tired of her miserable life. I don't wonder that she wanted to die." In asking readers: "Don't you think it would make you act like you was crazy if they should take your children away and you never see em any more," abolitionists affirmed white parents' reactions to real or imagined child death at the same time they encouraged them to identify with slaves and support abolitionism. Such stories undoubtedly reassured whites about their own family tragedies. For, as antislavery tracts reminded, while tyrannical masters routinely "tor[e] asunder" slave families "for sordid purpose," leaving a "thick cloud of utter darkness" between slave parents and their children, white children could only be taken "by the gentle agency of death . . . at the mild call of a Father of infinite love." As one abolitionist writer put it, "the grief of the bereaved Christian mother must seem as perfect bliss" when compared with the "agony" her enslaved counterparts experienced at the removal of their children by a different kind of "master's hand."[17]

Appearing as they did, and with such frequency, during a time of transitional domestic values, stories that detailed and justified desperate behaviors on the part of slaves separated from their children promoted sentimental ideas about children and gave those ideas political meaning. Through antislavery literature the white middle-class expressed its beliefs about the emotional value of families and the immorality of slavery. For abolitionists, the agony that slave parents experienced at the loss of their children provided evidence of blacks' humanity, validating sentimental definitions of children and families as well as the antislavery cause. That antislavery advocates so often used slave parents' attachments to their children to demonstrate the moral and civic virtue of blacks suggests that sentimental notions of children and families carried considerable weight on the scale of social values and in antebellum political culture. More than stories of personal grief, accounts detailing "the o'er flowing feelings" of separated slave families exemplified the domestic values of the emerging middle class and allied those values with antislavery politics. In accounts of distraught slave parents, abolitionists promoted sentimental ideas about children and families and offered a compelling condemnation of slavery.[18]

If domestic ideals and anxieties made the antislavery cause understandable to an otherwise apathetic nineteenth-century northern white public, then different beliefs and anxieties about families and children continued to help make slavery a defensible socioeconomic system in the minds of white southerners.

While Douglass, Stowe, and other abolitionists skillfully employed ideas about the family as an institution dedicated to the emotional well-being of its individual members, and childhood as a unique period of innocence and growth to challenge slavery, such ideas were open to question in antebellum America. And indeed, slaveholders defended the institution on the grounds that the master-slave relationship simply modeled the patriarchal order of families. As one of slavery's most ardent defenders, George Fitzhugh, insisted: "The father has property in his wife's services and may legally control, in some measure, her personal liberty. . . . The father has property in the services and persons of his children till they are twenty-one years of age. They are his property and his slaves." "What is the difference between the authority of a parent and of a master?" he asked. "Neither pay wages, and each is entitled to the services of those subject to him." For many of slavery's defenders, that it was "right and incumbent to subject children to the authority of parents and guardians," that fathers could sell the labor of their children until they arrived "at years of discretion," made slavery no more "hideous" than other proper family relationships. In the context of economic and hierarchically oriented ideas about children and families such arguments made perfect sense.[19]

Scholars have shown that despite shifts taking place among northern families, southern domestic realities did not fundamentally change during the antebellum period. While the average northern family size decreased to 4.9 by 1850 and to 2.9 within the next generation, white nineteenth-century southern households averaged 6 children and remained large, primarily economic units, with dependents important economic producers. According to Stephanie McCurry, demographic differences represented both ideological and lived differences; although aware of sentimental domestic ideals, hierarchical and economic notions of children and families continued to guide the lives of southern whites. Moreover, at the same time northern courts gave sentimental ideas about childhood legal backing, southern laws regulating families, apprenticeships, and other custodial relationships continued to reflect principles of patriarchy and hierarchy and to recognize the economic over the emotive value of children until after the Civil War. Peter Bardaglio suggests that the persistence of slavery explains why southern statutes did not change; the master-slave relationship continued to provide the model for other relationships. But southerners' use of childhood in slave debates indicates there may have been dialectical rather than one-way relationships between family law, slavery, and ideas about childhood. Slavery persisted in the South, in part, because economic and hierarchical ideas about childhood persisted. And slavery's demise was both a *causative* factor in transforming southern family law and a *result* of changing notions of childhood and families.[20]

Southerners' defenses of slavery suggest that they continued to believe that traditional domestic ideals constituted the natural order of social and political life; as one slavery defender explained: "Children are slaves to their parents, guardians, and teachers," and there is no "difference between the authority of a parent and of a master. . . . Neither pay wages, and each is entitled to the services of those subject to him." Like abolitionists, slavery's supporters made political use of domestic ideals—although a different set of domestic ideals.[21]

The white South, however, was not altogether unaffected by shifting sensibilities about families. Indeed, southerners revealed their anxieties about changing ideals when they defended slavery by warning that abolitionists planned to do away with marriage and parental authority as well as slavery, and in their assertions that "in our North . . . they hold that all men, women and negroes, and smart children are equals." But southern defenses of slavery in the years before the Civil War also reveal subtle changes in views of children and families. White southerners did not fully embrace sentimental notions of children and families, but they did attempt to negotiate changing ideals and incorporate new values into their own sense of proper domestic relationships and arguments for slavery.[22]

For instance, at the same time that slaveholders insisted fathers held property rights in their wives, children, and slaves, they also claimed "a prejudice and a weakness" for the modern quality of love and stressed the reciprocal nature of relationships between fathers or masters and their dependents. Southerners argued that hierarchical relationships reflected society's natural order and benefited slaves and other dependents for whom "the competition of the world would be too much." Arguments that the care, protection, and guidance masters provided slaves compensated for the labor they received had long been used to justify slavery (and child apprenticeships). But in the nineteenth century, as scholars have noted, slavery's defenders increasingly highlighted the *benevolent* nature of southern slave masters; "good" masters acted humanely and spoke kindly. Moreover, slavery's defenders condemned masters who did not fit this image—who treated their figurative children harshly.[23]

Slaveholders drew on traditional domestic ideals when they defended themselves by suggesting that the physical living conditions and mortality rates of their slaves compared favorably with those of other slave regimes and free workers in the industrializing North. But in addition to asserting a superior ability to provide "food, raiment, house, fuel, and everything necessary to the *physical* well being" of their workforce, southerners increasingly argued that slaves "identified . . . with the families in which they have been raised," and that "our slaves are cheerful, contented, and happy, much beyond the general condition of the human race." Such defenses reinforced hierarchical, economic, and practical notions of children and domestic relationships at the same time they appealed to new ideas about the importance of affectionate ties and emotional well-being. Arguments that stressed the relative ease of slave life also reflected new sentimental notions of childhood. Antebellum proslavery literature portrayed "light-hearted slaves" who seemed "the very prototype of children in their joys and sorrows" and "their indifference to the future." Why force the slave from "primeval innocence and ease," a proslavery poem asked. "Why peril the Negro's humble joys?" Instead of perverting childhood, slavery's advocates asserted that the institution guaranteed that blacks, who at any age were like children, would be able to live their lives as nineteenth-century children should—free from the worldly cares that confronted their masters and the anxieties of northern workers.[24]

White southerners also combined old and new conceptions of children and families when they argued that slaves lacked the ability to develop the kind of close family ties idealized by the middle class. Slaveholders did not generally deny blacks' kindly feelings toward family members, and, influenced by the "tender years" doctrine, some even supported the idea that young slaves should not be sold away from their mothers. But slaveholders did insist that slave parents' feelings for their children could be controlled and that the practical management of household (plantation) affairs should not be dictated by those sentiments. Such attitudes toward family relationships resembled traditional attitudes of parents toward children. Common colonial practices, including separating mothers from their children to aid the weaning process, or sending older children to live and work with other families, indicate that parents felt affection for their children but considered that affection secondary to families' practical needs and potentially dangerous to the proper functioning of society. Slaveholders used (and perverted) this model for thinking about families and children when they minimized slaves' feelings for their children and adapted colonial-era tactics, such as sending slave mothers away for the day when their children were to be sold, to ease the separation of slave parents from their children.[25]

Antebellum southerners likewise used traditional and modern domestic ideas to support slavery when insisting that blacks developed strong attachments to their masters instead of to one another. Defenses that endowed slaves with a childlike affection for white caretakers while denying them the capacity to develop significant attachments outside of the master-slave relationship drew on sentimental conceptions about children, on the idea that all blacks were like children, and on hierarchical notions of family relationships. In effect, such defenses channeled new domestic ideals into older models upon which slavery thrived. Arguments that merged an emphasis on emotional bonding with the idea that dependents "owed" love and respect to those who cared for them suggest that in the decades before the Civil War, southerners understood and defended slavery through the prism of both traditional and sentimental constructions of families.

Slave owners' increasing emphasis on the benevolent nature of slavery, criticisms of tyrannical masters, and attempts to build a "modern defense" of the institution by "drawing on the same domestic sensibility that appealed to their northern opponents" are suggestive of the growing nationwide cultural and political power of sentimental domestic ideals. But perhaps slavery was not "domesticated" during the nineteenth century, as one scholar has argued. Instead, domesticity itself changed during that period. Changing defenses of slavery and even seeming inconsistencies between slaveholders' ideals and behaviors reflect differences between competing domestic ideals; they reflect, in part, slaveholders' attempts to combine traditional frameworks for thinking about children and families with new sentimental ideals.[26]

Slaveholders' continued use of the lash to discipline slaves, for example, may have contradicted the benevolent image of slavery that its defenders tried to portray. Yet it also reflected society's ambivalence toward new views of children and the proper way to instill correct behavior and values in them. Indeed, popular literature continued to stress "the need to subdue the child early and at almost any cost" and did not completely reject "the belief in depravity or innate tendencies to wickedness [in children] . . . until just before the Civil War." Northerners as well as southerners tentatively held to traditional forms of discipline that correlated with negative views of children. In the same years that abolitionists began decrying the harsh physical punishment of slaves, northerners publicly debated the use of corporal punishment in schools and homes. In the 1830s and 1840s, educational reformers increasingly voiced their opposition to "punishments that mortify" and urged that whipping be used only when moral persuasion or other gentle modes of training failed. Lyman Cobb's book *The Evil Tendencies of Corporal Punishment* (1847) reflected what were becoming widespread views on the topic when it denounced thoughtless and frequent whippings (not all corporal punishment) as evidence of tyrannical parents instead of devilish children. Magazines, literature, and diaries additionally suggest that although progressively influenced by sentimental notions of children in their approach to child discipline, parents throughout the country still believed in the efficacy of whipping. Antebellum abolitionists generally advocated a more "rational system of discipline." Yet Miss Ophelia in *Uncle Tom's Cabin* insisted that "children always have to be whipped. . . . I never heard of bringing them up without," and kindly St. Clare agreed, in principle, with whipping. He clarified his own refusal to whip by explaining that under slavery, normal "whipping and abuse" by otherwise benevolent masters invariably grew into "the horrid cruelties and outrages . . . [in] the papers" because of a "hardening process on both sides."[27]

Abolitionists considered it highly unlikely, but some admitted that if a system of slavery could be designed "in which the slaves should be instructed and made wise"—if slaves would be brought up like children should be—"there might be some excuse for the slaveholder." And Stowe presents the Shelby and St. Clare plantations as nearly ideal domestic environments. But in antebellum America, more traditional models only remained valid provided they did not conflict with the new sentimental order. And abolitionists made clear that masters operating under traditional domestic ideals but still providing the kind of care and protection for slaves required by middle-class standards could fall into debt or die, leaving slaves subject to masters who did not uphold those standards. Despite white southerners' attempts to incorporate sentimental values into defenses of slavery, its legitimacy depended, in part, on economic and hierarchical notions of children and family relationships, notions that abolitionists pointed out ultimately clashed with ascendant domestic ideals.[28]

Indeed, abolitionists repeatedly drew on the rising cultural and political power of sentimental childhood, turning southern defenses of slavery on their head by showing the ways that slavery degraded *American* childhood. Whether it was the figurative childhood of slave adults, the "tender years" of actual slave children, or the pampered childhood of little white masters and mistresses, whom slavery taught to be thoughtless, violent, proud, and idle—like Eva's cousin—the institution clearly did not serve the interests of any child. The distance between old and new ideals about children and families meant that as America made the transition from traditional to sentimental domestic ideals, slavery became increasingly difficult to justify.

1. Frederick Douglass, *My Bondage and My Freedom* (Chicago: Johnson, 1970), 334–35, 37, 35.

2. Ibid., 37; Theodore Weld, *American Slavery as It Is: Testimony of a Thousand Witnesses* (New York: American Anti-Slavery Society, 1839), 7–9; First Annual Report of the American Anti-Slavery Society, "Declaration of the American Anti-Slavery Society" (New York, December 1833), reprinted in *The Negro in American History* vol. 3, ed. Mortimer Adler (Chicago: Encyclopaedia Britannica Educational Corporation, 1969), 265; James Pennington, "Slave Narrative" (1849), reprinted in *Childhood in America*, ed. Paula Fass and Mary Ann Mason (New York: NYU Press, 2000), 221.

3. Robert Bremner, ed., *Children and Youth in America*, vol. 1 (Cambridge: Harvard University Press, 1970), 316.

4. Ronald Walters, *The Antislavery Appeal: American Abolitionism after 1830* (Baltimore: Johns Hopkins University Press, 1976), 61.

5. Weld, *American Slavery*, 7; "An Appeal," *Anti-Slavery Examiner* 1 (September 1836): 13; "Selections: On the Duty of Promoting the Immediate and Complete Abolition of Slavery,"*Non-Slaveholder* 1 (February 1846): 27–28.

6. See Jean Fagan Yellin, *Women and Sisters: The Antislavery Feminists in American Culture* (New Haven: Yale University Press, 1989).

7. "Mother," *Non-Slaveholder* 1 (March 1846): 48. For a scholarly assessment contradicting slave owners' claims, see Richard H. Steckel, "A Dreadful Childhood: The Excess Mortality of American Slaves," *Social Science History* 10 (Winter 1986): 427–65.

8. Wilma King, *Stolen Childhood: Slave Youth in Nineteenth-Century America* (Bloomington: Indiana University Press, 1995); Harriet Beecher Stowe, *Uncle Tom's Cabin* (New York: Bantam Books, 1981), 364–65; Harriet Jacobs, *Incidents in the Life of a Slave Girl, Written by Herself* (Cambridge: Harvard University Press, 1987), 62; Louis J. Hall, "Birth in the Slave Hut," *Liberty Bell* (1849): 42–44.

9. Joan Hedrick, *Harriet Beecher Stowe: A Life* (New York: Oxford University Press, 1994), 191; Nina Baym, *Women's Fiction: A Guide to Novels by and about Women in America, 1820–1870* (Ithaca: Cornell University Press, 1978), 16.

10. Hedrick, *Harriet Beecher*, 193, 192; Pennington, "Slave Narrative," 221.

11. Stowe, *Uncle Tom's Cabin*, 260, 286.

12. Jane Elizabeth Jones, "A True Tale of the South," *Liberty Bell* (1847): 258–65; Marie Weston Chapman, "A Sonnet," *Liberty Bell* (1841): 99–100; "Testimony of Mr. John M. Nelson—A Native of Virginia," in Weld, *American Slavery*, 51; Walters, *Antislavery Appeal*, 97.

13. *Liberty Bell* (1841): 93–98.

14. *The Child's Anti-Slavery Book: Containing a Few Words about American Slave Children and Stories of Slave Life* (New York: Carlton and Porter, 1859), 9–10; Hedrick, *Harriet Beecher*, 191, 192–93. See Sarah Roth, "The Mind of the Child: Images of African Americans in Early Juvenile Fiction," *Journal of the Early Republic* 25 (2005): 79–109.

15. Matter of M'Dowles, 8 Johns (N.Y. 1811); *US. v. Bainbridge*, 1 Mason 71, 73 (U.S. C.C. Mass. 1816), Fed. Cas. no. 14,497; The Etna, 1 Ware 474, 476–77, 481 (U.S. C.C. Me. *1938)*; Grossberg, *Governing*, 260–64.

16. Hedrick, *Harriet Beecher*, 192. See also Elizabeth B. Clark, "Sacred Rights of the Weak: Pain and Sympathy in Antebellum America," *Journal of American History* 82 (September 1995): 463–93.

17. See *Anti-Slavery Reporter* (July 1834): 99–100; Marcus Wood, *Blind Memory: Visual Representations of Slavery in England and America* (Manchester: Manchester University Press, 2000), 181–83; Colman, "Little Lewis," 34; *Anti-Slavery Reporter* (July 1834): 100; Martineau, "A Child's Thought," 28; Colman, "Little Lewis," 35; Charlotte H. Coues, "An Appeal to Mothers," *Liberty Bell* (1845): 6–7..

18. Susan Wilson, "The Fugitives in Boston," *Liberty Bell* (1844): 207.

19. George Fitzhugh, *Cannibals All!* 235, and *Sociology for the South*, both *Ante-bellum Writing of George Fitzhugh and Hinton Rowan Helper on Slavery*, ed. Harvey Wish (New York: Capricorn Books, 1960), 92.

20. Stephanie McCurry, *Masters of Small Worlds: Yeoman Households, Gender Relations, and the Political Culture of the Antebellum South Carolina Low Country* (New York: Oxford University Press, 1995), 59; Peter Bardaglio, *Reconstructing the Household: Families, Sex, and the Law in the Nineteenth-Century South* (Chapel Hill: University of North Carolina Press, 1995).

21. Fitzhugh, *Sociology*, 90, 92.

22. Fitzhugh, *Cannibals*, 190, 244.

23. Ibid., 192, 235; Fitzhugh, *Sociology*, 91; Thomas Dew, "Dew on Slavery ," in *The Pro-Slavery Argument as Maintained by the Most Distinguished Writers of the Southern States Containing the Several Essays on the Subject by Chancellor Harper, Governor Hammond, Dr. Simms, and Professor Dew* (Charleston, SC: Walker, Richards and Co., 1852), 456-.

24. Fitzhugh, *Cannibals*, 1; Joseph Ingraham, "Planter and Slaves" (1835), in Adler, *The Negro*, 243; George McDuffie, "The Natural Slavery of the Negro," in ibid., 235; George Tucker's *Valley of Shenandoah*, quoted in William Taylor, *Cavalier and Yankee: The Old South and American National Character* (Cambridge: Harvard University Press, 1957), 303; William Grayson, "The Hireling and the Slave" (1854), reprinted in Adler, *The Negro*, 13.

25. See *Lawrence v. Speed*, 2 Bibb 401 (1811), reprinted in Bremner, *Children and Youth*, 1:332; John Demos, *A Little Commonwealth: Family Life in Plymouth Colony*, 2nd ed.(New York: Oxford University Press, 2000).

26. See Taylor, *Cavalier and Yankee*, 17, 304–11; Jeffrey Robert Young, *Domesticating Slavery: The Master Class in Georgia and South Carolina* (Chapel Hill: University of North Carolina Press, 1999).

27. Bernard Wishy, *The Child and the Republic: The Dawn of Modern American Child Nurture* (Philadelphia: University of Pennsylvania Press, 1967), 22, 43–48; Carl Degler, *At Odds: Women and the Family in America from the Revolution to the Present* (New York: Oxford University Press, 1981), 86. See also Richard Broadhead, "Sparing the Rod: Discipline and Fiction in Antebellum America," *Representations* 21 (Winter 1988): 67–96; Carl Kaestle, *Pillars of the Republic: Common Schools and American Society, 1780–1860* (New York: Hill and Wang, 1983), 67; *Abolition Intelligencer and Missionary Magazine* 1 (May 1822): 21; Stowe, *Uncle Tom's Cabin*, 245–46.

28. *Abolition Intelligencer and Missionary Magazine* 1 (May 1822); *Anti-Slavery Reporter* 1 (February 1834): 1.

2

"Train Up a Child in the Way He Should Go"

The Image of Idealized Childhood in the Slavery Debate, 1850–1870

ELIZABETH KUEBLER-WOLF

In the first half of the nineteenth century, the rise of sentimental domesticity and idealized childhood in American culture coincided with the intensification of sectional tensions over slavery. The effect of the slave system on children, in particular on white free children, had been a topic of interest to observers of the American slave system at least since Thomas Jefferson's famous lament about slavery's effect on master-class children in *Notes on the State of Virginia* (1781).[1] By the mid-nineteenth century notions of slavery were so entwined with ideas of family that discussions of one aspect of the national culture was often embedded in any discussion of the other. Most famously, *Uncle Tom's Cabin* deployed tropes of sentimental domesticity to argue that slavery effectively destroyed the cherished institution of family life and corrupted childhood's innocence.[2]

Novelized responses to *Uncle Tom's Cabin* used the same sentimental language to make exactly the opposite argument. Rather than destroying families, ruining children's innocence, and making them violent, the argument went, childhood familiarity between slaves and masters resulted in adult relationships governed not by violence but by mutual affection. As more than one postbellum white Southerner would claim, "Above all, there was a strong attachment between the master and the servant, the natural result of closest association from childhood, which made cruelty foreign to the very nature of the owner."[3] In these "competing rhetorics of home and family," childhood was central both as a rhetorical device and as a target of reform efforts.[4]

Antislavery forces typically depicted naturally innocent children who were irrevocably corrupted, damaged, and destroyed by slavery, while proslavery advocates represented childhood acculturation to slavery, for enslaved and free alike, as a necessary ingredient of a benevolent, hierarchical, organic plantation society.[5] In the years immediately surrounding the Civil War, images of childhood produced on both sides of this debate over slavery's effect on childhood reflect the influence of contemporary thought about childhood itself. In this essay I will consider three images that reflect the larger debate about slavery, in particular the alleged effects each side in the debate claimed that slavery had upon white children.

While none of these three images was in wide circulation, it is important to consider them as evidence in an ongoing investigation into the rhetorical importance of childhood in American culture, just as we might treat diary entries or private letters as evidence of wider social attitudes. Images, like other texts, are governed by conventions, conditioned by the surrounding culture in which they are produced, and reflect both directly and indirectly the concerns of their creators and their social contexts. By treating images of all sorts as a type of historical "text" that can be dissected for rhetorical and ideological content, this essay argues that childhood was an important battleground for interpreting and understanding the effects of slavery and race on society in America in the years just before and well after the Civil War.

David Claypoole Johnston (1799–1865), a prolific satiric cartoonist, weighed in on the antislavery side in 1863, when he produced a small watercolor titled *The Early Development of Southern Chivalry*. By this time, "Southern chivalry" was a term that could be understood to mean that the plantation system was an organic hierarchy that produced a tiered, family-like structure, akin to the grand manor houses of feudal England. Black dependents in this system may be enslaved, proslavery writers argued, but they were part of a structure that also produced caring, responsible, paternalistic masters.

For defenders of the system, it was a good thing for children to be raised as slave owners, to be familiar with and therefore affectionate toward their dependents, and to learn early the burdens and responsibilities of mastery.[6] Reverend C. K. Marshall addressed the Southern Convention at New Orleans in 1855 with a speech full of concern that Southern children were being ill served by having Northern teachers, Northern university educations, and Northern books to read. In Marshall's opinion, "it was not possible for Southerners to be safely educated at the North. They cannot come back with proper feelings towards their families and their people" but, instead, "return to us…poisoned by fanatical teachings and influences against the institution of slavery." In a further elaboration of this argument in a later issue, Marshall went on to call for a Southern publishing industry

Figure 2.1. David Claypoole Johnston, *The Early Development of Southern Chivalry*, American Antiquarian Society.

that would produce books fit for Southern children. The recently published novel *A Southern Home* won praise because

> its pictures of southern life truly paint the relation between the two races. The old servant loves the children of the old master, who, in their turn, protect and cherish as heir looms the dependent members of another and bygone age. Her sketches of the intercourse between the various personages of the family, white and black, exhibit the affection, and kindness, and sympathy which animate them. They are far more just and faithful than the hideous caricatures of Mrs. Stowe. We heartily commend it to southern parents.[7]

In children at play in the parlor, D. C. Johnston could not have chosen a more fitting scene, or more fitting characters, to critique explicitly the commonly deployed defense of slavery as benign owing to childhood acculturation.

In Johnston's caustic image of childhood play in the Southern parlor, a young white boy raises a cat-o'-nine-tails in the act of striking the bare back of a black female doll that is tied to a chair. By placing not just a whip but a cat-o'-nine-tails in the hands of the young brute, Johnston has increased the violence of the picture, as this instrument of the naval punishment known as flogging was the subject of public outcry throughout the 1840s and had just been outlawed by Congress in 1850.[8] At the boy's side, his smiling sister watches and grips by the hair a black male doll, stripped to the waist like its female counterpart. On the floor below the doll being whipped sits a chamber pot, positioned to catch the pretend flow of blood and bodily fluids, suggesting the shocking degree to which this make-believe play is based upon real-world observations of slave whippings. Indeed, with the boy whipping a stripped female and the girl preparing to whip a stripped male, the image cannot suggest any more powerfully the extent to which the institution of slavery befouls and perverts the parlor, the hallowed chamber of nineteenth-century sentimental domesticity.

Childhood exposure to the slave system, in Johnston's reckoning, had turned the children into vicious tyrants even in their most playful moments. Charles Dickens articulated the same belief in his *American Notes*, where he described a Southern mother "who smiles her acquiescence . . . as she reads the paper in her cool piazza, [and] quiets her youngest child who clings about her skirts, by promising the boy 'a whip to beat the little niggers [*sic*] with.'" Dickens himself was giving voice to a complaint that antislavery writers had long made. The Manumission Society of North Carolina warned in 1830 that "the children of . . . parents who own slaves, and think, or seem to think it not amiss to storm and drive, with all the hurry and fury of which they are capable, learn to act in a similar manner," an admonition that echoed antislavery writers at least as far back as the eighteenth-century Quaker John Woolman.[9]

Whipping itself was a powerful visual motif in the antislavery movement, with which Johnston was familiar as a resident of Boston and the designer of the first masthead for the abolitionist paper the *Liberator*. Tales of the whip appeared frequently in stories and pictures published in the *Slave's Friend* and other abolitionist literature, often in autobiographical accounts of ex-slaves. An 1840 narrative of an escaped slave, published in the *Liberator*, informed its readers:

> I played with my master's children, and we loved one another like brothers. This is often the case in childhood, but when the young masters and misses get older . . . the love of power is cultivated in their hearts by their parents, the whip is put into their hands, and they soon regard the negro in no other light than as a slave.[10]

Johnston's image of young children engaging in "Southern chivalry" is consonant with such criticisms of the slave system. Whipping appeared frequently in abolitionist discussions of the slave system, as the most potent symbol of the morally disastrous effects of being raised a slave owner. An ex-slave in 1862 explained that his mistress's daughters were raised not only watching their mother whip slaves for her own amusement but also whipping slaves themselves. Citing an often-quoted proverb about children, he remarked, "Thus she brought up her children in the way they should not go, and in consequence, when they were old they did not depart from it."[11]

It is in light of these common criticisms of the slave system's degrading and corrupting effect on young master-class children that images of white and black Southern children together should be considered. Though the number of these images still extant are unknown, the genre of white and black "playmate" and nursemaid photographs is a culturally significant product of late antebellum and postbellum visual culture.[12] They are embedded in, conditioned by, and respond to a larger national conversation about childhood and slavery that was ongoing in the years surrounding the Civil War. Two examples will represent the genre: an 1858 photograph from Missouri of the young H. E. Hayward on the lap of his slave nurse, Louisa, and an 1867 image of Magby Peterson from Florida. These photographs, although created for private reasons and certainly not in direct response to Johnston's cartoon, for which there is no record of publication, nevertheless offer a visual rebuff to the vision of childhood innocence corrupted by slavery, race, and unequal power relations so often repeated in abolitionist materials and codified in Johnston's image. In essence these photographs give a version of the argument of a Southern wartime polemicist, who claimed "how impossible it was, under . . . circumstances of habitual life-association, for the same feeling of repulsion toward the degraded race to exist here, which prevails and is fashionable in the Northern States."[13]

Such defenses of slavery and of postwar relationships that resembled slavery partook of the same language of sentimental domesticity that the Northern middle class used to reimagine parental discipline of children. As Richard Broadhead has noted, in the antebellum decades in Northern middle-class culture, discipline was transformed from a physical act— whipping—to a relational act of love and dependence. Rather than beating or threatening to beat a child, middle-class culture introduced the idea of "disciplinary intimacy, or simply discipline through love." Brodhead demonstrates how this notion pervaded the culture of childhood, in particular in advice books aimed at parents as well as in juvenile literature.[14]

In relationships of "disciplinary intimacy" both parties are governed by internal constraints of affection rather than by an externally imposed set of rules and punishment. Children wish to do right in order to please their parents, whom they love, while parents' gentle, loving guidance replaces threats, beatings, and physical coercion. In proslavery thought, the notion of disciplinary intimacy extended well beyond the immediate family and actual children, to include all those people who made up "the family, white and black," on the plantation.[15] One postbellum writer

Figure 2.2. H. E. Hayward and nurse, Missouri Historical Society.

Figure 2.3. Magby Peterson and nurse, Florida State Archives.

described the effect of his own childhood familiarity with slaves, which resulted "in those close bonds of confidence and interest, [in which] the old master and the old mistress were indeed the veriest [sic] slaves on the estate," and whose oversight of their slaves took on a paternal and familial, affectionate nature.[16]

Photographs like that of H. E. Hayward sitting on the lap of his caretaker Louisa, then, are not simple visual records of two individuals. Photographic portrait compositions of the middle nineteenth century were not spontaneous snapshots; technological limitations mandated that poses were carefully coordinated and could be held for several minutes. Certainly, technological necessity made it expedient to place a child on the lap of an adult who could keep the child relatively still. The physical proximity and closeness of nurse and child, though in part manufactured, is not only a product of necessity; after all, the child could just as easily been placed on the lap of his mother for this photograph. Rather, Hayward's portrait offers, however obliquely, a visual counterargument to antislavery's conviction that slavery warped white children, who would grow up to be callous and cruel adult slave owners or, worse, begin their tyranny as infants. After all, the image of young children brutally whipping others and exercising tyrannical cruelties was disturbing not only to abolitionist sympathizers but also to Southerners who had adopted middle-class sensibilities about childhood and family.

Nestled back into the bosom of his young nurse, the infant Hayward is embraced and contained. Louisa's chin rests on the baby's head, helping to keep him still but also suggesting a degree of familiarity and ease. Little H. E. Hayward in turn grasps two of Louisa's fingers in a gesture, familiar to parents everywhere, of the casually intimate connection between a child and his or her caretaker. Such a photograph offers a visual counterargument to the common antislavery complaint, voiced powerfully by one ex-slave, that "I have seen a child, before he could talk a word, have a stick put into his hand, and he was permitted to whip a slave, in order to quiet him. And from the time they are born till they die, they live by whipping and abusing the slave."[17]

Hayward and his nurse appear frozen in time in a photograph that could be read as presenting the proslavery vision of children learning early to love their slaves. White postbellum memoirists were particularly adamant about the positive qualities of their childhood experiences of slavery, insisting that their memories demonstrated that the Old South had been much misunderstood. As the Reverend Robert Q. Mallard, born in 1830, explained in a memoir published in 1892, "As a babe, I drew a part at least of my nourishment from the generous breasts of a colored foster mother, and she and her infant son always held a peculiar place in my regards."[18]

In the photograph of Magby Peterson taken just a couple of years after the end of the Civil War, the white child also leans back into his nurse.[19] While this photograph dates to the years immediately after the conflict, its rhetorical significance on the issue of race, childhood, and even slavery (though no longer a legal reality) should not be dismissed. After all, the young nurse was in all likelihood born into slavery, though no longer technically a slave. Indeed, while the war had in principle ended slavery, the social systems and racial stratifications inherited from the slave system did not end with the war. Such images of children with their nurses would persist well into the twentieth century and continued to function to obscure the power dynamics of race relations by casting them as familial, as Laura Wexler has eloquently described in *Tender Violence*.[20]

The baby is front and center, and his nurse is relatively marginalized; no one can be confused about who is the portrait's intended subject. Following a long-standing convention for child portraits, the baby is wearing only one shoe (the other is in his nurse's hand), signifying his youth and innocence.[21] Though their poses are governed by both convention and technology, contact between the children can be read as explicitly emotionally inflected. The two children are cheek to cheek in a pose suggestive of psychological as well as physical closeness.

In the little universe of this photograph, which of course captures only a constructed moment of time, the social order is imagined as hierarchical and, because of that hierarchy, benevolent. The very fact that the parents of this white child chose to include his black companion in a studio photograph is significant. It is a sort of utterance, through visual rather than textual cues, that says in the words of a wartime proslavery writer, "The Slave [sic] children and their young masters and mistresses, are all raised up together. They suck together, play together . . . and every other kind of amusement that is calculated to bolt their hearts together when grown up."[22] Again, although Magby Peterson was born immediately after the war, his slightly older nurse would have been born a slave, and Peterson would have been raised in a household whose break from the social and racial conventions of prewar society could hardly have been significant.

To proslavery writers, sentimental childhood friendships precluded white children from whipping black ones and even allowed for enslaved children to do the whipping of their masters. In one proslavery polemic of 1860, the narrator describes his relationship with his slave called Buck:

> He is slightly older than myself, but was my playmate in childhood; when he was almost indispensable to my happiness—though he occasionally administered a threshing to me. On one of these occasions I informed my father of it. He inquired into the circumstances, found that I had been to blame in the quarrel, and decided, that it was wrong in Buck to strike me, and he must not do it again; but that I had deserved all that I had got.[23]

The incident recounted here by a proslavery writer is intended to refute—and indeed reverse—the violent role of whipping in the socialization of master and slave children posited by abolitionist thinkers and illustrated in Johnston's *Early Development of Southern Chivalry*. It is this imagined close, intimate friendship that is at the heart of images like those of H. E. Hayward and Magby Peterson. These images respond to and reflect the contemporary interest about childhood, racial hierarchy, and slavery.

As seen in these images, childhood was a potent rhetorical device for slavery and antislavery arguments, arguments that continued well after the end of the Civil War and slavery itself. Visual representations like Johnston's cartoon and the photographic portraits of children like Hayward and Peterson were intended for grown-up audiences. The negative or positive effect of the racially stratified system begun under slavery is the point of these images; they are not didactic tools meant to create a change in children's behavior or beliefs but to persuade adults about the nature of the slave (and later racial) system of ordering society. At the same time as these images were created for adult audiences, however, children themselves also became targets of reform and education efforts by both proslavery and antislavery forces. In these efforts affection and discipline, love and cruelty—the subjects at the heart of the pictorial rhetoric considered here—were constant refrains.

Famously, the American Anti-Slavery Society published the *Slave's Friend*, a juvenile magazine, for a brief time in the 1830s. In the *Slave's Friend*, images of slaves being whipped appear in conjunction with texts imploring small readers to "remember them that are in bonds" and to donate money to the American Anti-Slavery Society.[24] The *Anti-Slavery Alphabet* of 1847 featured whip-related entries such as, "L is the Lash, that brutally / He swung around its [a slave baby's] head, / Threatening that 'if it cried again, He'd whip it till 'twas dead,'" and "W is the Whipping post, / To which the slave is bound, / While on his naked back, the lash/Makes many a bleeding wound."[25]

Savage whipping figures continued to appear in literature aimed at the juvenile audience after the publication of *Uncle Tom's Cabin*. In fact, Hammat Billing's illustration of Simon Legree beating Uncle Tom, which appeared in the first edition of *Uncle Tom's Cabin*, was later reused in *The Child's Anti-Slavery Book*, although the image was relabeled as a generic scene of "Whipping a Slave."[26] Through repeated representations of the suffering slave in text and image, antislavery literature called for children to empathize with the slave and to become antislavery activists themselves. In this way the whip became a doubly coercive device. In the pictured world of the "poor slave" the whip literally coerced work and compliance from the slave, and in the affective world of the child reader, the whip's effects would ideally produce little abolitionists.[27]

In this battle over hearts and minds, defenders of slavery turned the abolitionist argument that slavery exposed children to mind-warping cruelty back on itself. They argued that abolitionists were guilty of exposing youngsters to more horrors than any slave owner. While Southerners were personally acquainted with slaves, and believed that the affectionate bonds that developed between the races during childhood ameliorated the slave's condition, abolitionists

> frightful pictures to the children show'd,
> of monsters holding lashes in their hands,
> Of darkies tied or chain'd to whipping-posts,
> Till infant tears were trickling down their cheeks;
> And pictures on the mind engraved for life.[28]

Slavery's advocates argued that the practice of telling youngsters about slavery's worst excesses was far more damaging and distorting than growing up as a slave master in a relationship of mutual affection, or, in Brodhead's term, disciplinary intimacy, which would constrain an adult master from violence. Defensive Southerners often seized upon *Uncle Tom's Cabin* as the most egregious of antislavery literature to which children were exposed, warping its smaller readers in a variety of ways, and argued that Northern youngsters enthralled by the glamour of violent tales of slavery would grow up to be obsessed with and titillated by vicarious violence.

In her 1890s memoir, children's author Frances Hodgson Burnett gave evidence that *Uncle Tom's Cabin* inspired children to the kind of vicious, violent play that Johnston and others accused Southern chivalry of producing. Like many children of her era, Burnett read *Uncle Tom's Cabin* in the mid-1850s. One day, Burnett's mother found the little girl "apparently furious with insensate rage, muttering to herself as she brutally lashed, with one of her brother's toy whips, a cheerfully hideous black gutta-percha doll who was tied to the candelabra stand and appeared to be enjoying the situation."[29]

It is important to note that, although the scene Burnett describes matches quite closely the scene in Johnston's abolitionist drawing, the inspiration for Burnett's childish frenzy of whipping-play was actually abolitionist literature. In the illustration to this scene, the playing girl strikes the same posture as the boy in Johnston's cartoon. While Burnett is not typically considered a proslavery writer, and she recounted this tale simply as an amusing anecdote about her childhood imagination and ability to enter a realm where "*anything* can be pretended," this account of her childhood reaction to *Uncle Tom's Cabin* matches up surprising well with proslavery criticisms of Beecher's novel and other abolitionist literature as spectacles of violence that inspired just the sort of play violence that abolitionists accused slavery of producing.[30]

In the years leading up to the Civil War, Southern writers such as Rev. C. K. Marshall worried that there were not enough positive images of the slave system in the typical textbooks produced for teaching children geography and other subjects. During the Civil War, a response to the call for Southern schoolbooks came in the form of geography and spelling books published in the South, as well as revision of the school curriculum to support the Confederate cause.[31] Many texts contained passages aimed specifically at socializing young white Southerners with a vision of slavery as disciplinary intimacy. In *The First Dixie Reader; Designed to Follow the Dixie Primer*, white Southern children could learn to read by parsing short paragraphs like the following, titled "Our Babe":

1. We have a new babe at our house. It is a sweet babe. We call him Tom-my.
2. Bob is his nurse. Bob loves Tom-my. He says he may ride in his wag-on.
3. Tom-my will soon learn to love Bob, and then what fun they will have![32]

The young (white) readers of this book, then, would be conditioned not only to reading but also to thinking of themselves and their relationships with slaves in a particular way. Whether this sort of socialization would have much real effect on ameliorating a slave-owning child's behavior is moot; what is certain is that this rhetoric of love and affection fostered through childhood association was a common refrain of proslavery writers into the war years and continued to shape white Southerners' interpretations of their own experience well after the end of the war.

For decades after the end of the Civil War and slavery, white Southerners would continue to publish "correctives" to the picture painted in the public imagination by *Uncle Tom's Cabin*. J. Motte Alston, son of a distinguished South Carolina family, would exemplify this memory of white childhood under slavery in his postwar autobiography. He described coming home from boarding school to find that "even the old servants among whom I had lived from infancy were profuse in their manifestations of love, and I too well remember how my heart beat in love for them." Alston was an adult by the time slavery ended, but his claim of mutual affection between black and white plantation dwellers was a common refrain after the end of slavery.[33]

White memoirists of the generation who had been children when slavery ended were particularly adamant about the positive qualities of their childhood experiences of slavery. Thomas Nelson Page, born in 1852 and eleven years old when slavery ended, was the child of a prominent Virginia family who grew up to write several novels and memoirs about life on the antebellum plantation. Page's *Social Life in Old Virginia before the War* celebrated the plantation yard, where "there were the busy children playing in groups, the boys of the family mingling with the little darkies as freely as any other young animals [sic], and forming the associations which tempered slavery and made the relation one not to be understood save by those who saw it."[34]

Page was only slightly older than Magby Peterson and H. E. Hayward, who were children when recorded in the photographs considered here. Like them, he grew up in an era in which children were a special focus of proslavery adult efforts to justify and shape the image of slavery as an institution based upon reciprocal affection. His memory, like those of other young Southerners of the late antebellum years, was likely colored by the lessons that were taught to young Southern minds in those years. Even after the war,

Southerners continued to emphasize the benefits of socializing black and white children. In 1866, a year before Peterson's photo was taken, a writer in *Debow's Review,* published in New Orleans, hoped that

> our former system may be replaced by one such as that which exists in England, where the playmate of childhood becomes the confidential agent of later years, resides at the old homestead, and dying leaves his children's children in the service of his original employer, and attached to their native spot by all the sweet and gentle associations of home, kindred and friends.[35]

The proliferation of photographs of white Southern children with their black caretakers in the years surrounding the Civil War owed its existence partly to the increasing availability of photographic technology. However, the choice to include a black child or nursemaid with the white portrait subject was not solely a pragmatic one, to hold the white child still long enough to properly expose a photographic plate. As sectional tension over slavery increased, childhood became a prime cultural site for the battle over the meaning of slavery. Photographs of white children on the laps of their nurses were part of the general antebellum trend in the South to understand, explain, and defend slavery and racial hierarchy. Because children were believed to be in a state in which morality or depravity could be inscribed, both proslavery and antislavery forces made arguments in visual as well as textual form that slavery had potent effects upon the young.

In the postbellum years, as Americans began to grapple with the legacy of slavery, white reminiscences of childhood days in the South became a popular genre. Stories of the Sunny South appealed to Americans in both sections as a healing balm for the nation's wounds. Memories of cherished "mammies" and childhood "playmates" populate the genre of postbellum white Southern memoirs at the same time that Americans began "binding the nation's wounds" with commemorations of the Civil War that glossed over the original causes of sectional conflict.[36]

The Documenting the American South collection at the University of North Carolina houses a large number of memoirs published by Southerners from the 1890s onward, all of which claim to be "correctives" to *Uncle Tom's Cabin.* While Stowe's novel continued to be an extraordinarily popular text, not only as a novel but as a stage play and in popular songs, vaudeville shows, and movies, Southerners penned an impressive number of memoirs meant to "correct" what they felt was an unfair picture of life under slavery. The postbellum memoirs of whites who had been children when slavery was ended as a legal system have yet to be studied in much depth, although they provide a wealth of information about how white Southerners continued to frame the childhood experience of slavery—both for themselves and for black "playmates"—into the twentieth century.[37]

Images such as the portraits of Magby Peterson and H. E. Hayward, or D. C. Johnston's fictional children playing a hideous parlor game, should be considered as an important reflection of both proslavery and antislavery rhetoric before the war, and the ways in which slavery was understood well after the war had ended. None of these images can be accepted at face value as presenting a lived truth; rather, they are all corollaries to the rhetoric of childhood, race, and slavery deployed by adults, for adults, in the years surrounding and after the Civil War.

NOTES

1. Thomas Jefferson, *Notes on the State of Virginia*, 288, e-text from University of Virginia, http://etext.lib.virginia.edu/toc/modeng/public/JefVirg.html (accessed May 21, 2004). There is evidence that enslaved parents worried a great deal both about the effect of slavery on their children and their ability to parent their own children, as well. See Marie Jenkins Schwartz, *Born in Bondage: Growing Up Enslaved in the Antebellum South* (Cambridge: Harvard University Press, 2000), and Wilma King, *Stolen Childhood: Slave Youth in Nineteenth-Century America* (Bloomington: Indiana University Press, 1995).

2. For the complex relationship between the sentimental, domestic, and political in *Uncle Tom's Cabin*, see Jane Tompkins, "Sentimental Power: Uncle Tom's Cabin and the Politics of Literary History," in *Ideology and Classic American Literature*, ed. Sacvan Bercovitch and Myra Jehlen (New York: Cambridge University Press, 1986), 267–92; Amy Kaplan, "Manifest Domesticity" *American Literature* 70 (September 1998): 581–606; JoAnn Morgan, *Uncle Tom's Cabin as Visual Culture* (Columbia: University of Missouri Press, 2007); a variety of primary sources available at the wonderful *Uncle Tom's Cabin & American Culture: A Multimedia Archive*, directed by Stephen Railton at the University of Virginia (http://utc.iath.virginia.edu/), as well as Rebecca de Schweinitz's essay "'Waked Up to Feel': Defining Childhood, Debating Slavery in Antebellum America" in this volume.

3. Robert Q. Mallard, *Plantation Life before Emancipation* (Richmond, VA: Whittet and Shepperson, 1892), 45, electronic edition, Documenting the American South, University of North Carolina.

4. Gale L. Kenney, "Mastering Childhood: Paternalism, Slavery, and the Southern Domestic in Caroline Howard Gilman's Antebellum Children's Literature," *Southern Quarterly* 44 (October 2006): 40. For historical overviews of proslavery thought, see Jeffrey Young, *Proslavery and Sectional Thought in the Early South, 1740–1829* (Columbia: University of South Carolina Press, 2006), and Paul Finkelman, *Defending Slavery: Proslavery Thought in the Old South: A Brief History with Documents* (New York: Bedford St. Martin's, 2003); the older and still controversial Larry Tise, *Proslavery: A History of the Defense of Slavery in America, 1701–1840* (Athens: University of Georgia Press, 1987), is also very useful in this regard.

5. A sampling of essays and books that examine the debate about the effects of slavery on children and family relationships that have been important for this essay include Lesley Ginsberg, "Of Babies, Beasts, and Bondage: Slavery and the Question of Citizenship in Antebellum American Children's Literature," in *The American Child: A Cultural Studies Reader*, ed. J. S. Levander (New Brunswick, NJ: Rutgers University Press, 2003); David Roper, "Innocence Betrayed: Black and White Children on Antebellum Plantations," *Plantation Society in the Americas* 6 (1): 1–40; King, *Stolen Childhood*; Shirley Samuels, "The Identity of Slavery," in *The Culture of Sentiment: Race, Gender and Sentimentality in 19th Century America*, ed. Shirley Samuels (New York: Oxford University Press, 1992), 163–64; and Brenda Stevenson, *Life in Black and White: Family and Community in the Slave South* (New York: Oxford University Press, 1997), as well as bk. 1, pt. 2, "…and the Children Brought Up," in Eugene Genovese's *Roll, Jordan, Roll: The World the Slaves Made* (New York: Vintage, 1976), 113–58.

6. See note 4 for bibliography on proslavery.

7. Rev. C. K. Marshall, "Home Education at the South," *Debow's Review, Agricultural, Commercial, Industrial Progress and Resources* 18 (March 1855): 430–32; Rev. C. K. Marshall, "Home Education at the South," *Debow's Review, Agricultural, Commercial, Industrial Progress and Resources* 18 (May 1855): 655–68, quotation on p. 668. The review is of A Virginian [Clarissa Carr Woodson?], *A Southern Home* (Richmond, VA: A. Morris, 1855).

8. Myra C. Glenn, "The Naval Reform Campaign against Flogging: A Case Study in Changing Attitudes toward Corporal Punishment, 1830-1850," *American Quarterly* 35 (Autumn 1983): 408–25. See also the detailed meditation on slavery and whipping in visual culture in Marcus Wood, *Blind Memory: Visual Representations of Slavery in England and America, 1780–1865* (New York: Routledge, 2000), especially the chapter "Representing Pain and Describing Torture: Slavery, Punishment and Martyrology," 215–91.

9. Charles Dickens, *American Notes for General Circulation* (London: Chapman and Hall, 1850), 161–62; Manumission Society of North Carolina, *An Address to the People of North Carolina, on the Evils of Slavery: By the Friends of Liberty and Equality* (Greensboro, NC: William Swaim, 1830); John Woolman, *The Journal of John Woolman* (New York: Houghton Mifflin, 1909), 209–17.

10. James Curry, "Narrative of James A. Curry, Fugitive Slave," *Liberator*, January 10, 1840.

11. John Andrew Jackson, *The Experience of a Slave in South Carolina* (London: Passmore and Alabaster, 1862), 20.

12. Laura Wexler has discussed the extension of the nursemaid photograph and the racial dynamics of posing white children with black nursemaids, slave or free, and well into the twentieth century. See especially "Seeing Sentiment: Photography, Race, and the Innocent Eye," in *Tender Violence: Domestic Visions in an Age of U.S. Imperialism* (Chapel Hill: University of North Carolina Press, 2000), 53–93. In particular, see her discussion of George Cook's 1865 photograph of his own son with a black nursemaid who was technically free (pp. 61–74).

13. T. W. McMahon, *Cause and Contrast: An Essay on the American Crisis* (Richmond, VA: West and Johnston, 1862), 79.

14. Richard Broadhead, "Sparing the Rod: Discipline and Fiction in Antebellum America," *Representations* 21 (Winter 1988): 70. Laura Wexler has also written eloquently about this issue in *Tender Violence*, and Genovese has much to say on the subject in *Roll, Jordan, Roll*.

15. Rev. C. K. Marshall, "Home Education at the South," *Debow's Review* 18 (May 1855): 668–69. Though I am using a quotation from Marshall here, the refrain "our family, white and black" is a common trope throughout a great deal of Southern writing.

16. James Battle Avirett, *The Old Plantation: How We Lived in Great House and Cabin before the War* (New York: F. Tennyson Neely, 1901), 118, electronic edition, Documenting the American South, University of North Carolina.

17. Lewis Garrard Clarke, *Narrative of the Sufferings of Lewis Clarke, during a Captivity of More Than Twenty-Five Years, among the Algerines of Kentucky, One of the So Called Christian States of America. Dictated by Himself* (Boston: David H. Ela, 1845), 123.

18. Robert Q. Mallard, *Plantation Life before Emancipation* (Richmond, VA: Whittet and Shepperson, 1892), 9, electronic edition, Documenting the America South, University of North Carolina. In the preface Mallard explains, "The purpose of the author has been to portray a civilization now obsolete, to picture the relations of mutual attachment and kindness which in the main bound together master and servant, and to give this and future generations some correct idea of the noble work done by Southern masters and mistresses of all denominations for the salvation of the slave" (p. vi).

19. In the 1870 census, Magby Peterson is listed as a four-year-old-male. His father, Robert, was a livery stable keeper with real estate worth $5,000 and a personal estate of $300. If Peterson's birth year is 1866, this photograph was probably made in 1867.

20. Wexler, *Tender Violence*. See also Jennifer Ritterhouse, *Growing Up Jim Crow: How Black and White Southern Children Learned Race* (Chapel Hill: University of North Carolina Press, 2006); Grace Elizabeth Hale, *Making Whiteness: The Culture of Segregation in the South, 1890–1940* (Vintage, 1999), in particular the chapter "Remembering My Old Mammy," pp. 98–104..

21. Anita Schorsch, *Images of Childhood: An Illustrated Social History* (New York: Mayflower Books, 1979), contains several painted examples of this convention. See *The Torn Gazette*, unknown artist, n.d., fig. 103, and *Innocence*, ca. 1830, plate XX. In addition, Schorsch notes that a popular nursery rhyme repeats the theme: "Diddle diddle dumpling/my son John. / He went to bed with his socks on. / One shoe off and one shoe on. / Diddle diddle dumpling/my son John!"

22. Harrison Berry, *Slavery and Abolitionism, as Viewed by a Georgia Slave* (Atlanta: M. Lynch and Co., 1861), 22, electronic edition, Documenting the American South, University of North Carolina.

23. Ebenezar Starnes, *The Slaveholder Abroad; or, Buck's Visit, with His Master, to England: A Series of Letters from Dr. Pleasant Jones to Major Joseph Jones, of Georgia* (Philadelphia: Lippincott, 1860), electronic edition, Documenting the American South, University of North Carolina.

24. For example, a whipping scene appears as the preface to a story called "The Collection Box," in *Slave's Friend* 1 (1836): 1, reproduced online at http://www.merrycoz.org/slave/slave01/SLAVE01.HTM (accessed April 18, 2011). See also "The Cart-Whip," *Slave's Friend* 2 (1837): 9, reproduced online at http://digitalgallery.nypl.org/nypldigital/id?413070 (accessed April 18, 2011)

25. Anonymous, *The Anti-Slavery Alphabet Printed for the Anti-Slavery Fair* (Philadelphia: Merrihew and Thompson, 1847).

26. *The Child's Anti-Slavery Book: Containing a Few Words about American Slave Children and Stories of Slave Life* (New York: Carlton and Porter, 1859), 62. For a thorough discussion of these images, see Jo Ann Morgan, *Uncle Tom's Cabin as Visual Culture* (Columbia: University of Missouri Press, 2007); also Wood, *Blind Memory*, which devotes a chapter to images from *Uncle Tom's Cabin*.

27. Samuels, "The Identity of Slavery," 163–64.

28. Lacon, *The Devil in America: Spirit-Rapping—Mormonism; Woman's Rights Conventions and Speeches; Abolitionism; Harper's Ferry Raid and Black Republicanism; Defeat of Satan, and Final Triumph of the Gospel* (Mobile, AL: J. K. Randall, 1867), 139.

29. Frances Hodgson Burnett, *The One I Knew the Best of All: A Memory of the Mind of a Child* (New York: Scribner's, 1893), 55–56. A cursory visit to Stephen Railton's web archive "Uncle Tom's Cabin and American Culture" yields a bounty of contemporary Southern critical reviews that hone in on the corrupting nature of Stowe's novel upon children's imaginations.

30. Burnett, *The One I Knew the Best of All*, 59.

31. Elizabeth Joan Doyle, "Nurseries of Treason: Schools in Occupied New Orleans," *Journal of Southern History* 26 (May 1960): 161–79; O. L. Davis and Serena Rankin Parks, "Confederate School Geographies, I: Marinda Branson Moore's Dixie Geography," *Peabody Journal of Education* 40 (March 1963): 265–74.

32. Marinda Branson Moore, *The First Dixie Reader; Designed to Follow the Dixie Primer* (Raleigh, NC: Branson, Farrar and Co., 1863). The presumptive audience for Branson's work was white; it is reasonable to assume that Bob would have been a slightly older black child put in charge of Tommy. See both Schwartz, *Born into Bondage*, and King, *Stolen Childhood*, for discussion of the experience of black children being given to even younger white children as special nursemaids, companions, and caretakers.

33. J. Motte Alston, *Rice Planter and Sportsman: The Recollections of J. Motte Alston, 1821–1909*, ed. Arney R. Childs (Columbia: University of South Carolina Press, 1953).

34. Thomas Nelson Page, *Social Life in Old Virginia before the War* (Cambridge, MA: Charles Scribner's Sons, 1897), electronic edition, Documenting the American South, University of North Carolina.

35. L. Reynolds, "The South: Its Duty and Destiny," *Debow's Review* 1 (January 1866): 71–75.

36. David W. Blight, *Race and Reunion: The Civil War in American Memory* (Cambridge: Harvard University Press, 2002).

37. The postbellum Southern memoir is a seriously understudied genre in American literature. A number of these memoirs are now available online at the website "Documenting the American South" (http://docsouth.unc.edu/index.html) (several of them have been cited in this essay) and invite further investigation and examination by scholars. For some of the context in which such memoirs became popular, see Hale, *Making Whiteness*; M. M. Manring, *Slave in a Box: The Strange Career of Aunt Jemima* (Charlottesville: University of Virginia Press, 1998); and Rittenhouse, *Growing Up Jim Crow*.

3

"What Is a Person Worth at Such a Time"

New England College Students, Sectionalism, and Secession

KANISORN WONGSRICHANALAI

Amherst College was ablaze with excitement in the spring of 1861. Confederate forces had fired upon Fort Sumter in Charleston Harbor on April 12, and one week later, a pro-secession crowd in Baltimore had attacked Massachusetts troops on their way to Washington. With these events in mind, an eighteen-year-old student named Christopher Pennell told his father, "If excitement, and war feeling was high in all the rural districts, be sure it was higher still, if possible, at College." Books had been "laid aside, amusements neglected; scarcely anything has been doing, except the discussion of the events of the day, in private rooms, at the dinner-table & in impassioned knobs [*sic*] at the news-office & upon the College campus." At prayers one morning, Amherst's president, William A. Stearns, asked "for the success of the cause of the North" and was greeted with "deafening cheers from professor & student."[1]

When an Amherst professor hastily organized a company of volunteers, Christopher Pennell asked for his father's permission to go, writing that the men who joined were those "of the most talent, the soundest minds, *the men*, in short, of College." Washington was "surrounded by traitors. Lincoln's 75,000 is replied to by 100,000 from Jeff. Davis. Privateers are fitted out to harass our commerce. Our forts are shelled, our navy yards seized, & worse than all, our men have already fallen, while marching to defend the capital." Pennell asked, "What is a person worth at such a time, if he do not strain every nerve to uphold the stars & stripes[?]" Volunteering was a "sacred duty" because to "yield to the South" would be to allow "the blackness of the dark ages" to "overspread the whole land." "Life is all I have to offer," Pennell declared in the postscript. "I feel that I am ready."[2]

New England youth like Pennell who attended college between 1850 and 1865 saw the narrative of American history in sectional, northern-centric terms. Despite their varied political opinions and party loyalties, they believed in an American future without slavery. Although some scholars have studied the ideas, experiences, and challenges of southern undergraduates during this time, no corresponding work has been done on New Englanders who were just as engaged with national issues and, when the war came, also volunteered in large numbers. Understanding how New England's young leaders conceived of their nation prior to the conflict helps to establish why they thought it was worth preserving.

Drawing on the antebellum and wartime writings—including compositions, diaries, editorials, and letters—of more than twenty students from four New England schools (Amherst, Bowdoin, Dartmouth, and Harvard), this essay examines the relationship between the righteousness of the values demonstrated in the history of the North (or, more specifically, New England) and the students' responses to the sectional conflict. Their section's history, they believed, provided the true narrative for the nation's past. They also demonstrated their interest in national debates by participating in political campaigns throughout the period. In many cases, the social and intellectual environment that pervaded New England colleges before and during the conflict continued to influence them after they graduated and went on to their professional positions in northern society.

As news of the fall of Fort Sumter broke across the North, hundreds of college students and graduates on campuses across New England volunteered to suppress the rebellion. Their engagement with the issues, however, was not merely a result of the war's outbreak. Political campaigns had sparked action on New England college campuses throughout the 1850s. Although not all students' beliefs about sectionalism and the South translated into sustained action during the antebellum period—after all, they had their own careers to consider—the wartime service of many of these young men demonstrated their commitment to northern ideology and principles. Additionally, the expression of their beliefs was not limited to participation in openly political events. College compositions and orations likewise became a venue for students to express their opinions on the issues of the day. Papers about slavery and sectionalism tended to appear at times of increased national interest to those topics. These college essays reflected a northern, New England–centric conception of progress, in which slavery would die out and the entire nation would develop similarly to the industrializing North. On a more personal level, these young men understood that their future success was dependent on the Union's survival. As the future political and business leaders of the nation, they believed in safeguarding their inheritance (the United States) and securing their positions within it. Ironically, the New England students themselves displayed regional biases in their views even as they derided southern slaveholders' defense of slavery as a sectional interest.

The sectionalist worldview of these New England students had been purposefully established by their parents' generation in order to combat the loss of northern political influence. After the War of 1812, Massachusetts's political leaders, who had once led the nation, struggled to maintain their power. Falling from political leadership and hoping to guarantee that their beliefs and values would remain dominant, they attempted to bolster their region's cultural dominance and disseminate a New England–centric version of American history. Their ideas were sectional in nature even if they claimed to espouse nationalistic views.[3]

By the 1850s, this New England–centric narrative had taken root in the region's intellectual societies. Many of the students who came of age during this period never recognized their own biases. They simply accepted the narrative as fact and portrayed, in their writings, New England as the most righteous section of the United States. To these undergraduates, the New England version of American history was the most authentic.

The young men who attended college at this time viewed their experience as a rehearsal for their adult leadership of the nation. This was consistent with the ideas of the Founding Fathers, who believed that an educated citizenry was vital to the maintenance of liberty and republicanism. Sunday schools, first established in the 1790s under the belief that a person's habits and character were formed in childhood, tried to train youth to resist corruption and temptation. The first public schools, established in the 1830s, also attempted to impart good habits like punctuality and basic skills such as literacy. After public education, most youth had no choice but to work in the adult world. Some of those with enough money, however, opted to extend their education at college.[4]

Those fortunate enough to go to college were taught that they had a greater responsibility to act like good citizens because they would become the economic and political leaders of the nation. In addition to teaching the students about civic responsibility, postsecondary schools also exposed students to a classical curriculum and provided opportunities for them to revel in their youthful energy. The world of college allowed young men to learn, play, and make mistakes. "If the world has been compared to a stage," Harvard student William Colburn declared, "so college life may be compared to a stage with curtains drawn, and prompter and critic at their posts, upon which we rehearse the part we are afterwards to play." If students succeeded in this rehearsal, "we go forward with confidence when the curtain rises and the *probability* is that we shall also succeed in the representation."[5]

Such opportunities were complemented by a set of expectations. College men knew that their education was supposed to train them to act with knowledge, confront challenges, and guide the less fortunate members of society. Colleges, in short, were responsible for training society's leadership class. In an essay written during the Civil War, Harvard student William H. Appleton described how colleges prepared "men to be rulers." He pointed out that "the best legislators, & the best rulers are the men of the best education," and such educated individuals helped "raise the standard which the people require in their rulers." Appleton then acknowledged the military service of his college-mates. "Amid all the sacrifice which the present conflict between loyalty & rebellion has called forth," colleges had "sent forth from ancient halls of learning their sons as did the Spartan mothers of old." College students, as he described them, were not spoiled sons but rather key players in the defense of the nation's liberties and laws.[6]

In an era when few Americans attended college, men who did were members of an elite class. Despite the rising number of students in higher education, their proportion of the total number of youth in American society remained basically unchanged. In 1800, a mere 2 percent of young men attended college. In 1840, there were 16,233 students in 173 institutions of higher learning nationwide. By 1880, a total of 85,378 students attended college—still less than 2 percent of Americans between the ages of eighteen and twenty-one. The age of students ranged from their teens to late twenties; generally, the older students were men from poorer backgrounds who had to work to pay for their education.[7]

Although southern students attended New England colleges up to the eve of the Civil War, their population had declined throughout the first half of the nineteenth century. Southern parents did not appreciate some of the lessons being taught to their sons. For example, some "moral philosophy" classes, required of all seniors and designed to instill "an enlightened respect for basic Christian beliefs and virtues," touched on sensitive issues like slavery. By the 1850s, many southerners had already begun to push for a more independent southern education system. Southern leaders argued that the sons of the South ought to be educated in their own region so as not to expose them to Yankee values. These leaders promoted educational facilities that already existed but also advocated the creation of new schools to compete with the North. As historian Peter S. Carmichael has observed, college-trained Virginians were "groomed to become the state's next generation of leaders." An additional benefit of encouraging a uniquely southern education was the ability to transmit region-specific cultural values. Robert F. Pace has demonstrated how southern colleges served as training grounds for young men to learn about honor.[8]

Southern parents had reason to worry about their children's educational environment in the North, since sectional issues seeped into the everyday activities of the undergraduates. Chauncey Nye, a student at Dartmouth, recorded that the student lyceum had debated during the political crisis of 1850 whether the "Northern States should cecede [*sic*] from the Southern." The students resolved that the northern states ought to go their own way. A few months later, Nye recorded that a local minister "preached from Acts 4:14 directing most of his discourse against the *Fugitive Slave Law* taking the ground that human law is null and void when it clashes with divine law."[9] Incidents like this did not sit well with southerners who did not want their children learning antislavery values.

The very themes that New Englanders emphasized when they told the story of American history also seemed to challenge the foundations of southern life. Written for class or public orations on the topics of American history and national events, most college essays followed a particular historical narrative, celebrating the United States as a whole but emphasizing New England's contribution to the republic's success. For example, John Marshall Brown, a student at Bowdoin College, wrote glowingly about the swift development of the United States. He observed that "where now are crowded thoroughfares and populous cities" was untouched forest a few hundred years earlier. "Where now lofty manufactories rise and the hum of numberless spindles mingle with the din of business," he continued, "the stream flowed along to the ocean in silence 300 years ago." These expressions of regional pride were often unconscious, coming as they did from young men who had grown up in New England. They were not necessarily intended as attacks upon the South, although some authors did condemn slavery as uncivilized.[10]

Not surprisingly, the essays became more damning of the South during the war. By this point, the South was no longer just viewed as a region of the nation that would eventually reform its ways; it was now seen as an aggressor that threatened the progress of the United States. In 1861, Harvard student Leonard Alden called slavery "an organized system of the most odious injustice,—an oppression the most cruel that had ever disgraced a Christian land" and blamed the politicians who had been willing to compromise their morals to attain sectional peace. Slavery, he declared, had been a bane to the United States from its founding. In 1865, Flavius Cook, another Harvard student, accused slaveholders of having "planned secretly for the Rebellion" for decades.[11]

This selective and sectionalized narrative served as a unifying story for young New Englanders who grew up hearing heroic tales of their region's prominence in the establishment of the United States. According to this version of history, the United States had originated with Plymouth and the Puritans rather than Virginia. Most of southern history was excised from their national narrative, and what remained lacked the noble ideals of New England; for example, the first New England settler had sought religious liberty, whereas the Virginians had emigrated to seek economic gain. New Englanders drew a straight line between the piety of the Puritans and America's commitment to freedom.[12]

Some New England students, ironically unaware that their own ideas were biased, expressed their concern with the divisive sectional language emanating from the southern states. Not only did they believe such rhetoric threatened national harmony, they also saw it as a challenge to their narrative of American history, which condemned the spread of slavery. In his 1855 commencement address, Dartmouth student David Quigg noted that "it was most noble & glorious for the founders of this republic to obtain & transmit to us this precious inheritance—a free country." It was, therefore, "equally illustrious and praiseworthy to maintain & guard" the Union "as it was bequeathed to us, but most base & shameful if we prove incapable to discharge the duties necessary to fulfill this trust." Vaguely referring to contemporary issues—perhaps the violence in the Kansas Territory—Quigg warned that the "anarchy & civil war, that destroyed the ancient republics & which is the destruction of all nations without God & conscience," might yet reach American shores. "Indeed," he continued, "there has been going for the past few years in this land so boastful of peace & happiness[,] a civil warfare, more odious & more to be deprecated than any other history has yet recorded."[13]

Because, like most Americans, they believed slavery would die out if restricted to the South, most of the New England students in this sample favored a free-soil ideology. As Joanne Pope Melish has suggested, New Englanders had written African Americans out of their past, providing a less ambivalent version of the history of New England race relations than antebellum writers acknowledged. Yet students often wrote of slaves and slavery in the contemporary South. Bowdoin student Joseph Wingate, for example, demanded that governments stand up for workers, guarantee them good wages, protect their hard work, and end the degrading practice of slavery. "The time is approaching," he declared, "when the world shall acknowledge the social equality of man; when labor, no longer degraded by slavery, shall be a blessing rather than a curse." Some forward-looking students, such as Harvard's Charles Gregory, were concerned about the prospects of the nation if slavery were allowed to expand. Writing as the Kansas-Nebraska Act was sparking vigorous debate, Gregory calculated that there would be 300 million Americans by the turn of the century. The world had "never seen the splendid spectacle of a hundred millions of free people united into a democratic republic." Gregory urged caution because there "exists one cause of alarm; one institution yet remains which renders us obnoxious to keen reproach and the charge of inconsistency." That threat was slavery, of course, but Gregory trusted that "the moral conflict which has commenced, and the gentle but powerful influence of Christianity will render the institution. . . obsolete before the opening of the twentieth century."[14]

Although often ambivalent toward the abolitionist community, most New England students had a uniform distaste for slavery and southern slaveholders. By and large, northern students viewed slavery's advocates as aggressive expansionists who hid behind federal laws. Slaveholders' constant attempts to spread slavery worried students who saw such actions as morally repugnant, especially in the context of the American narrative of expanding liberty. Harvard student Robert Babson worried about the fate of the Union, seeing similarities between ancient Rome and the nineteenth-century United States. "If we ever needed men wise in the wisdom of experience," Babson wrote, "it is in the present position of our country." He complained that Americans were, like Romans, "too fond of territory." They "look with secret longings to Nicaragua," "have ogled the . . . Antilles," "robbed, or as good as robbed, Mexico of her fairest lands & their have been certain suspicious whisperings about the Sandwich Islands." All this could be tied to the American system of slavery, which was "unparalleled in the History of the race." "To enumerate" the "evils" of slavery "would be to count the sands on the sea shore." A proslavery mob, he pointed out, had "just controlled a territorial election," in the Kansas Territory.[15]

Whatever their beliefs about slavery and sectionalism, most New England college students hoped to maintain peaceful relations among all regions of the country. Although they recognized sectional differences, they blamed radicals within each region, including the North, for stirring up controversy.

Students condemned abolitionists in the North and slaveholders in the South for inciting sectional animosity. Dartmouth student Osgood Johnson, advocating the notion that lasting change came slowly, condemned "reformers of the present day." "Time," he argued, "is requisite to alter the whole tone of Society." Therefore, the "roaring of fanatics & crazy women has not relieved the condition of the slave" and had, in fact, strengthened the chains of slavery. The problem was that revolutions could not "advance farther than the intelligence of the people," and the reformers were merely appealing to "the worst passions of the multitude—not their sober & better feelings."[16]

College-age essayists and letter writers blamed contemporary politicians for failing to bring peace and stability to the nation. According to Dartmouth student Willard Heath, "The sectional jealousies so rife in America, and the source of so many conflicting parties result from no collisions of local interest . . . but from the multifarious passions inseparable from so great a diversity of climate, habits and institutions." What was needed was a breed of "true statesmen" who would transcend these various influences on the nature of the country. The statesman was supposed to "liberalize the adverse parties, till nothing but a . . . love, linked with the memory of a common origin, suffering and destiny, shall actuate the American people." Only when this had been accomplished could "their united affections cluster around the constitution—that hallowed monument of human reason." "It was the loss of this Constitutional affection," Heath explained, "that plunged Rome from the height of universal sovereignty into the gulf of infamy and slavery." He concluded that "the manifest destiny of America demands Statesmen thoroughly liberal in spirit" and "mindful of party spirit."[17]

Because they recognized the need for "statesmen" to lead the nation, college men paid close attention to national elections, especially for president. Although the contests were not entirely about sectional issues, Whig, Democratic, and Republican platforms always contained topics of regional contention, particularly about the expansion of U.S. territory and the extension of slavery. During the presidential contests in 1852, 1856, and 1860, college students enthusiastically engaged in debates, marched in rallies, and participated in other campaign-related activities. In June 1852, Dartmouth student Edwin Thomas recounted exciting scenes from Hanover. Referring to the Democratic and Whig nominees for president, he told his parents, "There is little thought of or talked about except politics. Pierce and Scot [*sic*] furnish almost the entire subject of conversation." When jubilant Whigs, celebrating Winfield Scott's nomination, asked the cadets at neighboring Norwich Academy to fire a salute, the soldiers "formed a procession to march to a small eminence north of the college, where the salute was to be fired, with two six pound pieces." Just as they were about to commence, however, "the bell began to toll, as for a funeral procession." This tolling distracted the Whigs for almost an hour. They eventually had to cut the rope to the bell and seal the belfry so that the culprits, college Democrats, could not further interrupt the proceedings. Freed from the disturbance, the cadets "fired 44 guns which is thought by some to indicate the number of electoral votes which they expect at the Nov. election."

Later that day, the college Democrats rallied in the chapel and "listened to about a dozen quite spirited speeches, and then adjourned having given nine hearty cheers for Pierce and King [their party's nominees]." Despite this display of force, Thomas acknowledged the presence of "a large majority of whigs [sic] in the college." A Democrat "finds a hard time unless he is posted up and can show the documents to maintain his principles." He thus asked his parents to forward "any speeches sent you last winter relating to internal improvements or any other part of the democratic platform" and declared his intent "to look into political matters . . . as I do not care to be run over by the whigs [sic]."[18]

The political discourse for the election of 1852 was equally animated at Bowdoin College, the alma mater of Democratic candidate Franklin Pierce. Joseph Emerson Smith, a student and secretary of the pro-Democratic "Granite Club," reported to his father that "politics never runs higher here than they do this campaign; every student in college thinks it his duty to *rave* about some of the great principles of party." The rival Whigs, however, "find it rather hard to do so, they having no principles." The pro-Whig "'Scott & Graham' club," Smith continued, was "stronger in numbers, but far inferior in ability," while the Democratic meetings, although "more thinly attended," were "characterized by much more unanimity, and much better speeches. The Whigs have about 3 to our 2 but two of their men aren't worth one of ours."[19]

In 1856, the presidential contest was even more intense because of the national debate over the fate of the Kansas Territory. Appalled by the threatening rhetoric in Congress and elsewhere, college students called for a more civil discourse. These young men despised mob rule and blamed agitators in the North—abolitionists among them—for instigating sectional strife. Although the students opposed slavery, they preferred a more gradual solution that did not threaten the Union. Bowdoin student Galen Clapp Moses noted in his diary that the issue of slavery was supposed to have been settled by the Compromise of 1850, but due to "the fanatic and disorganizing efforts of the free soil party [] the agitation was again renewed in all its fury upon the proposition about 1 year ago to organize the territories of Kanzas [*sic*] and Nebrasca [*sic*]." Despite his disapproval of Free Soilers' tactics, he believed that "no true lover of his country desires that Kanzas [*sic*] should be a Slave state." The men were equally critical of southerners who employed violence. After hearing the news of Senator Charles Sumner's "maltreatment" at the hands of southern congressman Preston Brooks, Dartmouth student Daniel Wild lamented northern politicians' constant retreat in the face of southern aggression, asking, "How long *will* northern blood *creep* in the veins of the sons of the Pilgrims?"[20]

What college students would not tolerate was a proslavery man at the head of their institution. During the 1840s, Nathan Lord, president of Dartmouth College since 1828, decided that his previous antislavery stance was untenable. In 1854 and 1855, widely distributed publications spread what was already local knowledge: Nathan Lord had become proslavery. Lord publicly stated that he believed slavery to be "a divine institution" sanctioned by God. Not surprisingly, the president's beliefs drew heated criticism from abolitionists (but correspondingly led to an increase in the number of southern students). The uproar following Lord's declaration eventually led to calls for his resignation during the war. Even before that, however, Dartmouth's students had quite a lot to say about their president's unpopular views.[21]

In 1855, the *Dartmouth Œstrus*, a satirical student paper, published a cartoon of President Lord as a slave catcher and put the president's family up for auction, copying the style of an advertisement for enslaved laborers. In a corresponding editorial, the paper complained about the president's position. Ever since Lord's views became widely known to the general public, parents were "beginning to hesitate about sending their hopeful young scions where their precarious intellects will be blasted and contaminated by such damnable doctrines as the Rev. Prex. seems bound to promulgate on the slavery question." The paper claimed to represent the views of a vast majority of the students and begged the trustees to "give us a man, so that when away during vacation, with our friends, we need not feel *ashamed* of the President of Old Dartmouth."[22]

One year later the *Œstrus* again pleaded with the trustees to replace their president. Lord had recently been known to "hobble into the chapel . . . like some hypochondriac old granny" and lament "over the 'irregularities' of students, for which he has mistaken the night horrors of his own guilty conscience." Predictably, he reminded the students "of his advancing age; and then relat[ed] the thread-bare tale of his 'retiring early the previous evening, to get rest for the *accumulating labors* of the morrow, but could not sleep, for there was a sound of revelry by night.'" Indeed, the "revelry" that the president

A few words to the Trustees.

Figure 3.1. *A Few Words to the Trustees* depicts the college president, Nathaniel Lord, as a slave catcher. The president's proslavery views clashed with the students' antislavery positions. *Dartmouth Œstrus*, July 1855. Dartmouth College Library.

claimed to hear was merely political activity concerned with the presidential contest. How, the paper asked, could "Dartmouth College . . . be made to suppress every noble and generous impulse of a manly nature" when "the whole country" was "alive in the cause of freedom of man." The students would not "withhold their voice in the general shout for *liberty*; and refuse to sing at night even one song for 'freeman and Fremont'—all out of *mere slavish respect, bare* sympathy for a childish, supercilious, *pro-slavery* old Fogy whom they, at the bottom of their hearts *hate*." The authors pleaded "in the name of *God* and *humanity* . . . take off from among us the cold, case-hardened, green-eyed monster who now fills the Presidential chair, and give us in his stead a *man*, who resides somewhere in the neighborhood of the rest of mankind in thought, sentiment and in feeling." Despite these passionate calls for Lord's ouster, the proslavery president remained in his position until 1863.[23]

During the election of 1860, the final presidential contest before the war, young Republicans sensed the momentum on their side and expected a victory at the polls. At Bowdoin College, Sam Fessenden reported to his father,

Senator William Pitt Fessenden, that interest in politics was increasing ahead of the Republican Party's nominating convention. The "contents of newspapers," he noted in May 1860, "are devoured with avidity." He believed potential Democratic nominee Stephen A. Douglas's "stock was 'below par'" and observed that Bowdoin Democrats were "rather mum on the subject." Feeling optimistic about the contest, Fessenden continued, "I don't see anything to prevent the success of Republican principles if a good man is put up, and we can only hope for such result, as the only thing which would tend to bring back our country to the right course of things." After hearing of Lincoln's nomination, Fessenden wrote that the college Republicans were organizing "a club for the campaign" and would "try to do something towards the cause." "Any good campaign speeches," he added, "will be joyfully received. I am a little behindhand as to politics, and want to be posted up."[24]

When the war began, college students instinctively held politicians responsible, blaming them for their failure to keep the peace. During the first summer of the war, Harvard student William H. Pettee wrote that "the personal ambition of the leaders has had more to do in exciting this present rebellion than any fears, naturally arising among the people, of aggressive action from the North." Northern politicians were at fault because they had yielded to southern demands so often that the slaveholding states had "gained the courage to make an open attack upon the government." The northern people "whose right it is to manage the government" had "allowed themselves to be led by a small number of active politicians" who were "men of inferior talents." All the while, "the best men, those who best understand the principles and difficulties of our complicated government, and who would have taken the most intelligent view of important questions, have been kept out of political life." Pettee expressed a theme common with his fellow students: that the previous generation of politicians had failed in their duties and that younger men would have to stand up and lead.[25]

For college students attempting to fathom the cause of secession, slavery was the obvious culprit. When describing the South as a hierarchical and aristocratic society, they thought of themselves as champions of republicanism and the true heirs of the Revolution. Slavery, they argued, had corrupted their fellow countrymen. According to Harvard student Stephen Emerson, southerners claimed "that work is dishonorable and their hands are free from the contamination of labor." This view allowed slaveholders to portray themselves as having "a more gentle and patrician quality than the northern people, who from the disadvantage of not having a servile race under them, perform many menial functions themselves." Emerson claimed instead that the South was "rich in self esteem and confident claims; poor in dignity, honor, truth and manliness; lofty in the patrician assumptions; of a type of character almost peculiarly low, almost vulgar in essential particulars, as the world will judge it, when tried by rules and principles unwarped [] by the influences of a system of wrong and oppression." Slavery had "corrupted the springs of their [southerners'] character, and sent selfishness through all its streams and courses."[26]

The war's outbreak allowed advocates of the sectional New England identity to assert an ideological victory. Their side had stood by the Union and could claim to be the true nationalists. Harvard student Henry Sheldon noted that secessionists had "rebelled against a government which had never failed to give them all the protection they had a right to expect, which had even watched over their interests with a partiality offensive to many at the North, often yielding to their demands even though justice forbade compliance." Furthermore, the federal government had hardly ever refused "to give up all its wide domains to that gigantic system of oppression[,] that relic of barbarism, which all the civilized world but the Southern States themselves united in condemning." The "ringleaders" of the rebellion had drawn "State after State into their base conspiracy." Sheldon claimed that "the flames of hatred to the Union, flames kindled by a series of misrepresentations whose ingenuity and success could be eclipsed only by their baseness," might "blaze" so high that they would "consume the whole nation, and leave only a smoldering pile of cinders and ashes to tell posterity that here had once been the home of a mighty people."[27]

At war's end, the New England version of American history had triumphed. Having fought the war, preserved the Union, and emancipated the enslaved, New England students could draw a straight line between the origins of their region and the ultimate progressive vision of a triumphant United States. Harvard student Charles Souther could tell that victorious narrative when he made the distinction between the "Slave Ship of 1619" and the "Pilgrim Ship of 1620." Souther described the arrival of a "Dutch man-of-war" to the colony of Virginia. This ship, bearing enslaved laborers, had allowed the "feudal system of the old world" to gain "a foothold in the new." Slavery, having been brought to the New World, "sapped the foundation of this rising civilization" by giving it "a selfish, an oppressive, and a barbarous character." Following this tainted beginning of the American story, there came, upon the decks of the *Mayflower*, those who "bade the long farewell to their homes & kindred, and set sail in search of an asylum in the known Western world." These intrepid voyagers had sought liberty when they crossed the Atlantic. The two founding stories represented the beginnings of incompatible civilizations. And, indeed, the experience of the war proved that "each of these civilizations" had remained "true to its original instincts."[28]

The price of saving the Union was not cheap. Hundreds of young college men rallied around the flag, and many of them paid the ultimate price. Harvard, Bowdoin, and Williams lost ninety-two, forty-four, and twenty-two of their sons, respectively. Amherst lost thirty-five of its sons, among them Christopher Pennell. When initially denied permission to enlist, Pennell wrote again to his father, rejecting the idea that his "sudden burst of patriotism" was "the result of wild excitement." Pennell wholeheartedly disagreed with his father's assertion that volunteers for the war should come "among a class which will not be missed, whose lives are not worth so much as yours or mine." Was it not a tragedy, he asked, when soldiers "be they Irish, Dutch or Yankee, shall be mown before the enemies' cannon in ranks, even though they come from the very humblest classes[?]" Pennell demanded, "Do not say they are not missed, that their lives are worth nothing." A long war meant that "the ranks of both armies shall be decimated, & wearied out, with toil & fighting," and there would be "a need of men who shall fight treason from principle, & not from desire for spoils, of educated soldiers who understand what they are fighting for. Tom Dick & Harry will not be so ready to enlist then." Ultimately, Pennell got his wish and joined the Union army. He was killed at the Battle of the Crater in 1864.[29]

New England college students witnessed the vindication of their national narrative. The threat of slavery had been ended, and the nation once again was set on the righteous path of freedom. The Union victory also demonstrated to the young men that their positions about politicians and slavery were correct. Whereas older politicians had bungled their way into a war, the younger generation of New England's leaders had succeeded in saving the Union. Slavery had proved itself to be a real threat since it had inspired secession. With its death, however, that threat to the Union was gone, the actions of bad politicians had been rectified, and New England's young sons had shown their mettle and proved themselves worthy of inheriting the republic.

NOTES

The author acknowledges generous funding from the New England Regional Fellowship Consortium and thanks the special collections staffs at Amherst, Bowdoin, and Dartmouth Colleges.

1. Christopher Pennell to Lewis Pennell, April 21, 1861, in Alumni Biographical Files, Amherst College Archives and Special Collections, Amherst College Library, Amherst, Massachusetts (hereafter cited as Pennell papers, ACL).

2. Ibid.

3. Harlow W. Sheidley, *Sectional Nationalism: Massachusetts Conservative Leaders and the Transformation of America: 1815–1836* (Boston: Northeastern University Press, 1998), xi–xii, 87, 118–24.

4. Carl F. Kaestle, *Pillars of the Republic: Common Schools and American Society, 1780–1860* (New York: Hill and Wang, 1983), 3–7; Steven Mintz, *Huck's Raft: A History of American Childhood* (Cambridge: Belknap Press of Harvard University Press, 2004), 90–92, 139.

5. William Gardner Colburn, "College Life a Rehearsal," not paginated, July 18, 1860, general information about Harvard commencement, Class Day, and exhibitions in academic year 1859/1860, Harvard University Archives, Cambridge, Massachusetts (hereafter cited as HUA).

6. William Hyde Appleton, "The Functions of Colleges in Our Democracy," not paginated, July 20, 1864, general information about Harvard commencement, Class Day, and exhibitions in academic year 1863/1864, HUA. For a discussion of the regular curricula of undergraduates and attempts at reform during the first half of the nineteenth century, see George P. Schmidt, *The Liberal Arts College: A Chapter in American Cultural History* (New Brunswick, NJ: Rutgers University Press, 1957), especially chapter 3, 43–75; John S. Brubacher and Willis Rudy, *Higher Education in Transition: A History of American Colleges and Universities* (1958; New Brunswick, NJ: Transaction, 1997), 100–111.

7. Helen Lefkowitz Horowitz, *Campus Life: Undergraduate Cultures from the End of the Eighteenth Century to the Present* (Chicago: University of Chicago Press, 1987), 4–5.

8. Wilson Smith, *Professors and Public Ethics: Studies of Northern Moral Philosophers before the Civil War* (Ithaca: Cornell University Press, 1956), 8–9, 14–15, 18–19, 24–25; D. H. Meyer, *The Instructed Conscience: The Shaping of the American National Ethic* (Philadelphia: University of Pennsylvania Press, 1972), vii, 4–5, 12, 63–69; John McCardell, *The Idea of a Southern Nation: Southern Nationalists and Southern Nationalism, 1830–1860* (New York: Norton, 1979), chap. 5, esp. 200–226; Peter S. Carmichael, *The Last Generation: Young Virginians in Peace, War, and Reunion* (Chapel Hill: University of North Carolina Press, 2005), 48, 101–3; Robert F. Pace, *Halls of Honor: College Men in the Old South* (Baton Rouge: Louisiana State University Press, 2004), 4–10.

9. Chauncey Nye, Journal Entries, May 18, 1850, and December 6, 1850, Journal 1850–55, vol. 1, Rauner Special Collections Library, Dartmouth College, Hanover, New Hampshire (hereafter cited as DCL).

10. John Marshall Brown, "A Companion of the Past with the Present," not paginated, undated, John Marshall Brown Papers, Maine Historical Society, Portland, Maine; Stephanie Kermes, *Creating an American Identity: New England, 1789–1825* (New York: Palgrave Macmillan, 2008), 184–85. Not surprisingly, the students in this sample neither discussed nor acknowledged their own region's complicity in the slave trade.

11. Leonard Case Alden, "Compromise," not paginated, May 7, 1861, general information about Harvard commencement, Class Day, and exhibitions in academic year 1860/1861, HUA (hereafter cited as Harvard 1860/1861, HUA); Flavius Joseph Cook, "The Penalties of Treason," not paginated, July 19, 1865, general information about Harvard commencement, Class Day, and exhibitions in academic year 1864/1865, HUA (hereafter cited as Harvard 1864/1865, HUA).

12. Sheidley, *Sectional Nationalism*, 120–24; Kermes, *Creating an American Identity*, 2–4, 8–9, 21, 169; Joseph A. Conforti, *Imagining New England: Explorations of Regional Identity from the Pilgrims to the Mid-Twentieth Century* (Chapel Hill: University of North Carolina Press, 2001), 188–89, 195.

13. Joanne Pope Melish, *Disowning Slavery: Gradual Emancipation and "Race" in New England, 1780–1860* (Ithaca: Cornell University Press, 1998), 2–3; David Quigg, "The Relation of the New States to the Old," not paginated, July 26, 1855, Commencement Parts, DCL.

14. Joseph Charles Augustus Wingate, "The Right to Labor for Remunerative Wages," not paginated, May 1851, Class Records (Class of 1851), George J. Mitchell Department of Special Collections and Archives, Bowdoin College Library, Brunswick, Maine (hereafter cited as BCL); Charles Augustus Gregory, "The Last Census," not paginated, October 17, 1854, general information about Harvard commencement, Class Day, and exhibitions in academic year 1854/1855, HUA.

15. Robert Edward Babson, "Ancient History as Applied to Illustrate Modern Politics," not paginated, July 16, 1856, general information about Harvard commencement, Class Day, and exhibitions in academic year 1855/1856, HUA.

16. Osgood Johnson, "The Slow Progress of Useful Revolutions," not paginated, July 29, 1852, Commencement Parts, DCL.

17. Willard S. Heath, "Necessity of a Liberal Spirit in American Statesmen," not paginated, July 29, 1858, Commencement Parts, DCL.

18. Edwin Alonso Thomas to his parents, June 23, 1852, Student Letters, DCL.

19. Joseph Emerson Smith to Samuel E. Smith, July 25, 1852, Smith Brothers Student Letters, BCL.

20. Galen Clapp Moses, diary, [April 10, 1855, entry], Student Journals, Letters and Scrapbooks, vol. 138, BCL; Daniel G. Wild, diary, [May 24, 1856 entry], vol. 1, D. G. Wild Diary, DCL.

21. John King Lord, *A History of Dartmouth College, 1815–1909* (Concord, NH: Rumford Press, 1913), 251–55, 321–26.

22. *Dartmouth Œstrus* 1, no. 3 (July 1855), DCL.

23. Ibid., no. 4 (July 1856), DCL.

24. Samuel Fessenden to William Pitt Fessenden, May 14, 1860, and May 21 or 18, 1860, Fessenden Collection, BCL.

25. William Henry Pettee, "How Political Influence Can Be Made Effective to Individual Citizens in This Republic," not paginated, July 17, 1861, Harvard 1860/1861, HUA.

26. Stephen Goodhue Emerson, "The Plebs," not paginated, July 17, 1861, Harvard 1860/1861, HUA.

27. Henry Newton Sheldon, "Our National Vanity," not paginated, October 21, 1862, general information about Harvard commencement, Class Day, and exhibitions in academic year 1862/1863, HUA.

28. Charles Edward Souther, "The Slave Ship of 1619, and the Pilgrim Ship of 1620," not paginated, July 11, 1865, Harvard 1864/1865, HUA.

29. Phillip Shaw Paludan, *A People's Contest: The Union and Civil War, 1861–1865* (1988; Lawrence: University Press of Kansas Press, 1996), 133; Christopher Pennell to Lewis Pennell, April 29, 1861 (Pennell papers, ACL; Daniel A. Cohen, "The Passions of Lieutenant Pennell," *Amherst*, Fall 1978), 24, 28.

PART II

Children of War

One need not be a grown-up to imbibe the peculiar feeling that hangs over everything in time of war. It was something like that sensation that goes about when a contagious disease suddenly breaks out in a peaceful community and the infected houses are placarded and streets barricaded. Young and old felt it weighing down like an incubus.
　　　　—Hermon W. DeLong Sr., *Boyhood Reminiscences*

The war was continually rising in front of me to bar me from something I wanted, whether food, clothes, or playthings.
　　　　—Robert Hugh Martin, *A Boy of Old Shenandoah*[1]

　　Civil War children and youth continued playing, going to school, arguing with their families, doing chores, and celebrating typical coming-of-age markers. Yet, as revealed in the recollections of these two boys—one a Yankee living safely in upstate New York, the other a young rebel living close to the fighting in Virginia—show, the lives of children and youth were inevitably altered by the conflict. It added to their chores, took away, sometimes forever, fathers and brothers, closed schools, and offered unprecedented distractions. Part II looks at some of the ways that the war intruded on and, in some instances, changed the lives of children and youth in both sections.

　　Teenagers have always challenged their parents; even though adolescence was not identified by name until late in the nineteenth century, its characteristic tumult and the resulting prickly relationships with parents were recognized for centuries before it had a name. The war provided yet another way for youths to rebel, and Thomas Curran offers the example of one Confederate boy whose confrontation with family and other authority figures took a special form due to the war.

Although many northern boys also ran off to war without their parents' permission—the famous drummer boy John Clem is just one prominent example—most Yankee children and youth enjoyed a more distant relationship with the war. Two essays offer very different accounts of the ways in which juvenile magazines adapted their customary content to the developing interests of wartime readers. Paul Ringel shows how the war gave the entrepreneurial editor of the *Youth's Companion* the opportunity to provide sensational adventure stories—the war would, he argues, permanently change the nature of juvenile periodicals—while at the same promoting patriotism and piety. Sean Scott examines the ways in which the near obsession with death in prewar Christian magazines for children may have prepared children to accept the unbearable human cost of war by infusing catastrophic loss with spirituality and providing a language for expressing and processing grief.

The most jarring experiences for American children and youth occurred, of course, in the Confederacy, where encounters with Union troops, the destruction of the institution of slavery, and the disruption of the southern economy reached into virtually every corner of their lives. Young Confederate women experienced the same hardships as their mothers, but their particular needs and desires were further interrupted by the absence of young men and the appearance of Yankee soldiers. As they tried to retain a grip on their traditions and values, they had to navigate wartime exigencies that often reshaped or, at times, exaggerated southern assumptions. As Victoria Ott shows, courtship rituals transcended biological imperatives and social niceties to become a political statement for elite Confederate teenagers, while Lisa Tendrich Frank's essay suggests that the lives of Confederate girls exposed to the trials and horrors of Sherman's March were altered materially but also psychologically; it is no coincidence that some of the most fervent believers in the Lost Cause were women who had lived through the war, formed memorial societies, and published books of reminiscences with evocative titles like *Our Women in the War: The Lives They Lived; the Deaths They Died.*[2]

NOTES

1. Hermon W. DeLong Sr., *Boyhood Reminiscences (Life in Danville, 1855–1872), with Other Sketches* (Dansville, NY: Dansville Press, 1913), 70; Robert Hugh Martin, *A Boy of Old Shenandoah* (Parsons, WV: McClain, 1977), 46.

2. *Our Women in the War: The Lives They Lived; the Deaths They Died* (Charleston, SC: Weekly News and Courier, 1885).

4

A "Rebel to [His] Govt. and to His Parents"

The Emancipation of Tommy Cave

THOMAS F. CURRAN

In mid-1862, despite his father's opposition, fifteen-year-old Tommy Cave ran away from his home in Boone County, Missouri, and joined the Confederate army. Six months later the boy was captured just a few miles from his father's farm and, like other prisoners of war taken in the state, was sent to St. Louis. It was not uncommon for Federal authorities in St. Louis to release prisoners under the age of eighteen to their parents, but not so with Cave. After investigating the facts, Provost Marshal General Franklin Dick determined that Cave had rebelled against his parents in the same way that he had rebelled against the Federal government. Instead of returning the boy to his parents, Dick decided that the army would continue to hold Cave as a prisoner of war. By doing this, Dick essentially freed Cave from his parents' control and treated him as any other adult prisoner. In fact, Cave did not want to be released to his parents. "I want to be Exchanged & sent South," Cave informed his captors, so that he could remain in the Confederate army. He received his wish. Dick sent Cave to the military prison in Alton, Illinois, with other rebel captives until an exchange of prisoners could be arranged. The boy would be paroled and exchanged with about a thousand other Confederates from Alton in mid-1863. He quickly returned to active duty, and a year later he died far from home on a battlefield in Virginia.[1]

The Civil War was more than a contest of brother against brother. As Amy Murrell Taylor shows in her recent study, the conflict divided families in many ways. Arguably, nowhere were the wartime divisions more complex than in Missouri. For Tommy Cave, joining the Confederate army meant rejecting the authority of his parents (despite the fact that his father sympathized with the South) in the same way that he rejected the authority of the U.S. government. James Marten has noted that when Civil War–

era boys became soldiers, "their military service made them de facto adults; their experiences resembled the exploits of the men with whom they served more than those of the children who stayed at home."[2] While this is certainly accurate, one can see from the records that boy soldiers belonging to the Confederate army were not always treated by Federal authorities the same as their adult counterparts. This was particularly true for young Confederate prisoners of war in Missouri. The decisions of Union authorities in the case of Tommy Cave and other underage detainees shed light on the complicated familial issues generated by the war, as well as on the broad discretion Union authorities had in carrying out their duties. In particular, the provost marshals general responsible for deciding these cases found themselves acting, in a way, as proto–family court judges. Although they could hardly have predicted that the twentieth century would see the rise of a judicial system intended solely for juveniles and their specific problems, the cases of underage soldiers in conflict with their parents over military service provide dim foreshadowing of the juvenile justice system. In cases such as that of Tommy Cave, the provost marshal general would have to weigh the interests of the community or the nation against the interests of the boy and his family.

Tommy Cave's family background made him a likely supporter of the Confederate cause. The Cave family could trace its roots back to colonial Virginia. Both of Tommy's parents, Major William S. Cave and Margaret Harrison Cave, came from prominent families that made their way to Missouri in the early nineteenth century. It is unclear how William obtained the sobriquet "Major." A "William S. Cave" served briefly as a private in a unit of Missouri volunteers during the Black Hawk War in 1832. William would have been twenty at the time. Nevertheless, he probably received the title from peacetime militia service. William Cave's farm was located only one mile north of the town of Columbia in Boone County, which sat at the center of the state on the north bank of the Missouri River. Visible from the cupola of the Columbia courthouse, the Cave farm on the eve of the Civil War was home to a growing family of six children. They included five sons and one twelve-year-old girl, who was probably Margaret's niece. Of the six children, thirteen-year-old Thomas Henry was the oldest. The Cave estate also included about a dozen slaves, accounting for much of William's $13,500 in personal property. At that time the average slaveholder in the county owned five or six slaves in a region with a vibrant and growing slave-based economy. According to the 1860 census, the elder Cave owned an equal amount of real property, making his one of the wealthiest families in Boone County.[3]

Through the 1850s, William Cave paid attention to the growing sectional crisis, especially on the border between Missouri and nearby Kansas. In fact, he contributed money "to sustain the Pro-Slavery Men in Kansas" during the height of the bloody struggle. Whatever Cave's sympathies before the war, once fighting broke out in the spring of 1861, the "Major," now nearly fifty years old, did not offer his services to the Confederate cause. Nevertheless, evidence suggests that Cave at least privately sided with the rebels. In fact, in March 1862 the elder Cave was required to give a bond of $2,500 dollars to Union authorities to guarantee his good behavior. Young Thomas Henry, also known as Tommy, proved to be less hesitant to act on his Southern proclivities. Whatever political ideals they shared concerning slavery, secession, and the Confederacy, William Cave apparently did not believe that sectional loyalty and the national crisis trumped his authority. He did not want his fifteen-year-old son putting himself in harm's way by joining the Southern army, and he forbade him from volunteering. Nevertheless, when Missouri Confederate Colonel John Poindexter sent recruiters throughout the northern counties of the state to raise troops for a regiment of cavalry in the summer of 1862, Tommy Cave eagerly answered the call.[4]

Cave lied about his age when he enlisted, claiming to be eighteen. A month before the attack on Fort Sumter, the Confederate government passed an act to establish and organize its army. Rather than creating new rules for the conduct of the army, Confederate legislators adopted the "Rules and Articles of War established by the laws of the United States of America for the government of the Army," with a few modifications. According to those rules, "Any free white male person above the age of eighteen and under thirty-five years . . . may be enlisted," although those under twenty-one needed written consent from a parent or guardian. Once the war began, one doubts that such particulars were enforced by either side. Eighteen remained the official age of service until 1864, when the Confederate Congress revised its conscription law, first passed in 1862, which lowered the age of service to seventeen. The Union army, on the other hand, maintained an eighteen-year-old threshold for enlistment except early in the war, when seventeen-year-olds could join with the permission of their parents. Despite these policies, underage boys donned uniforms to fight for both the North and the South during the war.[5]

Cave's record of activities in the Confederate service prior to his capture is a bit sketchy. According to a statement given by Cave on February 12, 1863, while in the Gratiot Street Prison in St. Louis, the boy admitted that he had his first taste of being "in arms" at some point early in the summer of 1862, when he "was out about 3 days with Capt. Simons." After this brief adventure, Cave "went home." The document gives no explanation why, but soon the rebel cause drew Cave back. According to the sworn statement that the boy wrote just after his capture, he enlisted with one of Poindexter's recruiters "about the 1st of August," although other documents suggest that it was on July 28. Cave claimed that he was with Poindexter for "about a month." In fact, not long after Cave's enlistment, a portion of Poindexter's regiment joined Joseph Porter's 1st Northeast Missouri Cavalry. This included Cave's Company N, under the command of Amos Hulett.[6]

When Porter's cavalry disbanded with plans to regroup in Arkansas, Cave remained with Hulett's company for a few months, but it is unclear from his record whether or not he ever made it to Arkansas. Whatever the case, by the end of the year, Cave had returned to the Boone County region, still looking for a fight. According to his February 12 statement, Cave was once again "sworn into the rebel service," this time by a Captain Robert Maupin, "for 3 years or the war." After this enlistment, he glibly noted, Cave had been "knocking round the county most everywhere" with a Lieutenant John Brown—apparently his cousin—and a Benjamin Batterton. He admitted to taking part in "the raid on Columbia" with Brown and about a dozen other rebels during the night of January 11, 1863. They unsuccessfully attempted to free from the Columbia jail several Confederate soldiers and guerrillas who had been captured recently.[7]

Three weeks later, on January 31, 1863, Cave, Brown, and Batterton robbed several local militiamen on a road outside of Columbia, only to be confronted by a patrol from the 61st Enrolled Missouri Militia sent out in search of the thieves. About six miles from Columbia the militia patrol found the perpetrators. According to the report of Lieutenant Colonel Francis T. Russell, who led the expedition, they encountered the rebels in question and chased them "10 or 12 miles & overtook them in full flight." They captured Cave and Batterton, but Brown managed to make his escape. Just as the militia arrived back in Columbia with their captives, Batterton yelled out a hurrah for Confederate president Jefferson Davis. Enraged at this defiant outburst, one of the captors shot and killed Batterton on the spot. Russell's report made no mention of Brown's escape; furthermore, it cryptically mentioned that Benjamin Batterton was "since dead." The report also noted that Cave and Batterton had in their possession clothing and other items stolen earlier that day. After holding Cave at Columbia for just over a week, Federal officials sent "him forward to St. Louis . . . to be disposed as the Provost Marshall General shall see proper."[8]

As a prisoner, Cave exhibited few signs of fear or intimidation. He freely, indeed defiantly, admitted his involvement with the Confederates, as shown in the statement he wrote just after his capture and in his February 12 statement. In the latter document he revealed that since joining the Confederate service he had consistently been in arms against the U.S. government with weapons he provided himself. He acknowledged assisting in "taking or pressing horses, arms, or other property" on more than one occasion. More important, when asked if he was a "southern sympathizer," Cave curtly answered, "Yes." Then when queried if he "sincerely desire[d] to have the southern people put down in this war, and the authority of the U.S. government over them restored?" Cave emphatically replied, "No." Finally, Cave, who identified himself as a "Confed. Soldier," made the request "I want to be Exchanged & sent South."[9]

In this statement, Tommy admitted that his father opposed his enlistment in the Confederate service. "When I went out twas against my father's wish," Tommy attested. "[H]e told me never to come back." A postwar memoir based on Margaret Cave's recollections of events confirms that William Cave did not want Tommy to join the army. Unable to deter the lad from signing up, however, she claimed that William "outfitted" Tommy "well with all the necessary equipment." Of course, one may question the veracity of this account. It was written by a third party and published half a century after Cave's capture. Furthermore, the volume in which it appears was produced by the United Daughters of the Confederacy at the height of their drive to reshape the memory of the war in the form of the "Lost Cause." If this account is accurate, it may explain how the youth was able to remain armed. Whatever the case, it is evident that Tommy Cave's father disapproved of the boy's desire to enlist but could not stop him. Perhaps this is why there is no evidence that Cave's parents pursued Tommy's release while he was held as a prisoner in nearby Columbia or after he was removed to St. Louis.[10]

One thing not made explicit by his statements is why Tommy Cave supported the Southern cause so strongly that he felt compelled to fight for it. A growing body of literature has investigated why men, and boys, chose to enlist during the 1860s conflict, suggesting that there was a multitude of factors. As one might suspect, for those who joined the Confederate army, protecting the institution of slavery stood prominently (albeit not exclusively) among the reasons that men fought. Circumstances in Missouri proved even more complex, as many who rebelled against the Federal government did so because they resented the intrusion of the government in the form of the Union army into their state, and not necessarily from Confederate sympathies. That was not the case with Tommy Cave, who openly identified himself as a "southern sympathizer" and a "Confed. soldier" and unabashedly admitted that he desired victory for the South. As the oldest son of a slave-owning family, it may have been only natural for Cave to support the Confederacy. Of course, the lure of adventure may have attracted him to the army, as it did many other young men who harbored a romanticized vision of war. According to historian Edmund Drago, "In the South underage boys, living in a slave society circumscribed by a code of chivalry and honor, knew instinctively that military service in this war was an opportunity to manhood, freedom and glory they could not reject." If that was the case, then nothing Cave saw or did during the half year of his initial enlistment, even being captured and imprisoned, and witnessing Batterton brutally shot down, served to dissuade him from continuing the fight.[11]

In addition, Cave's enlistment may have been an attempt to gain autonomy from his father. In her study of divided families during the Civil War, Taylor asserts that "coming-of-age struggles between sons and their fathers . . . were part of everyday life in midcentury families." During the war, such generational "rebellions" were commonly played out by sons leaving home to fight, against their fathers' wishes and usually against the side with which their fathers sympathized. Such family divisions were most common in the border states and usually entailed a Confederate son leaving a Unionist family. "The Confederacy's call for independence," Taylor explains, "meshed well with this young generation's desire for autonomy." In the case of the Caves, both father and son supported the same side, yet for whatever reason, William Cave chose to remain, at least overtly, a passive observer in the war. Marten points out that during the war children "saw themselves not merely as appendages to their parents' experience but as actors in their own right in the great national drama." For Tommy, it was not enough to observe the war from home with his father. Whatever his own involvement, William Cave did not want his son to enlist in the Confederate service and let his son know this. Tommy's disobedience, therefore, represents a form of rebellion against his father, as well as an assertion of independence from him. This fact would not go unnoticed by the Federal army officers in whose hands Tommy Cave's fate rested.[12]

On February 14, 1863, W. J. Masterson, the commander of the Gratiot Street Prison in St. Louis, sent a letter to the Department of the Missouri Provost Marshal General Franklin Dick about "the case of Thos. H. Cave, a boy only fifteen years of age." "The extreme youth of the prisoner," Masterson continued, "is my reason for this specially calling attention to his case." Cave, in fact, had turned sixteen twelve days earlier while in custody in Columbia. Nevertheless, Masterson considered that Cave's age warranted him special consideration. Cave would not be unique in this respect. Less than a week after Masterson wrote to Dick about Cave, Dick ordered the release of Clement H. Knott, a sixteen-year-old prisoner who had also been with Porter's 1st Northeast Missouri Cavalry. A resident of Ralls County, Missouri, Knott entered the service of the Confederacy in July 1862, about the same time as Cave. Knott was captured in neighboring Monroe County the following October and, like Cave, would be sent to the Gratiot Street Prison. Knott's release from custody in February 1863 came with expectations. First, the youth had to swear an oath of allegiance to the Federal government and promise not to take up arms in rebellion again. Second, he had to enlist in the Enrolled Missouri Militia, a local home guard designed to try to the keep the peace in the factionalized (and fractured) state. Finally, Knott had to report on a regular basis to the provost marshal in Monroe County to affirm his continued good behavior, and otherwise "to obey [the provost marshal's] orders."[13]

In fact, there were several other young prisoners from Missouri who, like Knott, gained their release in this way. For instance, sixteen-year-old Samuel Henley ran off to join the Confederate army in 1862. Once the boy was captured, his father managed to secure Henley's release on the condition that the youth swear to the oath of allegiance and that a bond of $1,000 be paid to guarantee the boy's future good behavior. Likewise, seventeen-year-old Thomas Shearer enlisted in Porter's 1st Northeast Missouri Cavalry in early August 1862 and was captured five weeks later in Shelby County, Missouri. Like Knott, Shearer gained his release on his oath and a $1,000 bond along with his agreement to join the Enrolled Missouri Militia. And seventeen-year-old Manlius R. Suggett of Callaway County, who was arrested "In the Bush" in the late summer of 1863, was released after giving his oath and paying a bond for his good behavior because "of his youth (but 17), and the absence of testimony to convict him of any Overt act."[14]

Such releases continued as the war progressed, even after James O. Broadhead replaced Franklin Dick. Fourteen-year-old Ferdinand Mindrup, sixteen-year-old John G. Craft, and eighteen-year-old James M. Hutton all entered the Confederate army as conscripts during Sterling Price's fall 1864 raid and soon fell prisoner to the Federals. Broadhead, like his predecessor, decided it best to return these boys to their parents rather than keep them as prisoners. And there would be others.[15]

In these cases, the provost marshal general of the Department of the Missouri made a decision to release these young men from Federal custody because of their age. Of course, loyalty mattered, too, or at least showing a change of heart about siding with the rebels. But it does not appear that loyalty was absolutely required for release of an underage soldier. Two factors may help explain why these army officers proved willing to release the young men, even when the boys' loyalty remained in question during time of rebellion. The first reason relates to the value Americans placed on the unity of the family. Even though the boys were caught in arms against the Federal government, the government felt an obligation to return the children to their parents. Second, nineteenth-century American society witnessed a new understanding of childhood, which recognized the teen years as a critical time of growth and development while at the same time reinforcing the notion of the family. As Steven Mintz and Susan Kellogg have observed, "According to an emerging consensus" among nineteenth-century middle-class parents, "only a gradual process of maturation within the protective confines of the home could ensure a smooth transition to adulthood." Thus, minors increasingly remained in the home under the supervision and guidance of their parents until they reached their late teens or early twenties. Therefore, it would appear that for younger prisoners of war during the Civil War, at least in the St. Louis area, Union authorities often respected this parental relationship and in many cases returned their underage charges to their parents.[16]

To be sure, in the nineteenth century state and local governments at times intervened in the raising of children, even to the point of removing children from the custody of their parents. Custody law shifted from viewing children as property to treating them in a way that recognized and protected their best interests. Whether the best caretaker be the father or the mother, the courts honored the sanctity of parenthood as long as the parents were competent. Certainly, these governments never left the children on their own. Instead, they created institutions specifically designed to protect, reform, and/or punish the children in question. Aside from the brief intervention of the Freedmen's Bureau in black families immediately after the Civil War, the Federal government would not involve itself with such family matters on a permanent basis until the late nineteenth and early twentieth centuries with the advent of Progressivism.[17]

Once Union authorities released young prisoners to their parents, responsibility for the youths' behavior rested on the parents' shoulders. Why, then, was Tommy Cave kept as a prisoner while others like him were returned to their families? The answer may lie with Cave's relationship with his father. In the nineteenth century, the authority of fathers contracted somewhat. The expansion of the marketplace meant that boys would be much less dependent on their fathers for their future livelihoods. According to Mintz and Kellogg, fathers became "the symbol of public and external conceptions of authority" whose responsibility it was to "prepare a child for a life of disciplined independence." Tommy Cave, it appeared, desired the independence of an adult but lacked the discipline that went with it. He had rejected the authority of his father, despite the Confederate sympathies they shared. N. D. Randall of the provost marshal's office in Columbia, Missouri, probably captured the situation best when he noted in Cave's file that the boy was a "Rebel to [his] Gov't. & to his Parents." Rather than fearing that Cave's Confederate-sympathizing father would let the boy run off again to rejoin the rebels, Franklin Dick assumed that once again William Cave would not be able to stop his son from disobeying. Therefore, Tommy Cave's status as a minor would not lead to his release. But the question remained, what to do with Cave if not release him?[18]

Cave's fate rested in the hands of Franklin Dick. Unlike Clement Knott, who was returned to his family, Cave would be retained as a prisoner. Dick's decision actually guaranteed that Cave eventually would be released. Once designated as a run-of-the-mill prisoner, the teen would be eligible for prisoner exchange, as he desired. Cave was transferred to the Alton Military Prison in Illinois on March 24, 1863. A day later, the St. Louis–based *Missouri Democrat* reported among the names of Confederates recently sent to Alton one "T. H. Cave, of Boone co." Instead of listing him with his regiment or unit, as others appeared in the news item, the paper identified him with the term "rebel."[19]

In the cases dealing with underage prisoners of war, Dick acted, in effect, as a family court judge, a function that fell well outside of the normal role of the provost marshal general. By returning youths to their parents, Dick acted as a protector of the family, entrusting the boys' fathers in particular with the responsibility of maintaining their sons' good behavior. With Tommy Cave, Dick acknowledged the lad's past disobedience of his father and the likelihood that Tommy would disobey his father again. Whether intentionally or not, by deciding to keep Cave as a prisoner, Dick emancipated the teen from his parents' control. This came more than a century before the child liberation movement, which paved the way for children to sue their parents for their freedom. Doubtless, Franklin Dick's intention was not to establish innovative policy in the field of family law or children's rights. Rather, he faced a tough decision generated by the divisive conditions of civil war.[20]

Dick's choice allowed Cave to be exchanged eventually and to return to the Confederate army to continue the fight for the Southern cause. In June

1863 Union authorities paroled Cave with about a thousand other prisoners from the Alton Prison and sent them to City Point, Virginia, to be turned over to Confederate authorities for exchange. At this point Cave united with about seventy other Missourians under Captain Charles Woodson to form Woodson's Cavalry, also known as Company A, 1st Missouri Cavalry. The only Missouri unit to serve in the Virginia theater under Robert E. Lee, Woodson's Cavalry spent the next year either on garrison duty or attached to the 62nd Virginia Mounted Infantry. During the Battle of New Market on May 15, 1864, Woodson and his Missourians earned distinction for the key role they played in that Confederate victory, despite incurring heavy casualties. One of them was the now seventeen-year-old Tommy Cave.[21]

Today a marker describes the actions of Woodson's Cavalry in the 1864 battle at New Market. The marker includes Tommy Cave's last words, purportedly uttered to an officer as he fell to the ground: "Good-bye, Lieutenant, I am killed." After the battle, Cave's body was moved to nearby Harrisonburg in the Shenandoah Valley, where it was put to rest. Months later, Mrs. Cave learned of the fate of her oldest son. She now mourned not only for Tommy but also for husband, William, who just weeks earlier had been killed by Federal soldiers who suspected him of aiding and abetting rebel guerrillas at his Bone County farm. Tommy Cave gave his life in the name of the rebellion against the Federal government. He could do so only because of the rebellion he first carried out against his parents' authority.[22]

NOTES

1. T. H. Cave, "Woodson's Cavalry," Compiled Service Records of Confederate Soldiers who served in organizations from the State of Missouri (RG 109), National Archives (hereafter cited as Compiled Service Records).

2. Amy Murrell Taylor, *The Divided Family in Civil War America* (Chapel Hill: University of North Carolina Press, 2005); James Marten, *The Children's Civil War* (Chapel Hill: University of North Carolina Press, 1998), 2.

3. Mary Harrison Claggett, "Memoirs of Mrs. Margaret Harrison Cave," in *Reminiscences of the Women of Missouri during the Sixties* (Jefferson City, MO: United Daughters of the Confederacy Missouri Division, 1913), 153–54; William S. Cave, Soldiers' Records, War of 1812–World War I, Missouri Digital Heritage Collections, Missouri Office of Secretary of State, Missouri State Archives, Jefferson City, Missouri, http://www.sos.mo.gov/TIF2P-DFConsumer/DispPDF.aspx?fTiff=/archives/AdjutantGeneral/Black_Hawk_War/ServiceCards/s914/1743.tif&Fln=S141.pdf; William F. Switzler, *History of Boone County, Missouri* (St. Louis: Western Historical Company, 1882), 423–24; 1860 United States Census, Missouri, Boone County, Columbia Twp, 781; T. H. Cave, "Woodson's Cavalry," Compiled Service Records; James William McGettigan Jr., "Boone County Slaves: Sales, Estate Division and Families, 1820–1860," *Missouri Historical Review* 72 (January 1978): 176–77.

4. *Missouri Statesman* (Columbia), September 5, 1856, and September 9, 1864; Claggett, "Memoirs of Mrs. Margaret Harrison Cave," 155; Switzler, *History of Boone County, Missouri*, 741; Janice A. Toms, *Oaths and Bonds for Boone County Missouri* (Independence, MO: Two Trails Publishing, 2008), [35]; James E. McGhee, *Guide to Missouri Confederate Units, 1861–1865* (Fayetteville: University of Arkansas Press, 2008), 127–28; Thomas Cave, "1st Northeast Missouri Cavalry," Compiled Service Records. Cave's records are spread out among at least three Confederate units: Woodson's Cavalry, the 1st Northeast Missouri Cavalry, and the 6th Missouri Infantry. For Missourians' response to the Missouri-Kansas border war, see Michael Fellman, *Inside War: The Guerrilla Conflict in Missouri during the American Civil War* (New York: Oxford University Press, 1989), esp. 3–22.

5. *War of the Rebellion: A Compilation of the Official Records of the Union and Confederate Armies*, 70 vols. in 128 books (Washington, DC: Government Printing Office, 1880–1901), 4: 1, 131; 4: 1, 1095; 4: 3, 178; U.S. War Department, *Revised Regulations for the Army of the United States, 1861* (Philadelphia: J. G. L. Brown, Printer, 1861), 130; Steven Mintz, *Huck's Raft: A History of American Childhood* (Cambridge: Belknap Press of Harvard University Press, 2004), 121; Emmy E. Werner, *Reluctant Witnesses: Children's Voices from the Civil War* (Boulder, CO: Westview Press, 1998), 9.

6. T. H. Cave, "Woodson's Cavalry," Compiled Service Records. For more on Porter's regiment, see Joseph A. Mudd, *With Porter in North Missouri: A Chapter in the History of the War between the States* (Washington, DC: National Publishing Company, 1909); and McGhee, *Guide to Missouri Confederate Units*, 51–54.

7. T. H. Cave, "Woodson's Cavalry," Compiled Service Records; McGhee, *Guide to Missouri Confederate Units*, 53; Switzler, *History of Boone County, Missouri*, 428–29; Nichols, *Guerrilla Warfare in Civil War Missouri*, vol. 2, *1863*, 25.

8. T. H. Cave, "Woodson's Cavalry," Compiled Service Records; Nichols, *Guerrilla Warfare in Civil War Missouri*, vol. 2, *1863*, 26.

9. T. H. Cave, "Woodson's Cavalry," Compiled Service Records.

10. Ibid.; Claggett, "Memoirs of Mrs. Margaret Harrison Cave," 155.

11. Fellman, *Inside War*, esp. 23–80; T. H. Cave, "Woodson's Cavalry," Compiled Service Records; Edmund L. Drago, *Confederate Phoenix: Rebel Children and Their Families in South Carolina* (New York: Fordham University Press, 2008), 16. For a broader discussion of why soldiers fought, see Reid Mitchell, *Civil War Soldiers: Their Expectations and Their Experiences* (New York: Viking, 1988); and James M. McPherson, *For Cause and Comrades: Why Men Fought in the Civil War* (New York: Oxford University Press, 1997).

12. Taylor, *Divided Family in Civil War America*, 5, 13–34; Marten, *Children's Civil War*, 5. The elder Cave may have been a clandestine aider and abettor of rebel guerrillas during the war until he was killed by Unionist militia who accused him of such activities. See *Missouri Statesman* (Columbia), September 9, 1864; Claggett, "Memoirs of Mrs. Margaret Harrison Cave," 155; Switzler, *History of Boone County, Missouri*, 741.

13. T. H. Cave, "Woodson's Cavalry," Compiled Service Records; Thomas Henry Cave in "Harrison Genealogy Repository," http://freepages.genealogy.rootsweb.ancestry.com/~harrisonrep/Harrison/d0044/g0000087.html; *Missouri Democrat*, February 21, 1863; Clement Knott, "1st Northeast Missouri Cavalry," Compiled Service Records.

14. Samuel Henley, Union Provost Marshals' File of Papers Relating to Individual Civilians, Roll 192 (RG 109), National Archives (hereafter cited as PM Papers); Thomas Sherer

[*sic*], "1st Northeast Missouri Cavalry," Compiled Service Records; Thomas Shearer, PM Papers, Roll 243; Manlins [*sic*] Suggett, "Miscellaneous, Missouri," Compiled Service Records; Manlius R. Suggett, PM Papers, Roll 260.

15. Ferdinand Mindrup, PM Papers, Roll 192; John G. Craft, PM Papers, Roll 61; 1860 United States Census, Missouri, Ray County, Grape Grove Town, 209; James M. Hutton, PM Papers, Roll 138; 1860 United States Census, Missouri, Franklin County, Beouff Township, 43.

16. Michael Grossberg, *Governing the Hearth: Law and the Family in Nineteenth-Century America* (Chapel Hill: University of North Carolina Press, 1985), 3–4; Steven Mintz and Susan Kellogg, *Domestic Revolutions: A Social History of American Family Life* (New York: Free Press, 1988), 58–60.

17. Mary Ann Mason, *From Father's Property to Children's Rights: The History of Child Custody in the United States* (New York: Columbia University Press, 1994), 49–73, 85–96; Mintz, *Huck's Raft*, 145–99; Barbara Finkelstein, "Uncle Sam and the Children: A History of Government Involvement in Child Rearing," in *Growing Up in America: Children in Historical Perspective*, ed. N. Ray Hiner and Joseph M. Hawes (Urbana: University of Illinois Press, 1985), 255–66. During Reconstruction the Freedmen's Bureau collaborated with state courts in the South to allow African American children to be apprenticed as laborers for former slave owners, effectively removing the children from their parents. See Rebecca J. Scott, "The Battle over the Child: Child Apprenticeship and the Freedmen's Bureau in North Carolina," in Hiner and Hawes, *Growing Up in America*, 193–207; and Mintz, *Huck's Raft*, 113–15.

18. Mintz and Kellogg, *Domestic Revolutions*, 54–55; Grossberg, *Governing the Hearth*, 7; T. H. Cave, "Woodson's Cavalry," Compiled Service Records.

19. Thomas H. Cane [*sic*], "6th Missouri Infantry," Compiled Service Records; *Missouri Democrat*, March 25, 1863.

20. Thomas H. Cane [*sic*], "6th Missouri Infantry," Compiled Service Records; Joseph M. Hawes, *The Children's Rights Movement: A History of Advocacy and Protection* (Boston: Twayne, 1991), 115–17; Mintz and Kellogg, *Domestic Revolutions*, 231.

21. For the best study of Woodson's Cavalry, see Thomas F. Curran, "Memory, Myth, and Musty Records: Charles Woodson's Missouri Cavalry in the Army of Northern Virginia," pts. 1 and 2, *Missouri Historical Review* 94 (October 1999): 25–41; (January 2000): 160–75. For more on New Market, see William C. Davis, *The Battle of New Market* (New York: Doubleday, 1975).

22. "The Historical Marker Database," http://www.hmdb.org/marker.asp?marker=13197 (accessed February 25, 2010); Claggett, "Memoirs of Mrs. Margaret Harrison Cave," 157–58; Switzler, *History of Boone County, Missouri*, 741; *Missouri Statesman* (Columbia), September 9, 1864. Cave's last words were supposedly recorded by Lieutenant Edward Herndon Scott in his diary. The passage containing the quotation was then cited in *Memorials of Edward Herndon Scott, M.D.* (Rockingham Co., VA: Ruebush, Kieffer and Co., Printers, 1973), 15. The whereabouts of the original diary is unknown.

5

Thrills for Children

The Youth's Companion, *the Civil War, and the Commercialization of American Youth*

PAUL B. RINGEL

The week after the Confederate guns fired on Fort Sumter, the Boston children's weekly the *Youth's Companion* opened its issue with a didactic tale called "The Counterfeit Quarter," and its editorial column discussed "Good Friday in Brazil."[1] After the first battle at Bull Run, the paper led with a story called "The Suicide," and the editorial considered "The Notches in the Osiers."[2] Finally, on December 19, 1861, the *Companion* acknowledged the existence of the conflict when "William Walker, a Story of the War" appeared on the front page. The story recounts the internal struggles of the fatherless title character regarding whether to enlist in the Union army or stay home and attend to his mother and sisters. Eventually, he determines that his duty is to join the army, and he dies in his first battle. At the conclusion of the story, the narrator ruminates over the reasons for and consequences of war:

> The great hearts o' all times are those which rise above the thoughts of personal interests, and feel that wrong must be put down and right vindicated at any cost.
>
> But why not do it some other way? Why must men maim and murder each other like wild beasts? Why not settle their differences like rational beings? These are hard questions, too. We only know that every war and every change among the nations is helping to work out God's great plan for the redemption of the world.
>
> And is it worth all this? . . . Yes it *is* worth it, and the mother felt so, in all her grief and desolation, or rather she felt that this is a time when we must not stop to count the cost; when we have nothing to do but go straight forward and leave everything to God.[3]

Thus even as the *Companion* turned toward the war, its concerns were neither public nor political. Instead, the paper's editor, Daniel Sharp Ford, used stories such as "William Walker, A Story of the War" to turn his audience's attention inward to the intensely personal and spiritual question of where an individual's primary responsibility lay during this time of crisis.

Within fifteen months, however, the *Companion*'s approach to the war had shifted dramatically. By early 1863, Ford began to insert stories on the inside pages of the paper that not only presented an overtly pro-Union political stance but also offered explicit and sensational violent details about the war and its effects, the likes of which had rarely appeared in the paper. Some of these stories celebrated Union soldiers as brave and intelligent individuals who could regularly trick Southerners into surrender or death. In "Vermont's Strategy," for example, a "crafty, hard-working, rough-sinewed" young soldier created a device that allowed him to fire a gun from a distance; when the Confederate sentry stood up to fire at the position from which the gun discharged, the Vermonter shot him in the side of the head.[4] Others detailed the moral depravity of slaveholders who tied up slaves so rats could eat their feet or whipped a woman and then soaked her cuts in brine in order to prevent scarring.[5] Thus over the course of the war, the *Companion* moved from ignoring the conflict to using it as an instrument to inspire moral introspection, and finally to presenting it as a moralistic drama suitable for both the instruction and entertainment of its young audience.

This wartime shift was a pivotal stage in Ford's longer struggle to transform the *Companion* into a more widely marketable publication without sacrificing its reputation as a respectable conveyor of conservative Protestant values. Ford and a partner had purchased the *Companion* in late 1856, at a time when the paper was a struggling publication with a circulation of approximately 4,800 subscribers, most of whom resided in or near Boston or Portland, Maine. Before the war, the new owners' commercializing campaigns had confronted resistance, uncertainty, and outright failure. The *Companion*'s antebellum audience, which was mostly affiliated with Congregationalist and other churches still deeply influenced by Puritan theology, proved unwilling to embrace fully Ford's attempts to integrate their children into the nation's emerging culture of consumption and leisure. The conflict itself initially drove Ford even further from his original agenda. Yet wartime circumstances, including displacement of families and a consequent intensification of fears of juvenile delinquency, the financial success of the dime novel industry, and a surge of patriotism on behalf of the Union cause, combined to diminish popular resistance to commercially oriented publications for children. Dozens of children's periodicals emerged in the decade after the Civil War seeking to benefit from this shift, but the *Companion*'s brand of moralistic sensationalism, which Ford had unsuccessfully introduced during the 1850s and gradually reintegrated into the paper during and after the war, drove it to unmatched success during the postwar era. By the 1870s, the paper reached a national audience of more than 100,000 mostly middle-class subscribers, and by the 1890s it had become one of the best-selling periodicals of any genre in the country, with a weekly circulation that allegedly reached over half a million.[6]

The *Companion*'s history during this period, along with the proliferation of periodicals and books for children during and immediately after the Civil War, suggests that the conflict strengthened the connection between children and the nation's market economy. This trend, which parallels the politicization of childhood identified by James Marten, resulted from the greater exposure children received to events happening outside the protected realm of the home during the war.[7] Yet at least in the *Companion*, the commercial connection had a more sustained impact than its political counterpart; while politics largely disappeared from the paper soon after the conclusion of the war, the social issues raised by the growth of the American economy became an increasingly central concern of the publication for the remainder of the nineteenth century.

The unique success of the *Companion*'s moralistic sensationalism also indicates that despite this commercializing trend, many postwar Americans remained decidedly ambivalent about integrating children and youth into the nation's commercial culture. Gail Murray, a historian of children's literature, has argued that during the mid-nineteenth century, "the construction of childhood moved from society's need to redeem the child to one in which the child became the redeemer," but the *Companion*'s continuing presentation of childhood as a time of great physical and spiritual peril offers a prominent counterpoint to the pattern she identifies.[8] Ford's primary challenge was to find a commercially appealing method for conveying those traditional values without alienating an audience that feared the encroachment of such commercialism into the lives of American youth. The Civil War made the drama and violence he employed to this end acceptable to a broad constituency of American families, but the paper's postwar success also derived from Ford's recognition that the conflict had not eradicated fears about the influence a modernizing American society might have on their children.

When Ford took over the *Companion* in January 1857, the paper had been controlled for three decades by Nathaniel Willis, a printer and deacon at the Congregationalist Park Street Church in Boston. Willis's *Companion* presented society outside the home as a physically and morally hazardous place for children, and thus kept its worldview narrow; for the most part, the paper limited its content to Bible stories such as "Young Samuel, a Servant of God" and domestic stories about children's deaths and misbehaviors such as "Emma Winifred; or, The Little Girl Who Was Punished for Sabbath Breaking."[9] By midcentury, though, this approach had begun to lose its appeal with the *Companion's* audience; profits during 1856, Willis's last year as editor, were down over 75 percent from their peak in the early 1840s. In his seventies and without an apparent successor, Willis sold the declining paper to Ford and his largely silent partner, John W. Olmstead, who together had turned the *Christian Watchman*, a Baptist weekly, into one of the most successful publications in New England.[10]

Ford immediately sought to recast the *Companion* as less of a "supplement to the lessons of the public and church schools."[11] "Feejee Islanders," the lead story of Ford's first issue of the *Companion*, opened with an illustration of a sixty-foot hollow man made of wicker who towered over a religious ceremony. As one group of islanders forced living men, women, and children inside the figure, another covered the captives with "combustible materials," preparing to burn them alive. On the margins of this ritual, the community elders selected the victims for the sacrifice while young men speared those who resisted. Other islanders hung their heads or writhed in anguish on the ground, grieving the impending loss of their loved ones. Below the picture, a brief article condemned this society as "very ignorant, superstitious and cruel." However, the story also exposed additional horrors, quoting the Roman poet Lucan's description of a sacred grove filled with "multitudes of altars on which they sacrificed their victims," and the historian Pliny's impression that the islanders "consider it a part of their most solemn and most obligatory religion to put men to death; and to feed on their dead bodies they esteem most wholesome."[12]

"Feejee Islanders" launched Ford's effort to make the *Companion* more commercially appealing by borrowing the strategies of sensationalism and exoticism from the story papers and penny press of the era and recalibrating them for his young audience by presenting thrilling narratives (accompanied by dramatic pictures) as cautionary tales that reinforced the *Companion's* traditional values by highlighting the dangers of life in societies different from readers' own American Protestant culture. The stories covered topics such as trench warfare in the Crimea, with a picture of a soldier's head and bayoneted rifle emerging from a foxhole as cannonballs landed on either side of him; *bastinado*, a Turkish method of torture, with an illustration of a man in a fez and military uniform raising a whip to a bound and cowering prisoner while a group of turbaned and robed men looked on with great interest; and the Pocahontas story staged as a romance of betrayal and deception, with a picture of the doleful girl who died of a broken heart.[13] Through this unique brand of moralistic stories, Ford attempted to appeal to a broader audience by expanding the *Companion*'s worldview without alienating his existing readers.

Apparently this strategy failed, for after three months this campaign abruptly ceased. The reasons for this policy change remain unclear; no complaints from customers or the public about the *Companion*'s new direction have surfaced, but clearly either the audience or Ford's partner found this material inappropriate for young readers.[14] Yet this initial setback did not cause Ford to abandon his commercialization campaign. Instead, he sought to redefine the paper's relationship with its audience in other ways. He redesigned the layout of the *Companion* to make it look more like the popular adult story papers of the era, with larger illustrations and more columns of text. He began to accept advertising, disregarding Willis's concern that the practice had "a tendency to injure public morals."[15] He also introduced a premiums program that enabled entrepreneurial young readers to earn prizes by selling new subscriptions of the *Companion* to friends, family, and neighbors. All of these changes emphasized a reciprocal commercial relationship between the paper and its young readers rather than the unilateral didactic affiliation that had predominated during Willis's tenure. In taking such an approach, Ford still sought to establish a connection between the cultures of American childhood and the market economy.

This strategy carried tremendous risk at a time when many Americans viewed the marketplace as a potentially hazardous influence on American youth, and Ford simultaneously moved to present the changes in the *Companion* as a vehicle for reinforcing and even expanding the paper's established reputation as a trustworthy publication for children. In the editorial of his first issue, he promised readers that the new publishers would continue to produce a paper designed to "best promote the good in your minds and hearts," and followed this pledge with a new argument:

> For thirty years it [the *Companion*] has gladdened many a family circle with its weekly visits, and it will be no fault of ours if its coming to a yet larger company than now, does not meet with greater pleasure than ever. We have no doubt it is your wish to get good from your reading, and also to impart good to others. With such aims in life you will be blessed and

happy. You will consequently, we trust, make an effort to introduce the
Companion to your friends, say a kind word for it, and induce them to
take it. You will thus do good, and thus also you will entitle yourself to
some one or more of the pretty and useful premium presents which we
have already offered you.[16]

Thus for the first of many times during Ford's tenure at the *Companion*, he
aligned the paper's commercial ambitions with its readers' interests as both
Christians and consumers. If young readers helped to increase the audience
of the *Companion*, they would not only spread upstanding values to their
peers but also receive more entertainment and (potentially) more rewards
through the paper's premiums program.

After the dissipation of his sensationalism strategy in April 1857, Ford even
continued to stretch the paper's ideological boundaries in a less dramatic but
potentially more resonant fashion. His sensational stories had maintained
Willis's perspective that the world outside the home contained a myriad of
physical and moral hazards for young Americans but radically diverged in
their approach to these concerns; rather than sheltering young readers, Ford
chose to educate them through carefully managed exposure to such threats.
Yet in stories such as "Feejee Islanders" and "The Bastinado," the danger had
remained minimal because their events were so distant from the actual experiences of the *Companion*'s readers. Ford's new twist on the sensational genre
kept the paper's traditionally cautionary perspective on public life and significantly reduced the thrills of the exotic stories, but it addressed a subject
much closer to the hopes and fears of the paper's subscribers: the increased
participation of young Americans in public life.

The new stories, which appeared regularly on the front page for the next
four years, highlighted the dangers of the urban commercial environment or
of settings dominated by peers rather than parents. "Wanted—A Boy from
the Country" presented a young man struggling to cope with an unscru-
pulous employer, while "Frank Norton, or, the Unheeded Admonition"
introduced a main character who tries (and fails) to handle the pressure of
classmates who urged him to smoke against his mother's wishes. Girls also
faced danger outside the home, particularly in the city, if they became overly
concerned with rituals of fashion and courtship, as in "Deception," in which
a young debutante's mistreatment of a respectable suitor in her pursuit of
a flashy but irresolute young man results in the destruction of her reputation.[17] While stripped of the violence and exoticism of their predecessors,
these stories placed young Americans at the center of the narrative, implic-

itly acknowledging that young Americans among the *Companion's* primarily northeastern middle-class audience were leaving the security of their local communities with increasing frequency.

Ford built this genre into a vehicle that served the *Companion's* commercial and ideological needs by accentuating the extremes of youths' public experiences. Not every young business clerk worked for an immoral employer, nor were many girls capable, as in "Grace Darling," of instigating a rescue in the midst of a natural disaster.[18] However, by sensationalizing situations that were becoming increasingly ordinary in the lives of many of his young readers, Ford fed adult subscribers' concerns about the encroaching negative influences of life outside the home, creating additional demand for assistance from a reputable children's publication such as the *Companion*. At the same time, such fears justified the presence of more stories identifying the dangers of nondomestic environments, which allowed Ford to present narratives with more entertainment value for his young readers.

The onset of war severely tested this formula. Even though he treated his young readers as active participants in aspects of the nation's culture that dealt with commerce and consumption, on the eve of the war, Ford was not yet prepared to perceive them as part of the American public when considering issues of politics or social change. As the sectional conflict increased during the 1850s and fighting broke out in 1861, Ford assiduously avoided addressing the topics of war or slavery in the pages of the *Companion*. Once he began to address the Civil War in stories such as "William Walker, A Story of the War," it was not presented as a hazard for young people along the lines of the dishonest employers or gossiping classmates. Instead, the crisis sparked Ford to return to the *Companion's* traditional role of directing young people's attention inward, toward reassessment of their own moral development and their duties to family and community in this time of national calamity.

Ford's own process of formulating the *Companion's* response to where young people's responsibilities lay during the war was clearly still in flux. Alice Fahs correctly notes that the *Companion's* attitude toward boys on the battlefield was mixed. "The Michigan Drummer Boy" glorified the "spunk" of the title character who, after having his drum "blown to atoms" by a shell, recovered to singlehandedly capture a rebel soldier, yet in "The Boy Soldier" the author directly warned readers not to become enamored by the supposed glory and romance of military service: "This is not your place. You are too young for that."[19] Ford would never again so overtly suggest that young men's duty was to enlist to support the Union cause as he did in "William Walker, A Story of the War." Instead, he skirted the issue by focusing on the responsibilities of children who remained at home. Literal examples of what children could do to aid the Union war effort included sending articles from home (such as books or clothing) or even just letters to men at the front, or wearing their old clothes for another year and sending the money saved to buy supplies for the army.[20]

The *Companion* also demanded more from its readers than simple economy or generosity toward those on the front lines; it expected Northern children to sacrifice personal interests in support of the war effort. In "The Patriot Boy," a child too young to go into the army took a job as a bookkeeper and relegated his studies to the evening hours in order to help support the families of soldiers who went off to war. The paper asked its girl readers, who, as members of prosperous families, typically would not have worked outside the home, to make emotional sacrifices. In "Myself or My Country?" a young girl slowly comes to the realization that she had no right to prevent her father from fulfilling his duty by enlisting, despite the potential damage to her own life. Children could also make basic behavioral modifications, such as those indicated by a soldier in "The Brother's Letter" who told his younger brother at home that the best thing he could do for the Union was to obey his mother.[21]

This concern about filial obedience to parental values had figured prominently in the paper before the conflict, but the pervasive displacement of fathers and older brothers from the home heightened many Americans' wartime fears of juvenile dissipation and delinquency. Marten cites a number of newspaper articles from both the North and the South bemoaning the immoral and criminal behavior of the nation's youth, which included truancy, gambling, petty theft, vandalism, and assaults on other children as well as African American refugees. The *Companion* attempted to fill the vacuum of absent role models by reinvigorating its traditional efforts to provide a supplementary source of moral guidance for its readers. Editorials urged children, particularly boys, to adopt behaviors ranging from punctuality to honoring their parents, all of which served to promote social stability in the midst of the war's upheaval. The *Companion* also evaluated military and political heroes as models of good and bad behavior. "General Mitchel and the Newsboys" informed the audience of the Ohio division commander's rise from an impoverished newsboy and suggested that they too could make an important contribution to society through diligence and proper conduct. The more equivocal tone of "General Grant's Boyhood" countenanced the Union hero's youthful propensity for fighting only in defense of his nation's honor. Most negative was the editorial that followed President Lincoln's assassination, in which Ford employed the tragedy as a cautionary tale about the dangers of improper amusements:

We are sorry that he should have received his death-wound in a theatre. For some reason it seems to be required of men of very high station, and much honored, that they should consent to receive some of their popular honors at the theatre, and probably Mr. Lincoln's education had not rendered him fully sensible of its wrong. But we are sorry he was there. The fearful opportunities for sin and crime afforded by the theatre have made it fatal for more than one.[22]

The presentation of such a critical editorial in the immediate aftermath of the national tragedy of Lincoln's assassination indicates the seriousness of Ford's commitment to helping his young readers avoid physically and morally damaging behaviors.

This commitment also allowed Ford to resurrect his genre of cautionary sensationalism, for the rising wartime fears of juvenile delinquency began to push the *Companion*'s ideological and commercial agendas back into alignment. In 1863, the paper gradually started to reintroduce stories about the dangers of the world outside the home (although not of the war). Peer environments became a particular focus of fictional narratives from this period, with front-page stories highlighting the cruelty of youths unsupervised by parents. More dramatic nonfiction stories about the dangers of town and city life remained buried on the inside pages of the paper, but titles such as "Ending on the Gallows" and "Twenty Years in the State's Prison" made the dire ramifications of juvenile misbehavior clear to regular readers, if not to casual observers or passersby at newsstands.[23]

Ford's return to sensationalism at this time reflected the nascent shift during the war toward a more commercialized approach to young readers within the publishing industry. The most prominent source of this change was the wartime success with boy readers of dime novels published by the firm of Beadle and Adams. Sales numbers for Beadle's dime novels are notoriously sketchy, but by all accounts sales of the books were huge; some scholars claim that the most popular of these weekly publications sold more than 100,000 copies. The publishers did not originally target juveniles as a primary audience for their books, but a flood of anecdotal evidence suggests that these adventure stories, which Beadle and Adams shipped by the tens of thousands to Union army camps, trickled down to become wildly popular with Northern boys too young to serve in the military. Moreover, this connection between young readers and sensational fiction aroused little apparent opposition during the war years. Even Charles Eliot Norton, the scion of Harvard and the liberal northeastern intellectual and cultural establishment, published an article in the staid *North American Review* in 1864 that noted the widespread popularity of dime novels among boys without any hint of the condemnation of the genre that would emerge during the 1870s.[24]

Only the occasional use of popular Beadle authors in the *Companion* directly links Ford's revival of sensationalism to the success of the dime novel industry, but by late 1863 Ford added a new type of thrilling fiction to his war coverage that mirrored the violence and drama of dime novels. Young people generally were not the focus of these stories; the pattern Alice Fahs describes in which "children's war novels and war histories invited children to imagine *themselves* as protagonists in the war" rarely occurred in the *Companion*. Instead, Ford made these exciting narratives appropriate for his juvenile audience by framing them as patriotic, moralistic celebrations of Northern skill and Southern vice. While stories such as "Vermont's Strategy" highlighted the ingenuity of Northern soldiers, other war tales portrayed Southern soldiers as war-weary cowards. For example, "A Brave Woman" related the adventure of a Kentucky mother who captured ten "secessionists" who had come to ravage her household. When Union soldiers mocked the captured Confederates for surrendering to a woman, the rebels "said they had been wanting to get captured for sometime past, and were heartily sick of the war, and did not care how they got out of it." *Companion* stories also disparaged Southern civilians as "slothful" and "deceitful," but most often this story genre presented the majority of Confederates as uneducated victims of aristocratic trickery; one example presented a young white Southerner astonished to learn that Union soldiers did not have tails.[25]

Such portrayals allowed the *Companion* to focus on Southern planters as the primary evildoers of the war, a stance that allowed Ford to once again align his theological and commercial interests. The stories that railed against Southern aristocrats offered another opportunity to reinsert violence and drama into the paper without appearing to exploit the horrors of the war for commercial gain. The details of slaveholder's atrocities served as a cautionary example of the depravities to which immoral beliefs and behavior could lead. Such articles provided evidence "that some good has been done by the wives and daughters of our land in sending their loved ones to deliver the oppressed from the hand of the cruel and tyrannical oppressor," but they also allowed Ford a patriotic reason to return to the sensationalism that helped to sell his publications.[26]

This surge of patriotic sensationalism did not extend much past the end of the war in the *Companion*, but Ford seized upon the new, more permissive standards established during the war and quickly transferred the drama and violence of this genre into stories and pictures on other topics. The week after the surrender at Appomattox, the paper brought back its sensational front-page illustrations, beginning with a picture of a lion biting a flailing man through his midsection. Three weeks later, the cover displayed a man scaling down a cliff while reaching out his hand to rescue a young girl, and over the next few months illustrations included an anguished woman covering an infant she had just pulled out of the roiling surf, three medieval knights arresting an affronted man while a mysterious stranger lurked in the background, and an "Italian bandit" and his crony ransacking a castle.[27]

While the emphasis on dramatic images and exoticism in these issues suggested a return to Ford's original antebellum editorial strategies, his postwar approach ultimately reversed the philosophy behind that initial campaign. Whereas in 1857 Ford presented drama distant in time and place from the experiences of his readers in order to distinguish such dangers from the cloistered domestic lives of American youth, by 1865 the Companion's sensational drama emerged from American homes and communities. "The Lighthouse on the Skeve Mhoil," one of the Companion's first postwar stories of this genre, recounted the story of a mother and son trapped in their island lighthouse home with two burglars, one of whom had sworn revenge on the woman because she spurned his proposal of marriage. While the son remained in hiding and thus undiscovered by the villains for most of the story, the mother faced repeated danger, including being tied to a post and left to drown in the incoming tide, before her husband and the crippled assistant who had escaped the burglars returned to rescue them.[28]

Domestic sensationalism such as that in "Skeve Mhoil" suggested that the horrors of war had blurred the divisions between private and public space that had seemed to guarantee children's safety in the antebellum period. As the Companion gradually shifted young Americans into more active roles in these stories, the impact of national issues on local communities seemed more direct. Thus in "Reclaimed," a troubled young boy who set fire to the barns of local farmers because he "hates rich people [who] have no mercy for poor folks" highlighted the class tensions of the Gilded Age, while "The Slave's Crime," which offered a melodrama in which a slave boy (fathered by his owner) and his master's adopted white daughter fell in love, personalized the social costs of slavery. When the mistress of the plantation discovered their affair, she had the daughter sent away and whipped the slave into apparent submission. The boy, with "crime in his heart," retaliated by inducing a rattlesnake to kill the mistress in her bed.[29]

Violent stories that weakened the division between the domestic and public realms left Ford freer to explore the hazards of the outside world in fictional stories about American youth, as long as those nondomestic stories retained the seemingly paradoxical view that home remained the safest place for the nation's children. He expanded his focus gradually, beginning with the schoolroom, where many members of the paper's audience were spending more time than ever before. The *Companion* presented schools as a place where children, free from the oversight of their parents and subject to the influence of peers of uncertain character, might collectively succumb to their basest instincts and veer away from proper standards of respectable behavior. Girls at school planned secret rendezvous with boys, gossiped inappropriately about their classmates, and generally treated each other cruelly; one author called them "savage beings." Schoolboys displayed excessive rowdiness away from the calming feminine influence of the domestic sphere, a problem exemplified through school hazing rituals, which provided the *Companion* with an opportunity to reiterate its traditional connection between children's immoral behavior and physical harm. In all these examples, children's misbehavior occurred because classmates exacerbated an individual's wayward impulses. One editorial from the period attributed such behavior to the period of life that psychologists were just beginning to call adolescence, arguing that "boys and girls who have been obedient, even-tempered and studious, often become at a certain age unaccountably peevish, rebellious and indolent"; bringing such youths together in poorly or unsupervised peer groups only exacerbated the threats to their physical and moral well-being.[30]

The city offered an environment more distant from the small-town hearth and thus more dangerous than the schoolroom, making urban stories the culminating example of Ford's cautionary sensationalism. These stories focused on the dissipation of country boys seeking economic opportunities in the city; the consequences of such dissolution often started as acute embarrassment, but increasingly these effects turned violent as the genre became more well established in the *Companion*. Stories about boys getting lost, robbed, or falsely accused of theft grew into tales of spending money impetuously, escorting disreputable young women to saloons and theaters, and skipping town in a drunken haze one step ahead of the law. Ultimately, the front-page illustrations for these stories focused on the young men's complete moral and physical dissipation; "Aunt Tennant's Wedding Present" displayed a young man reaching for a gun to commit suicide, while "The End of It" featured a youth in respectable clothing sprawled facedown on the stairs leading to a tavern.[31]

The *Companion's* renewed commitment to these genres of cautionary sensationalism after the war coincided with the paper's remarkable economic ascent. Despite greatly intensified competition from new juvenile publications created by nearly every major publishing house, including Harper's, Scribner's, and Ticknor and Fields, as well as by independent entrepreneurs like Frank Leslie, the *Companion's* circulation, which was estimated at 50,000 in 1868, rose by an average of 10,000 subscribers a year over the next ten years and 25,000 for the subsequent decade.[32] The expansion of the paper's premiums program and the hiring of big-name authors such as Harriet Beecher Stowe and Louisa May Alcott contributed to this transformation, but throughout this period, Ford continued to place sensational stories, combined with dramatic illustrations, at the top of the front page, an indication of his belief that these stories strongly appealed to both his current and potential readers.

The circuitous route taken by Ford's *Companion* from the failure of "Feejee Islanders" to the successful postwar stories of the violent decline of American youth reveals how the Civil War both loosened standards for children's literature and left certain cultural presumptions about youth intact. The violence and drama Ford tried to employ for commercial gain in the antebellum *Companion* failed to resonate with audiences, but the war broke down many of the barriers Americans had constructed to protect their offspring from the temptations and dangers of the marketplace. Yet even as those barriers came down, many Americans remained ambivalent about releasing children from the protection of the private sphere. Ford's postwar sensational stories succeeded because they employed thrilling drama and violence to reinforce traditional fears about the physical and moral susceptibility of American youth, pleasing both young readers who craved entertainment and concerned parents who remained wary about the impact such amusements might have on their children's moral development.

NOTES

1. "The Counterfeit Quarter," *Youth's Companion* (hereafter cited as *YC)* 35 (April 18, 1861): 61; "Good Friday in Brazil," *YC* 35 (April 18, 1861): 64.

2. "The Suicide," *YC* 35 (July 25, 1861): 117; "The Notches in the Osiers," *YC* 35 (July 25, 1861): 120.

3. "William Walker, A Story of the War," *YC* 35 (December 19, 1861): 199 (italics in original).

4. "Vermont's Strategy," *YC* 36 (February 19, 1863): 30

5. "Celia the Contraband," *YC* 37 (January 28, 1864): 14; "General Butler and the Slave Whipper," *YC* 36 (December 3, 1863): 196.

6. Circulation and audience information in this paragraph comes from Frank Luther Mott, *A History of American Magazines*, vol. 2, *1850–1865* (Cambridge: Harvard University Press, 1938): 266–68.

7. James Marten, *The Children's Civil War* (Chapel Hill: University of North Carolina Press, 1998), 3.

8. Gail Schmunk Murray, *American Children's Literature and the Construction of Childhood* (New York: Twayne, 1998), 54.

9. "Young Samuel, a Servant of God," *YC* 30 (December 18, 1856): 137; "Emma Winifred; or, The Little Girl Who Was Punished for Sabbath Breaking," *YC* 30 (November 27, 1856): 125.

10. Mott claims that "Ford was the real editor from the time that Olmstead and Company bought the paper. Mott, *History of American Magazines*, 266.

11. David Greene, "*Youth's Companion*," in *Children's Periodicals of the United States*, ed. R. Gordon Kelly (Westport, CT: Greenwood Press, 1984), 509; *YC* 13 (December 6, 1839): 120.

12. "Fejee Islanders," *YC* 31 (January 1, 1857): 1.

13. "French Riflemen in Russia," *YC* 31 (February 19, 1857): 29; "The Bastinado," *YC* 31 (February 26, 1857): 33; "Scene in the Life of Pocahontas," *YC* 31 (January 29, 1857): 17.

14. Mott suggests that Olmstead incited these changes. This argument makes sense, since they were known to disagree about the use of advertising and a premiums program designed to spur circulation, and Ford promoted all these aspects of the *Companion* more aggressively after he and Olmstead severed their partnership in 1867. Mott, *History of American Magazines*, 266.

15. This quotation appeared in the prospectus for the *Companion*, which appeared in Willis's newspaper, the *Boston Recorder*, on April 16, 1827. "Prospectus," *Boston Recorder* 1 (January 3, 1816): 1. It recurred periodically throughout Willis's tenure. For one of several other examples, see *YC* 13 (December 6, 1839): 120.

16. "To Our Friends," *YC* 31 (January 1, 1857): 3.

17. "Wanted—A Boy from the Country," *YC* 31 (June 25, 1857): 101; "Frank Norton, or, the Unheeded Admonition," *YC* 31 (April 2, 1857): 52; "Deception," *YC* 31 (January 1, 1857): 2.

18. "Grace Darling," *YC* 31 (June 18, 1857): 107.

19. Alice Fahs, *The Imagined Civil War: Popular Literature of the North and South, 1861–1865* (Chapel Hill: University of North Carolina Press, 2001), 263.

20. "Give to the Soldiers," *YC* 36 (February 5, 1863): 22; "Do Our Part for the Country," *YC* 36 (March 26, 1863): 50.

21. "The Patriot Boy," *YC* 36 (December 31, 1863): 209; "Myself or My Country?" *YC* 37 (June 9, 1864): 88; "The Brother's Letter," *YC* 36 (May 14, 1863): 78.

22. Marten, *Children's Civil War*, 168–69; "General Mitchel and the Newsboys," *YC* 36 (February 26, 1863): 34; "General Grant's Boyhood," *YC* 37 (January 28, 1864): 14; "The Great National Tragedy," *YC* 38 (April 27, 1865): 66.

23. Examples of the dangers of peer environments from this period include "Naomi Nightingale," in which the Jewish victim of the title character's cruel anti-Semitism dies after forgiving a chastened Naomi for her misdeeds (*YC* 36 [January 29, 1863]: 17), and "Stuttering Fielder," in which a group of boys led by a child from a well-to-do family dunk the poor title character into a pond on a cold March day, nearly killing him (*YC* 36 [April 30, 1863]: 69); "Ending on the Gallows," *YC* 36 (Oct. 29, 1863): 175; "Twenty Years in the State's Prison," *YC* 37 (August 11, 1864): 126. "The First Step" explicitly laid out the course of moral destruction, telling children that disobeying their parents constituted the beginning of their path to prison (*YC* 36 [March 12, 1863]: 44).

24. See, for example, Albert Johanssen, *The House of Beadle and Adams and Its Dime and Nickel Novels: The Story of a Vanished Literature* (Norman: University of Oklahoma Press, 1950), 33, 40; Norton calls the books "without exception, so far as we can judge, unobjectionable morally, whatever fault be found with their literary style and composition. They do not even obscurely pander to vice, or excite the passions." "Beadle's Dime Books," *North American Review* 49 (1864): 308.

25. Fahs, *Imagined Civil War*, 258 (italics in original); "Vermont's Strategy," *YC* 36 (February 19, 1863): 30; "A Brave Woman," *YC* 36 (March 12, 1863): 44; "The Trooper Captain," *YC* 36 (February 12, 1863): 25; "A Southern Boy's Idea of the Yankees," *YC* 36 (October 15, 1863): 164.

26. "The Iron Yoke," *YC* 38 (January 7, 1864): 4.

27. "Fight with a Lion," *YC* 38 (April 13, 1865): 57; "The Wronged Shepherd," *YC* 38 (May 4, 1865): 69; "Agnes Briarly," *YC* 38 (May 18, 1865): 77; "Lord Howth's Arrest," *YC* 38 (May 25, 1865): 77; "The Italian Bandit," *YC* 38 (June 29, 1865): 80.

28. "The Lighthouse on the Skeve Mhoil," *YC* 37 (July 20, 1865): 112.

29. "Reclaimed," *YC* 44 (August 17, 1871): 257; "The Slave's Crime," *YC* 40 (November 14, 1867): 180.

30. Ruth Chesterfield, "The Eagle's Nest," *YC* 46 (January 16, 1873): 17; "Nannie Hapgood," *YC* 49 (February 10, 1876): 43; and "'Aunty Di,'" *YC* 50 (August 16, 1877): 261. Edward Eggleston argued that this rough nature of boys naturally emerged when they formed a group, but particularly arose at boarding schools because "it doesn't do men any good to live apart from women and children." Eggleston, "Kitty's Forty," *YC* 47 (January 1, 1874): 1. "'Piggy,'" *YC* 46 (May 8, 1873): 143; "The Boys at Beechwood," *YC* 47 (August 27, 1874): 277; "Haunted," *YC* 52 (May 29, 1879): 176; "Our 'Dragon,'" *YC* 47 (May 21, 1874): 163; "Hints to Teachers," *YC* 55 (June 22, 1882): 258; "Clubs," *YC* 51 (October 24, 1878): 344.

31. Stories of embarrassment included Rufus Sargent, "Dandy Lyon's Visit to New York," *YC* 46 (June 5, 1873): 177; "'Prince Albert' and the City Girls," *YC* 46 (June 12, 1873): 186; Mrs. Denison, "Sally's Trip to the City," *YC* 48 (January 14, 1875): 10; Ruth Chesterfield, "Aunt Tennant's Wedding Present," *YC* 46 (September 25, 1873): 305; M. A. Denison, "The End of It," *YC* 52 (March 27, 1879): 96

32. Mott, *History of American Magazines*, 268.

6

"Good Children Die Happy"

Confronting Death during the Civil War

SEAN A. SCOTT

Willie was "a child of unusual promise," extraordinarily astute for his age and noted for his grown-up activities and interests. He planned a daily schedule and meticulously followed it in order to make the best use of his time, and in school he excelled at drawing and writing. A local newspaper had even published a poem composed by the lad. He faithfully attended his Sabbath school and on one occasion informed his class leader that he hoped to become a minister or teacher when he grew up. Yet like numerous other children of his day, Willie fell victim to typhoid, which brought an abrupt and sorrowful end to a life filled with expectation for a bright future. Instead of dwelling on this immeasurable loss, the author of Willie's obituary comforted his family and friends with the assurance that he now resided in a better place: "He has gone as an envoy to the court of the King of Heaven, and already wears ensigns of higher honors than earthly courts can confer."[1]

It might come as no surprise that leading newspapers would carry the obituary of William Wallace Lincoln, the eleven-year-old son of the president and first lady who died at the White House in February 1862. In fact, Willie Lincoln's obituary differed little from those of numerous other northern children who passed away between 1861 and 1865. At a time when reports of the heroic deaths of soldiers on the battlefield might have crowded out the presumably mundane accounts of the passing of children at home, religious newspapers continued to print weekly notices describing the passing of infants, children, and teenagers. According to these descriptions, nearly every deceased child possessed an exemplary disposition, demonstrated noteworthy skills, loved God and the church, and gained admittance into heaven at death. This relatively standard format followed by most obituary writers helped sanitize death and attempted to turn the thoughts of grieving family and friends away from their immediate loss to scenes of eternal bliss. Memorialists crafted idealized portraits of the experiences and final earthly moments of children and youths to comply with dominant social expectations and, more important, to provide models of the Good Death archetype for other children to emulate. Although it may be difficult to uncover entirely factual depictions of children through their obituaries, behind every romanticized rendering was a real child whose presence on earth was sorely missed. The following accounts, culled primarily from the pages of Cincinnati's *Western Christian Advocate*, clearly convey the theological assumptions of adults and constitute a neglected resource that provides a valuable, albeit not completely translucent, window into the lives of young people during the Civil War.

Indeed, for Americans of the Civil War era, the reality of death, according to Drew Gilpin Faust, was "the most widely shared of the war's experiences." Condolence letters, casualty lists, and mourning garb were standard features of life on the home front, and the challenges of retrieving, burying, and memorializing fallen soldiers weighed heavily on the minds of civilians while taxing the resources of the national government.[2] Newspaper columns were crowded with the obituaries of soldiers, many of which followed a formulaic pattern describing the deceased's devotion to family, country, and God, even if the latter emphasis sometimes stretched the truth. Stories of the deaths of brave drummer boys or teenage soldiers, whether based on actual events or completely fictionalized, underscored the importance of patriotic sacrifice for citizens of all ages. Yet while honoring Union dead, civilians did not neglect to remember children and youth who passed away on the home front during the war. In fact, the presence of children's obituaries alongside those of soldiers demonstrates the high value that society had come to place upon the lives of children by the middle decades of the nineteenth century. Although the Civil War may not have noticeably altered the content of children's obituaries in comparison with those written in the 1850s, it undoubtedly intensified children's cognizance of death. Whether describing the death of a child who succumbed to disease at home or an underage soldier who fell in battle, the importance of these obituaries and articles lies in their emphasizing to children the need to make spiritual preparation for death in order to enjoy the blessings of heaven and a familial reunion untouched by sickness and war.

Of course, children encountered death and recognized its nearness long before the outbreak of the Civil War. Most people died at home during the mid-nineteenth century, and the prominence given to the deathbed in many households enabled children to glimpse how their family members comported themselves at death. Christian denominations sought to impress upon children the gravity of dying and the need to prepare for eternity. Indeed, a recent analysis of letters and diaries written by children between 1770 and

1861 revealed death to be the most frequent topic of concern. This awareness of mortality not only persisted but oftentimes was heightened during the Civil War. For example, thirteen-year-old Hattie Pontius of Westerville, Ohio, pondered the brevity of life after the unexpected passing of a friend in the autumn of 1862. "How necessary it is to be prepared," she admonished another friend. "How careful we should be in life, for at . . . farthest we have only a few days to live." After two of her brothers enlisted in the Union army, she prayed that God would preserve their lives. However, she did not presume upon divine protection but reminded her brother Will to "be ready at all times to meet death."[3]

Nothing reveals the deliberate effort of adults to compel youngsters to contemplate the meaning of death like the numerous articles published in children's magazines and denominational weeklies during the Civil War. Both types of periodicals included moralistic stories that conscientious parents might employ for didactic purposes. Selecting titles such as "A Foolish Fear; Or, the Death-Watch," "How a Little Boy Can Die," and "Death of a Sabbath School Scholar," the authors of these pieces hoped to convince children that they could face the reality of their own mortality without apprehension. The war served as an ideal backdrop for stories that emphasized the patriotism and faith of drummer boys, and tales of their noble deaths conveyed to children the idea that dying for one's country was an admirable sacrifice. An agent for the Christian Commission recalled the poignant testimony given by a drummer boy from New York during religious meetings at Falmouth, Virginia, in the winter of 1863. The lad, probably about twelve years old, explained that he had entered the army because he was an orphan with no extended family to care for him, and he sincerely sought to meet his parents in heaven some day. After the engagement at Chancellorsville the following spring, as that same Christian Commission worker visited the wounded on the battlefield, he happened upon the body of the orphaned drummer boy. Although the boy's corpse was pale, a smile rested on his face, and his hand clutched a Testament. The religiously inclined observer interpreted this peaceful tableau as evidence that the child had reached heaven's shores and reunited with his parents.[4]

The aforementioned anecdote may have been true, but the story "The Drummer-Boy of Marblehead," which appeared in Henry Ward Beecher's *Independent* in March 1862 with an editorial vouching for the account's authenticity, bore only a slight resemblance to actual events. The romanticized rendering described how fifteen-year-old Albert Mansur, brimming with patriotism, convinced his reluctant parents to let him enlist as a drummer boy with the 23rd Massachusetts. Unwilling to let his only son leave his watchful care, the devoted father enrolled as a private. During the Battle of Roanoke Island in February 1862, Albert snatched a rifle from a fallen soldier and fought valiantly, not even stopping a moment to help his wounded father. With the rebels in retreat, the jubilant lad beat out the cadence of "Yankee Doodle," and a fleeing sharpshooter stopped running long enough to fell the unsuspecting drummer, whose sole dying concern was to know that his regiment had prevailed. Although the narrative emphasized the boy's patriotism and valor, it also conveyed an important religious message. The piece actually began with rambunctious children playing "gunboat" after the victories at Roanoke and Fort Donelson, and their father, intent on conveying the gravity of war, recounted the drummer boy's heart-wrenching tale. The story accomplished its desired effect, for the children abandoned their war games. More significantly, little Nellie demonstrated during bedtime prayer that she had learned a valuable lesson about the necessity of accepting death, for she supplicated God to "'make Albert's mother willing he should be dead.'"[5]

Whether the death of a child was due to natural or martial causes, parents, of course, sometimes struggled to cope with the loss. In order to alleviate this sorrow, some writers of popular fiction during the antebellum era suggested that the deaths of infants and young children might have a redemptive effect by drawing first the attention and ultimately the souls of family members to heaven. At least one Union chaplain found this to be the case after a grieving soldier came forward at the close of a prayer meeting in New Orleans and expressed "his desire to become a Christian." Devastated by news of the death his daughter Nellie, the soldier turned to religion to find solace for his anguished soul. Benjamin Whittemore, chaplain of the 30th Massachusetts, thought it remarkable that the decease of a cherished, innocent child proved more effectual in bringing a father to salvation than any ministrations of a clergyman or prayers of a devout wife or mother. Even death itself, Whittemore asserted, would not terminate Nellie's influence on her father, for her spirit, "like a ministering angel," would hover around him throughout the remainder of his life, "beckoning him ever towards the pure and holy."[6]

The chaplain's confidence that the soldier's daughter had reached heaven epitomized the almost universal assurance in the salvation of infants, children, and even older youths that existed among Protestants by the mid-nineteenth century. As a result of the Second Great Awakening, numerous churchgoers had rejected the rigid determinism of Calvinism and embraced the more liberating individualism of Arminian theology. The emphasis on free will and man's inherent ability to choose God's grace gave him control

HARPER'S
NEW MONTHLY MAGAZINE.

No. CLXX.—JULY, 1864.—Vol. XXIX.

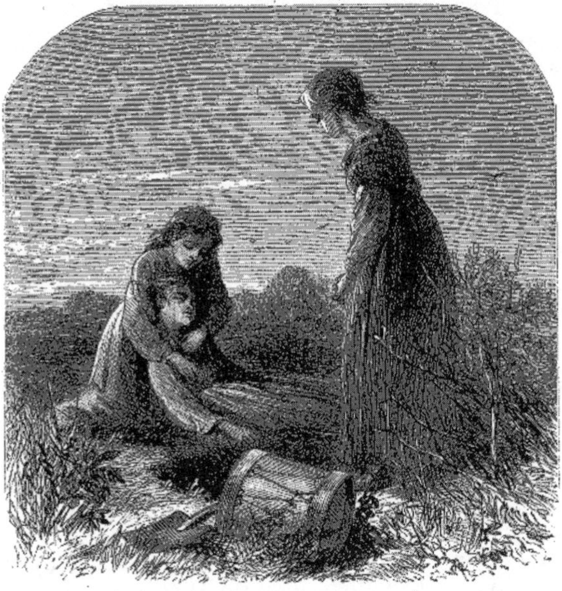

THE DRUMMER-BOY'S BURIAL.

ALL day long the storm of battle through the startled valley swept;
All night long the stars in heaven o'er the slain sad vigils kept.

Oh the ghastly, upturned faces gleaming whitely through the night!
Oh the heaps of mangled corses in that dim sepulchral light!

One by one the pale stars faded, and at length the morning broke;
But not one of all the sleepers on that field of death awoke.

Slowly passed the golden hours of that long bright summer day,
And upon that field of carnage still the dead unburied lay:

Entered according to Act of Congress, in the year 1864, by Harper and Brothers, in the Clerk's Office of the District Court for the Southern District of New York.

Vol. XXIX.—No. 170.—K

Figures 6.1 and 6.2. The Civil War brought a new image of children's deaths to Americans with poems and images dedicated to drummer boys dying in the line of duty. *The Drummer-Boy's Burial, Harper's New Monthly Magazine*, July 1864; *The Dead Drummer Boy, Harper's New Monthly Magazine*, February 1863.

THE DEAD DRUMMER BOY.

'Midst tangled roots that lined the wild ravine,
    Where the fierce fight raged hottest through the day,
And where the dead in scattered heaps were seen,
Amid the darkling forests' shade and sheen,
    Speechless in death he lay.

The setting sun, which glanced athwart the place
    In slanting lines, like amber-tinted rain,
Fell sidewise on the drummer's upturned face,
Where Death had left his gory finger's trace
    In one bright crimson stain.

The silken fringes of his once bright eye
    Lay like a shadow on his cheek so fair;
His lips were parted by a long-drawn sigh,
That with his soul had mounted to the sky
    On some wild martial air.

No more his hand the fierce tatoo shall beat,
    The shrill reveillé, or the long roll's call,
Or sound the charge, when in the smoke and heat
Of fiery onset foe with foe shall meet,
    And gallant men shall fall.

Yet maybe in some happy home, that one,
    A mother, reading from the list of dead,
Shall chance to view the name of her dear son,
And move her lips to say, "God's will be done!"
    And bow in grief her head.

But more than this what tongue shall tell his story?
    Perhaps his boyish longings were for fame?
He lived, he died; and so, *memento mori*—
Enough if on the page of War and Glory
    Some hand has writ his name.

over his own spiritual destiny, and some individuals even insisted that sin could be eradicated completely and Christian perfection attained in the present life. A religious economy that placed the possibility of holiness within man's grasp also enabled Congregationalist minister Horace Bushnell to assert that proper parental nurture would convince children that they were Christians from birth. With the concept of sin eliminated from a child's consciousness, there remained little reason to teach them that upon death they would go anywhere other than heaven. Although most Protestant ministers, of course, did not disregard sin to the same degree as Bushnell, many professed certainty in the salvation of all infants. In 1859, Methodist F. G. Hibbard took satisfaction in claiming that his denomination had formed the vanguard in declaring "the final salvation of all children dying in immature childhood," since "all alike are included in the redemptive plan and purpose."[7]

Since a primary function of obituaries is to memorialize an individual's life and noteworthy accomplishments, it is somewhat surprising to uncover numerous death notices of infants and children in religious newspapers such as the Methodist weekly *Western Christian Advocate*. Despite death's preventing them from achieving anything of lasting merit, at least as far as the world normally measures success, some children nevertheless became subjects of glowing and even lengthy obituaries that sought to demonstrate how each deceased child had actually been far from ordinary. Willie, a six-year-old boy who died of scarlet fever in August 1862, reportedly possessed a remarkable capacity to love, and all who knew the lad were amazed by his "fervent" affection. The obituary writer asserted that the boy had "a stronger hold upon the hearts of his parents" than his three sisters and probably had formed a closer bond with them than could be found in most parent-child relationships. Willie especially loved his father, who was absent during his son's illness due to military service. After learning that a letter summoning his father home had been mailed, Willie expressed appreciation for the gesture but realized that "'pa can't come for two or three days,'" a comment that his memorialist construed as evidence of the lad's preparation for death and acceptance that he would depart life before his father could return. While younger children may have endeared themselves to adults by means of an amiable disposition, older children received commendation for possessing maturity beyond their years. After her passing, twelve-year-old Alice Blair was lauded for preferring the company and conversation of her mother rather than engaging in "the ordinary sports of children" or interacting with her peers. According to her obituary, Alice's unusual inclination to reflect on more serious matters of life such as spiritual topics rather than to join in the frivolities of childhood made her seem almost otherworldly and marked her "as one too nearly allied to those above" to live among sinful mortals.[8]

Time and again, most writers interpreted a deceased child's ardent interest in religious subjects as confirmation of his or her exceptional nature. Because of his "sprightly mind" and proclivity to engage in "reflection beyond one of his years," eight-year-old Frank Dimmitt often queried his mother concerning God, heaven, and death. His eagerness to learn more about eternity, combined with a willingness to "pray and trust in the Lord," enabled him to be "patient and resigned" while suffering for several months from the effects of diphtheria. According to a few writers, the religious training of some children evidenced itself in actions that attested to their conspicuous concern for doing right. Five-year-old Thomas Jones expressed sorrow when he noticed other boys misbehaving and on more than one occasion hugged a naughty playmate and admonished, "'Don't do so'; or, 'Jesus won't love you, and you will not go to him when you die.'" Not to be outdone, one "remarkably conscientious" child even aimed his moralizing at adults. Charlie Heaton, who died three months before reaching his fourth birthday, gained notoriety for his awareness of "the temperance question," and his obituary writer recalled several "precious little anecdotes" that attested to Charlie's disapproval of alcoholic beverages.[9]

Modern observers might find it odd that a child of fewer than four years could be portrayed as something of a temperance crusader, but it makes perfect sense considering that many churchgoers, especially Methodists, would expect a young child, destined for eternal salvation if taken in death, to have more in common with the perfections of the next world than the evils of the present life. Declarations that dying children gained immediate admittance into heaven abound, such as minister W. J. Peck's assertion that his nearly four-year-old daughter, Clara, "gently fell asleep in the arms of Jesus" or J. E. Allison's claim that "the kind Shepherd saw fit to remove" his two-year-old son and "transplant him in the paradise of God." These writers emphasized Christ as the mediator who had provided access to heaven, while others cited scripture that attested to the Savior's interest in children. The synoptic Gospels record how the disciples tried to prevent people from bringing young children to Jesus, but their Master taught them a lesson by taking time to minister to the needs of a seemingly insignificant and neglected segment of society in the Roman world. One writer comforted the parents of five-year-old Mercy Anna Pool with the assurance that their daughter had gone "to Him who said, 'Suffer little children to come unto me.'"[10]

Some writers focused on Jesus taking an active part in ushering innocent babes into paradise, but others emphasized the role of angels as ministering spirits who transported children over the gulf between death and eternal life. After his nine-year-old daughter, Mary, breathed her last, Lewis Wiley avowed, "Then came the angels, and our darling child journeyed with them to her happy home above." Although Wiley, if pressed, likely would have admitted that he had not glimpsed ethereal beings but was employing poetic license to express an idea to which he gave personal credence, other writers reported that dying children claimed to see angels approaching. Shortly before expiring, three-year-old Emma Koonse smiled, pointed aloft, and exclaimed, "'Look, ma, do you see them?'" Buttressed by such an appealing testimony, her obituarist concluded, "Doubtless God sent his angels to carry her happy spirit to heaven."[11]

Older girls frequently reported seeing angelic hosts and gave more detailed accounts of their visions of the heavenly realm. Adults seemed little surprised that a departing child might be allowed to preview the eternal abode before departing life, and many parents and obituary writers considered these momentary revelations of paradise and its emissaries as proof that the end was near. Two days before her death, having suffered for more than three months, fourteen-year-old Mary Folsom called her mother to her bedside and engaged in the following exchange. "'Don't you see them?' 'See what, my child?' 'Why, see the angels; they are so pretty and white; and they are talking to me; they say they are coming for me before long.'" Sixteen-year-old Mary Bills detected a deceased relative among the ranks of those who called upon her before death. She reportedly exclaimed, "There they come now. They are angels come for me. They have such long white wings. Look! There is cousin James come from heaven, too." Based on her own testimony, few children observed such an amazing panoply of divine figures as thirteen-year-old Harriet Snyder. The author of her obituary explained that "she was permitted to have remarkable views of heaven" before dying. Not only did she claim to witness angels surrounding her bed, filling her last hours with beautiful music, but she also discerned "the spirits of departed friends" ready to "welcome her home." Most significantly, she testified that "the Savior also appeared to assist her through the valley and shadow of death."[12] These memorialists do not give the impression that a child imagined angels, dead family members, or Christ himself while in a state of delirium caused by a feverish condition. They clearly imply that children still possessed full command of their mental faculties when describing such otherworldly scenes. Although it is impossible, of course, to verify or disprove the authenticity of such beatific visions, their frequent inclusion in obituaries conformed to social expectations of the Good Death and assured watching family members that dying children had met a happy end.

In addition to being taught at an early age that angels would convey them to heaven at death, many Methodist children expected to become angels upon entering the celestial realm. A popular Sabbath school song entitled "I Want to Be an Angel" underscored this notion of angelic escorts and complete metamorphosis into a cherub. After expressing the desire to become an angel in the first verse and enumerating the benefits of possessing an angelic nature in the second stanza, in the penultimate verse the singer affirms the presence of myriad children in heaven and petitions Christ to commission an angel to carry him upward when death beckons:

> I know I'm weak and sinful
> But Jesus will forgive;
> For many little children
> Have gone to heaven to live.
> Dear Saviour, when I languish,
> And lay me down to die,
> O send a shining angel
> To bear me to the sky.

The final stanza repeats the first except for altering the initial line, in which the child's earthly desire to be an angel has been granted, and he exultantly declares, "O there I'll be an angel." Several obituary writers recorded that children loved this song, chanted it on their deathbeds, or spoke of becoming an angel. Having endured severe pain for several days, twelve-year-old Alfred Lockridge pondered what it might be like to live in a perfect environment and escape the tribulations of earthly life. "'Ma, I wish I was an angel,' he imagined, 'and then I would not have to suffer.'"[13]

Some children deflected attention away from their painful condition and directed their final thoughts and remarks to those they soon would leave behind. Last words always had been a central component of the deathbed, and loved ones made every effort to hear and take to heart the final earthly directives of children. Although it is possible that some older children, who in all likelihood had personally witnessed several deathbed scenes, simply conformed to custom by leaving a parting admonition, it seems just as probable that devout young people sincerely sought to point their family and friends toward spiritual matters. After professing his faith that Christ would take him to heaven, eleven-year-old Joseph Comer urged his unconverted father to seek the heavenly abode so that they could be reunited some day. In addition to last words, documentary evidence of a young person's preparation for death proved equally comforting to mourning family members. Convinced that her illness would result in death, seventeen-year-old Sarah Jane Idle composed a soul-revealing epistle three months before her departure from life. After affirming her spiritual preparation for death and willingness to exchange earth for heaven, she encouraged her loved ones not to weep, since she had gone to "shout around God's throne," reunite with deceased relatives, and "be at rest forever." Not all youths, of course, possessed such foresight, and in some instances the suddenness and disabling nature of death prevented last words from being spoken. In these cases, family members looked for evidence from the deceased's life to provide a measure of comfort. Although sixteen-year-old Emma Shobe was unable to communicate in her final moments, her recent decision to join the church on a probationary status was followed by her conversion, and she shortly would have been granted full membership.[14]

Indeed, the Methodist Church frequently received children into its membership, often regardless of whether or not the applicant had been converted prior to joining. This practice demonstrates the concurrent emphasis on and interrelation between conversion and Christian nurture. Unlike Horace Bushnell, Methodists did not expect proper nurture to make conversion unnecessary, but they nonetheless believed that official ecclesiastical attachment might stimulate a child's desire to be saved. Fourteen-year-old James Millison, who had regularly attended Sunday school for several years, officially united with the church after he had "experienced religion" during a protracted meeting one month prior to his death. To be sure, some children may have been caught up in the emotional atmosphere that characterized many revival meetings and made spiritual decisions based on feelings rather than reasoned understanding. Ohioan Mary Stork claimed as much after witnessing several youngsters aged ten to fifteen walk the aisles during a protracted Methodist meeting. "I don't believe a child ten years old has sense & judgment enough to know . . . [why] they are going to the mourners bench," she asserted. "The preacher says they do, but it is little more than I can believe." When recalling the life of fifteen-year-old Almira Wilson, Indiana Methodist Samuel Longden defended his effort to convert young people. At age eleven, Almira had "sought and obtained religion" during a revival, and her exemplary testimony since that day more than silenced critics who "objected to children seeking religion and joining the church, under the plea that they did not know what they were doing." At the tender age of nine, Anna Crawford joined the "infant class" of the Methodist assembly in Danville, Indiana, and received baptism and full membership in her twelfth year. Although Anna's death notice three years later lacked any reference to her having experienced conversion, her long-standing association with the church confirmed to her obituarist that she had been "emphatically brought up 'in the nurture and admonition of the Lord.'"[15]

In fact, the obituaries of several children entirely omit any reference to conversion but focus instead on their moral living and good works as sufficient grounds for their eternal salvation. Ten-year-old Sammy Longsworth, who died after falling thirty feet from a tree, "loved his Sunday school very much" and treasured his Bible. His determination to live uprightly was best exemplified by his assertion on one occasion that he "would sooner die when he was little, than to live to be a man and be wicked." Other children were described as paragons of virtue. According to his obituary, nine-year-old Frankie Long had never been caught lying, never squabbled with any other children, always obeyed his parents, faithfully attended Sunday school, and prayed regularly. Clergyman Evan Stevenson regarded his seventeen-year-old daughter Sidney as without peer, for after her death he expressed certainty that "she had never lost her infant justification," meaning that she had never sinned since reaching an age of accountability and being able to distinguish between good and evil. This claim of sinless perfection likely would have been too much for most Methodists to swallow, for few parents, despite loving their children unconditionally, would allege them to be completely faultless. Even five-and-a-half-year-old Alice Dobyns understood her own moral shortcomings and "seldom did wrong without asking her mother's forgiveness" or prayerfully imploring God "to make her a better child." When underscoring the moral qualities and exemplary behavior of children, few memorialists were as blunt as one writer, who matter-of-factly asserted that fourteen-year-old Thornton Jenkins "had never made a profession of religion nor become a member of the Church." Nevertheless, the boy's childhood baptism, attendance at Sunday school, and deathbed declaration that he "loved the Savior" and intended to meet his deceased brother satisfied his family that his departure had been heavenward.[16]

In rare occasions, a few candid obituary writers admitted that they lacked certainty whether or not a young person had entered heaven. These memorialists still garnered any available circumstantial evidence that pointed to preparation for eternity, but their unwillingness to make a definitive judgment based solely on moral living prevented them from asserting that the departed child had reached heaven's shores. Fifteen-year-old Albert Moore never united with the church, but his parents had endeavored to model Christian principles and instill virtue into their son's character. Albert had become "a pleasant, manly, and moral boy," but his obituarist could only "hope" that the lad "rests with God." The author of Bell Sparks's obituary similarly offered limited consolation. Although the nearly ten-year-old girl regularly attended Sunday school, this lone pious habit was insufficient grounds for placing confidence in her eternal salvation, and the writer could merely "hope she is with the good children in heaven."[17]

Instead of conveying a sense of ambiguity regarding a child's eternal status, most obituary writers found hope even in the most tragic circumstances. In cases of multiple fatalities in close succession, obituary writers oftentimes availed themselves of a prime opportunity to discuss the inscrutable nature of God's sovereignty. The three Woodrow children of Hillsboro, Ohio, aged between ten and fourteen, all succumbed to diphtheria during a two-week period in October 1862. With one heartrending blow, "this mysterious dispensation from God" deprived the grieving parents of their entire progeny. Yet because their children had "exercise[d] a pure, saving faith in the atoning merits of Christ" and now resided in heaven, the afflicted parents, according to the obituary, received "the sustaining grace of God." Four children of John and Catherine Garrett passed away while traveling with their mother to visit their father, a soldier with the 7th Illinois Cavalry. Although three of the children shared a grave in Corinth, Mississippi, the author of their obituary refrained from editorializing by blaming the war for indirectly causing the Garretts to embark on a rigorous journey and unnecessarily risk exposure to disease. One writer, in contrast, barely commented on the life of seventeen-year-old Calkins Bagel, who died from an injury suffered while jumping from a moving train. Instead, the Union-loving obituarist focused on the war and noted that Bagel's two brothers had entered the Federal army "to put down this unholy, unprovoked, and the wickedest rebellion which God ever saw, except the devil's rebellion in heaven," before vindictively adding that he hoped Confederate leaders would "share the same fate" as Satan and his minions.[18]

Although appropriating the death notice of a youthful noncombatant to make a political statement may have pushed the limits of propriety, nothing underscored the convergence of the war and child mortality like the obituaries of boy soldiers. Existing records, while far from complete, indicate that at least 10,000 boys between the ages of thirteen and seventeen joined the Union army over the course of the war. Some intentionally lied about their age in order to gain admittance, while others found accommodating enrollment officers who signed up any willing, able-bodied youth. Away from home for the first time, many adolescent soldiers fell prey to diseases for which they had no immunities. Still two months shy of his fifteenth birthday, William Havens volunteered with the 130th Indiana in December 1863, became ill in camp shortly thereafter, returned home to Cassville, and was dead by the end of February 1864. Before his passing, Havens summoned a minister, who conversed with him about eternity and expressed confidence that the boy "was happily converted" on his deathbed. Sixteen-year-old Noah Milam was eager to fight in the spring of 1862 and, after watching two relatives enlist, donned a uniform in August. In mid-September, his regiment, the 67th Indiana, participated in the Battle of Munfordville, and during the fighting Milam had three rifles shot out of his hands. Union forces defending Fort Craig and guarding the railroad bridge over the Green River performed well until General Braxton Bragg brought rebel reinforcements, surrounded the Federals, and captured nearly 4,000 bluecoats on September 17. Paroled and released, Milam marched from Kentucky to his home in Ellettsville, Indiana, and the physical strain, exposure to the elements, and lack of proper food and rest throughout the two-week trek contributed to his catching typhoid fever. Fully aware that his condition was perilous, the ailing lad, who had converted and joined the Methodist Church four years earlier, was grateful to spend his final five earthly days at home among family and friends. With his dying breath, he repeated the words to the hymn "There Is a Fountain Filled with Blood" and, according to his obituary, "passed triumphantly to the land where there is no war."[19]

Some boy soldiers, of course, died in camp or on the battlefield, far from loved ones at home. Sixteen-year-old Jeremiah Cunningham of the 61st Ohio, a probationary member of the Methodist Church, perished from an unintentional self-inflicted gunshot wound at Camp Falmouth in Virginia during the winter of 1863. Seventeen-year-old James Cooper of the 27th Indiana contracted measles and died at Camp Havelock in Maryland in January 1862. Even in the midst of physical suffering, the devout youth never grumbled but, in the presence of his comrades, publicly affirmed with the psalmist, "'The Lord is good, and his mercy endureth forever.'" Although Cooper's body was interred in a local Methodist church cemetery, possibly never to be visited by his family hundreds of miles away, the lad's obituarist expressed assurance that God would include the faithful soldier with the redeemed who would partake "'in the first resurrection.'" Often deprived of the closure associated with a funeral or burial, relatives of youths killed in combat had to console themselves with personal remembrances or recent tokens of the deceased's piety. After only three months of service with the 145th Pennsylvania, sixteen-year-old Lewis Heder was killed at Fredericksburg amid "an incessant storm of shell and balls." Fifteen-year-old Charles Disney of the 129th Indiana received a mortal wound at Kennesaw Mountain on June 27, 1864, and died six days later. Heder, a church member who had converted at age twelve, continued to faithfully read his Bible while in the army, and members of Disney's company attested to the fine character of the fallen Sunday school scholar. According to his obituary, Joseph Barnes, less than three weeks shy of his seventeenth birthday, was studying his Bible at the exact moment when the drumroll summoned him to form ranks at the end of August 1862. He never returned to camp, one of 16,000 Union casualties at Second Manassas.[20]

Obituaries of boy soldiers seldom if ever implied that the deceased might have thrown away his life for no purpose. To be sure, personal testimony sometimes confirmed a lad's willingness to die for the Union. When queried in 1861 why he desired to join the 3rd Iowa Cavalry, sixteen-year-old Wagoner Amon Jr., who died of pneumonia before year's end, bravely affirmed, "'My life is no dearer to me than the lives of my companions.'" Most parents, of course, did not think in these terms but sought to preserve the lives of their children at all costs. When the war commenced, the father of William Wirterstarret prohibited his fifteen-year-old son, a sickly youth who had been plagued with severe asthma for most of his life, from enlisting. After the summer of 1862, he permitted his boy to leave their small town in rural Ohio to clerk at a dry goods store in Cincinnati. After seven months away from the restraints of home, Wirterstarret, now seventeen, succumbed to the martial fever and joined the Mississippi Squadron, serving as master's mate aboard the gunboat *Champion* on the Tennessee River. Within two months, he contracted pneumonia and passed away in a Kentucky hospital. Despite the obvious paternal attempt to keep the lad from joining the military, the author of Wirterstarret's obituary refused to view his death as an unnecessary loss. Instead, he focused on the deceased's childhood piety and described him as "a victim to that laudable ambition and manly patriotism which ever glowed in his bosom." Downplaying the family's personal grief, the writer framed the obituary in terms of national meaning by depicting Wirterstarret as simply one of "many valuable sacrifices which have been offered on the altar of his country." During the war, patriotism became such an essential component of the Good Death that in some instances it even superseded the traditional spiritual emphases of obituaries. After being shot in the chest during the Battle of Atlanta in 1864, sixteen-year-old John Ball of the 123rd Indiana calmly declared, "'I die for my country,'" before expiring on the field. Rather than focusing on the spiritual qualities and hope of attaining heaven possessed by this minister's son, Ball's obituary writer instead praised his bravery and closed with a poem that extolled the "untarnished" names of valiant soldiers who had purchased earthly glory through their noble deaths.[21]

Perhaps no story conveyed the essence of the ideal death and depicted a proper spiritual response to the loss of a child like "The Drummer Boy: A Fact," a far-fetched account published in New York's Methodist weekly *Christian Advocate and Journal*. The tale opens with a tableau of a solitary twelve-year-old girl kneeling in the corner of a one-room New York City tenement house, earnestly praying and shedding tears for her brother. The scene then shifts to the battlefield, where a wounded drummer boy expends his waning energy testifying of his faith in God to an injured soldier lying nearby. Throughout the night they lingered unattended, tenuously hanging on to life while other sufferers expired around them. At daybreak, having given up all hope of obtaining aid, the soldier espied an ox charging directly toward the boy, who had fallen silent. Utterly horrified, the man was astounded when the animal stopped short of trampling the motionless form, lowered its head, and dropped from its horns a small carpetbag before darting off as mysteriously as it had appeared. With his remaining strength, the soldier dragged himself over to open the parcel, which contained bandages, crackers, and wine. Reviving the boy, who thanked God for deliverance, the once skeptical soldier began to seriously consider the existence of a watchful providence. One year later, still uncertain if her brother, the faithful drummer boy, had been captured or killed, the prayerful girl opened her door to a haggard-looking man. Recently exchanged, the soldier recounted this miraculous story and assured the girl's family that their drummer boy, despite suffering in a southern prison, had died nobly. More important, the lad's Christian testimony had resulted in the soldier's conversion. Thus comforted, the girl was willing to place her brother's life into God's keeping and to accept his death.[22]

Sentimental stories and obituaries of infants, children, and youths published in denominational newspapers during the Civil War sought to diminish the terrors of dying for a culture permeated with death. The relatively sanitized pages of the religious press helped convey this ideal picture of an eternal paradise that teemed with babies and youths who never reached maturity. Perhaps no obituary captured this optimistic anticipation of heaven better than that of thirteen-year-old Benjamin Delenbaugh. On his deathbed, he reportedly asserted, "Mother, don't take it so hard. I'm going to heaven, and expect to see Peter and James," his two deceased soldier-brothers. Such confidence that heaven offered the prospect of a joyous family reunion helped assuage the grief of many religious northerners whose children died during the Civil War. In all likelihood, they could concur with the sobering yet optimistic conclusion of Delenbaugh's obituary, "Rejoice on, ye sainted children! Your parents will soon be with you."[23]

1. *Washington Republican*, excerpted in *Western Christian Advocate*, March 5, 1862. The title quotation comes from *Zion's Herald and Wesleyan Journal*, December 21, 1864.

2. Drew Gilpin Faust, *This Republic of Suffering: Death and the American Civil War* (New York: Knopf, 2008), xiii.

3. E. Brooks Holifield, "Let the Children Come: The Religion of the Protestant Child in Early America," *Church History* 76 (December 2007): 752–53, 767–69; Hattie Pontius to Ann Morral, September 28, 1862; Hattie Pontius to William Pontius, June 2, 1865, in *Pontius Family Letters*, ed. James A. Thorson (n.p.: privately printed, 1998), 5–6, 36.

4. *Child's Magazine*, excerpted in *New York Observer*, July 30, 1863; *Examiner*, excerpted in *Western Christian Advocate*, December 9, 1863; *Zion's Herald and Wesleyan Journal*, October 7, 1863; April 20, 1864.

5. *Independent*, March 6, 1862.

6. *New York Evangelist*, June 30, 1864.

7. Nathan O. Hatch, *The Democratization of American Christianity* (New Haven: Yale University Press, 1989), 170–79; Robert Bruce Mullin, *The Puritan as Yankee: A Life of Horace Bushnell* (Grand Rapids, MI: Eerdmans, 2002), 117–20; F. G. Hibbard, "The Moral Condition of Infants," *Methodist Quarterly Review* 41 (1859): 633.

8. *Western Christian Advocate*, December 3, 1862; November 26, 1862. While the *Western Christian Advocate* regularly carried children's obituaries, southern Methodist weeklies such as the *Nashville Christian Advocate* and the *Southern Christian Advocate*, printed death notices of children only occasionally during the 1850s and the Civil War. Although this smaller sampling of southern obituaries contains similar themes to northern death notices, limiting this study to northern children allows for more thorough analysis of and greater representativeness within a designated region.

9. Ibid., August 19, 1863; April 15, 22, 1863.

10. Ibid., April 9, 1862; September 10, 1862; January 8, 1862. Matthew 19:13–15, Mark 10:13–16, and Luke 18:15–17 record Jesus receiving children.

11. Ibid., December 30, 1863; November 18, 1863.

12. Ibid., April 9, 1862; March 16, 1864; June 1, 1864.

13. "I Want to Be an Angel," in *A Manual for Infant Schools*, comp. S. L. Farr, ed. Thomas O. Summers (Richmond, VA: Soldiers' Tract Association, M. E. Church, South, 1863), available through "Documenting the American South," http://docsouth.unc.edu; *Western Christian Advocate*, June, 15, 1864.

14. *Western Christian Advocate*, July 6, 1864; August 5, 1863; July 13, 1864.

15. Ibid., April 6, 1864; January 7, 1863; August 3, 1864; Mary Stork to Rufus Dooley, February 14, [1865], Rufus Dooley Papers, Indiana Historical Society, Indianapolis.

16. *Western Christian Advocate*, September 24, 1862; January 13, 1864; August 26, 1863; December 10, 1862; April 8, 1863.

17. Ibid., April 29, 1863; April 26, 1865.

18. Ibid., November 5, 1862; March 11, 1863; January 21, 1863.

19. Bell Irvin Wiley, "Boys in Blue," *Abraham Lincoln Quarterly* 6 (December 1951): 421–22; *Western Christian Advocate*, April 13, 1864; December 3, 1862.

20. *Western Christian Advocate*, June 17, 1863; March 12, 1862; February 25, 1863; September 7, 1864; March 18, 1863.

21. Ibid., March 26, 1862; August 5, 1863; November 23, 1864.

22. *Christian Advocate and Journal*, April 27, 1865.

23. *Western Christian Advocate*, October 5, 1864.

7

Children of the March

Confederate Girls and Sherman's
Home Front Campaign

LISA TENDRICH FRANK

In January 1865, as word of the imminent arrival of Union troops filled the streets and homes of Columbia, South Carolina, Emma LeConte bemoaned her fate as a child of war. She was "dreadfully sick . . . of this war" and felt that "we girls whose lot it is to grow up in these times are unfortunate!" After all, the war "commenced when I was thirteen, and I am now seventeen and no prospect yet of its ending." As a result of the constant pressures of wartime shortages and war work, her adolescence and that of her peers revolved around "nothing but the stern realities of life." She resented that she had been forced to spend much of her girlhood worried about the safety of loved ones. "Those which should come later are made familiar to us at an age when only gladness should surround us. We have only the saddest anticipations and the dread of hardships and cares when bright dreams of the future ought to shine on us." Her childhood, she continued, had little in common with that of elite antebellum Southern girls whose carefree lives revolved around parties and socializing. The war denied LeConte the opportunity to enjoy the privileges of her gender or her transformation from a child to a young lady; LeConte complained that her adolescence had instead been filled with "nothing but rigid economy and hard work." As a result, "I have seen little of the light-heartedness and exuberant joy that people talk about as the natural heritage of youth. It is a hard school to be bred up in and I often wonder if I will ever have my share of [fun] and happiness." Even so, LeConte expressed her willingness to continue on the same path. Despite the fact that her last four years had been filled with constant fear, worry, and work, she did not relish the thought that the war might be ending. As she nervously awaited the approach of Union troops, she confessed, "I would far rather [work for a living] and bear much more than submit to the Yankees."[1]

This essay examines how Sherman's march through Georgia and the Carolinas in 1864–65 created and clarified the meaning of the war for elite Southern girls like LeConte. It explores both the social experiences that slaveholding girls faced during the invasion and the ways in which these experiences often became manifested as postwar anger and the fodder for the Lost Cause mythology. During the march, these privileged girls witnessed what they considered Yankee "depravity" and thereby found justification for secession and other decisions previously made by Confederate adults. In addition, their firsthand experiences—and the ways in which adults explained these experiences to them—provided elite Southern girls with ample material to later edit, dramatize, and craft into the Lost Cause interpretation of the war.

Recent scholars have recognized the centrality of the civilian experience during Sherman's march and other home front campaigns; the incorporation of children into this framework has occurred at a much slower pace. Children, however, hardly avoided the horrors of the campaign. As soldiers arrived in their area, they witnessed firsthand combat, death, disfigurement, and occupation. When Sherman marched 60,000 soldiers through Georgia and the Carolinas, he introduced a new face of war to children of all ages. Often caught in the crossfire, Southern girls and boys found their worlds turned upside down, their homes destroyed, and their treasures ransacked. Although sources tend to obscure the presence of girls behind phrases like "civilians" and "women and children," they experienced the war in a gendered manner. For girls, who were traditionally more sheltered from many of the harsh realities of life than their male counterparts, the arrival of the war on their doorsteps drastically changed their lives. The presence of enemy men led them to fear for their safety, both physical and sexual. Instead of primping for prospective beaux, young ladies often made themselves look "ugly" to hide from Union men. As a result, girls in the path of Sherman's march, as well as those in other invaded and occupied areas, were denied the opportunity to enjoy the freedom of childhood and the frivolities of young ladyhood. Girls had their bedrooms searched and their personal treasures revealed, destroyed, or mishandled. For girls still learning the rules of proper behavior, the enemy's breaches of feminine space provided gender-specific challenges, as "proper" ladies were expected to show restraint rather than respond to these perceived injustices. In addition, elite Southern girls became eyewitnesses to battles and sometimes, by necessity, became nurses. The war destroyed, or at least redefined, many of the protections and privileges that their race, class, gender, and age had previously provided them.[2]

As the war progressed, the Union army classified Confederate girls and other civilians as traitors and enemies, expanding the conventional understandings of warfare. In June 1864, Union general William Tecumseh Sherman emphasized to Secretary of War Edwin Stanton, "There is a class of people, men, women, and children, who must be killed or banished before you can hope for peace and order." With this statement, Sherman singled out the moral and material support that children and other civilians offered to the Confederacy. Civilians raised armies and kept them on the field, and they supplied food, medical supplies, medical personnel, and uniforms. Sherman's statement further suggested an end to the Union's policy that tended to keep civilians from direct or intentional military attacks. Although guerrilla warfare had directly involved some civilians from the outset of the war, prior to 1864 the Union armies generally focused their energies on the male military portion of the Southern population. Even when Confederate and Union soldiers met on battlefields adjacent to towns, civilian populations rarely faced deliberate or direct attacks. Shortly after Sherman made this statement, Union policy shifted as Sherman brought the war directly to white Southerners who remained in their homes—primarily women and children.[3]

Sherman's campaign grew out of a developing strategy to defeat the Confederacy. Union efforts to control occupied areas as well as continued guerrilla warfare ultimately led the military to categorize all white Southerners as enemies in their own rights. As a result, in 1864 some Union commanders turned their focus to the home front supporters of the Confederate war effort. Realizing that battles were won not only by the soldiers on the field, but also by the infrastructures at home, Union leaders pursued campaigns against Southern civilians and their worlds. Union general Philip Sheridan, for example, led a campaign in Virginia's Shenandoah Valley that intentionally burned the countryside to subdue its civilians. As one Confederate soldier recalled, Sheridan's "fame lay not in the soldier's hard-fought battles, but in burning farmers' houses and barns."[4]

During the march, Union soldiers waged "a hard war" campaign to target the war matériel and civilian resources of the lower South. Sherman's "bummers" confiscated property while other soldiers razed much of what was in their path. The nature of the destruction and the origins of many of the fires are hotly debated, but the destruction of private property shaped the ways in which civilians of all ages and sexes as well as many soldiers understood the march. During the campaign, Union troops destroyed railroad tracks, razed crops, and burned countless homes, barns, and businesses, all in the name of crippling the Confederate war effort. However, even when acknowledging the destruction on the home front, scholars have often ignored the civilian population, assuming that the destruction was largely confined to military targets, or have minimized the implications of the presence of a population made up primarily of children and women. This understanding has recently been questioned, and the campaign has been labeled as "an entire army on a raid," a significantly better way of understanding the mentality of Sherman's soldiers and the experience of civilians.[5]

Union soldiers recognized the effectiveness of bringing war to Southern civilians, and many willingly took the war to the playrooms of elite white children. Major General Henry W. Halleck, for example, applauded his commanders' efforts to make the war directly felt on the Southern home front. After Sherman proposed to evacuate Atlanta of its civilians and then destroy the city, Halleck noted both the nature of the civilian population and the benefits of dislocating it. "Let the disloyal families of the country thus stripped go to their husbands, fathers, and natural protectors in the rebel ranks" because the Union situation required "that we apply to our inexorable foes the severe rules of war." Sherman willingly applied those rules to the enemy, regardless of age or gender.[6]

Sherman could not have been too surprised by the reaction to his efforts against Southern civilians in Georgia and the Carolinas. In 1862, while in occupied Memphis, Sherman reflected to his daughter on vitriolic Confederate attitudes toward him. He acknowledged to Minnie, "Hundreds of children like yourself are daily taught to curse my name, and each night thousands Kneel in prayer & beseech the almighty to consign me to Perdition." However, it did not bother him because "such is War." The Southern antipathy toward him resulted, he knew, from Confederate fears as well as from his military tactics. "I have been forced to turn families out of their houses & homes & force them to go to a strange land, because of their hostility." He urged Minnie to "think of this and how cruel men become in war, when even your papa has to do such acts." In Memphis, unlike in the march, Sherman attempted to restrain his soldiers from indiscriminate destruction. "It now requires all my energy to prevent our soldiers from robbing & plundering the houses & property of supposed Enemies."[7]

Such "robbing & plundering" on the Confederate home front would, especially in 1864 and 1865, force white Southern girls in Georgia and the Carolinas to reconsider what war meant to their lives. Although they had already spent several years dealing with the so-called realities of wartime life, such as shortages, death, refugeeing, and aid work, with Sherman's arrival Confederate girls recognized that "the horrors of war are coming home to us now." Most elite Southern girls in these areas did not feel the full brunt of war until this point, as their gender and class shielded them from many of the hardships felt by others. They often acknowledged as much, especially as they awaited and later reflected upon their direct encounters with enemy soldiers during Sherman's campaign. With the arrival of Northern soldiers, girls who had earlier romanticized soldiers and the battlefield were now forced to deal firsthand with the terrors of an invading army. They suddenly had to face the constant threat of enemy soldiers in their towns and often in their homes. This experience was especially dramatic for girls who came of age during the war.[8]

The campaign's direct effect on children began during Sherman's bombardment of Atlanta and continued after the Union captured the city. On September 8, 1864, already chafing at the prospect of living under military occupation, Confederate girls experienced a new side of war with Special Field Order Number 67. Announced six days after the Union capture of the city, this order evacuated Atlanta's civilians, a group composed overwhelmingly of children and their mothers. To justify his order, Sherman stressed that he "was not willing to have Atlanta encumbered by the families of [his] enemies," who would be burdensome to feed and could even pose a danger to his men. A majority of this population was children, a reality often obscured by the ubiquitous use of the umbrella phrase "women and children." Girls and young ladies were by definition a significant portion of those labeled "women and children." According to Sherman's count, and confirmed by Confederate reports, the order expelled 867 children and 705 adults from the city. The evacuation was chaos. "Everybody seems to be hurrying off. . . . Wagons loaded with household furniture, and everything else that can be packed upon them crowd every street, and women, old and young children innumerable, are hurrying to and fro." These evacuees, some of whom had earlier fled other endangered areas of the Confederacy to take refuge in Atlanta, vocally protested their expulsion and traveled southward with what they could carry. The presence of girls and boys among the evacuated Atlantans further raised the ire of Southerners around the Confederacy who assumed that children and women remained a protected category of the population, even during wartime.[9]

The uprooting of families as official military policy shocked many in the North and South, in large part because of its effects on "innocent children." Hoping to prevent the evacuation, Confederate general John Bell Hood protested in a letter to Sherman. Criticizing "the unprecedented measure you propose [which] transcends, in studied and ingenious cruelty, all acts ever before brought to my attention in the dark history of war," Hood beseeched his Northern counterpart not to evacuate civilians. In particular, Hood hoped that Sherman would reconsider after he realized that he was "expelling from their homes and firesides the wives and children of a brave people." Hood's rationale resounded in some measure with several Union men who had misgivings about their actions. One casually noted that "the citizens are all being sent away, according to Sherman's order." Although he acknowledged that "it must make a trying time for women and children to be taken from home and put outside of our lines with very few things to do with," that did not change his attitude. It was, as he put it, "pretty rough, but cant help it." Another remarked that he "did feel sorry for the women and innocent children," but he dismissed his sympathy in favor of a larger cause. After all, he concluded, "our army is here and must be fed."[10]

Yankee civilians often had some sympathy for the plight of Confederate children, largely because of the gendered presumption that these civilians, especially the female ones, were helpless and had little understanding of politics or war. After the expulsion of civilians from Atlanta, a Northern woman made a distinction between the "rebels" and the civilians. She declared, "I do not sympathize at all with the rebels, but I do feel sorry for the women & children & those who have been drawn into this war through ignorance." Later in the campaign, another Northern mother empathized with Confederate children. After receiving news about the plight of Goldsboro, North Carolina, from a loved one in the Union army, she urged her daughter to not only "think of the beautiful cities and towns of N. and S. Carolina, sacked and burned," but also consider the "helpless women and children fleeing in terror, without a home to shelter them, without bread to feed them." The lack of food was especially poignant as she noted the similar plight of "our poor starving Union prisoners."[11]

Sherman recognized that his decision to treat children and women as enemies was controversial, but he did not shy away from defending his tactics. His most famous justification came after Atlanta's mayor and city council protested the evacuation of "helpless people" who were "mostly women and children" as inhumane and unnecessary. Sherman replied by asserting that "war is cruelty, and you cannot refine it; and those who brought war into our country deserve all the curses and maledictions a people can pour out." Sherman considered all Confederates culpable for the war, enemies of the United States, and acceptable targets of a military campaign who "all the curses and maledictions a people can pour out." In an earlier response to Hood's protests of the evacuation orders, Sherman rationalized his actions in terms that specifically appealed to the ideals of protecting children and women. "It is kindness," Sherman wrote, "to remove them now at once from scenes that women and children should not be exposed to." Despite the Southern uproar against his orders, Sherman tried to portray himself as the protector of, or father figure to, Atlanta's children and mothers.[12]

As Sherman stressed the necessity and benefits of removing civilians from Atlanta, numerous Union soldiers rationalized that Southerners, regardless of age and sex, deserved to suffer for causing the Civil War. Many enthusiastically supported the evacuation of the city. Edward Allen boasted about his commander's orders to evacuate Atlanta. He urged his family to "read . . . Sherman's letters to Hood in reference to the removal of the women & children of Atlanta," which accurately reflected "the sentiments of his whole army." Allen and his fellow soldiers praised Sherman because he was "not afraid to treat . . . them as they deserve." These Union men, some of them fathers, accepted the treatment of civilians because they had determined, like their commander, that the only way to end the war was to bring it home to the children and mothers of the South. They no longer viewed children and women as a protected class—although they still treated them differently than they did soldiers on the battlefield—but instead saw them as enemies who needed to feel the brunt of war.[13]

The girls of Atlanta were not the only ones to be dislodged from the comforts of their home or to worry about the war. For many children around the Confederacy, the worlds they knew changed as soon as their fathers and older brothers left home for the battlefield. As mothers moved their families to places that they presumed to be safer or as they combined homes to economize and lighten their loads, Southern children adapted to new surroundings, people, and daily routines. Although along the march Union soldiers did not frequently command families to leave their homes, thousands of families took flight immediately before and after the arrival of Sherman's men. As rumors about Sherman's advance circulated—especially those that referred to rape at the hands of the enemy soldiers—terrified mothers hoped to shield their daughters from the horrors of invasion by removing them to safer places. Others left when the invading Union soldiers destroyed their homes and foodstuffs. Some moved to the cities while others found places closer to home. Regardless of the place, however, refugee life proved both a challenge and a thrill.

Although Sherman's campaign, and the war as a whole, tended to force adolescents to mature quickly, it also encouraged a sense of adventure in younger girls. As Atlanta's civilians prepared to evacuate the city, ten-year-old Carrie Berry expressed surprise that "every one I see seems sad." She did not understand why all "the citizens . . . think it is the most cruel thing to drive us from our home." Her perspective on the prospect of leaving her home in Atlanta was quite different from that of the adults around her. As her parents worried about the family's future, Carrie enjoyed the excitement. "I think it would be so funny to move." Although she had hidden in basements to avoid the shells flying around the city during the bombardment, she still did not understand the gravity of the situation or the stresses of wartime relocation. Older girls typically had a better grasp on the dangers of wartime life.[14]

The decision to leave was not an easy one, and many girls witnessed their families' indecision on the matter but could do little about it. Even though her mother thought it the safest course of action, seventeen-year-old Emma LeConte did not want to leave Columbia, South Carolina: "I so dread leaving home, for I feel I would never see it again except in ashes." In the end, her family remained in Columbia because they felt comforted by the presence of Confederate troops and doubted that the city could "be taken by a raid." As a result, she witnessed the capture and burning of the town three days later. Emma described the many other families hurrying out of town just ahead of Sherman's arrival in Columbia: "The streets in town are lined with panic-stricken crowds, trying to escape. All is confusion and turmoil."[15]

Confederate girls who did not leave before the enemy arrived had to deal with the consequences of being in the middle of a battle zone. As the battle raged around them in Columbia, one woman wrote that her "children began to cry they did not want to stay here." Families who remained in threatened areas frequently crowded together. In Smithville, North Carolina, seventeen-year-old Janie Smith described how her extended family crammed into one house and tried to survive after the invasion. "We lived for three days on four q[uar]ts of meal. . . . Didn't pretend to sift it, baked up in our room where fifteen of us had to stay. Where & how we slept I dont [sic] know now." Others fled to the streets or their fields when soldiers forced them from the presumed safety of their bedrooms before raiding and then torching the homes.[16]

Meeting enemy soldiers face-to-face often reinforced earlier prejudices about the enemy. Girls who experienced the invasion decried the soldiers as "Sherman's 'hell hounds,'" "fiends incarnate," "Scoundrels," "hyenas," "scamps," "devils," and "blue coated fiends." Janie Smith's personal experiences near the Battle of Averasboro in North Carolina both terrified and enraged her. The soldiers charged "right into the house breaking open bureau drawers of all kinds, faster than I could unlock . . . cursed us for having hid [*sic*] everything and made bold threats if certain things were not brought to light, but all to no effect." In addition, Union soldiers "left no living thing in Smithville but the people." All chickens and livestock were killed. She fumed that "every nook and corner of the premises was searched and the things that they did'nt [*sic*] use were either burned or torn into strings." Accustomed to various shortages prior to the march, Confederate girls had to worry about adequate food supplies and other basic necessities afterward.[17]

Confederate girls routinely had their personal property destroyed or stolen, even items of little or no military or monetary value. The loss of sentimental property helped magnify girls' impressions that Union soldiers were unduly cruel. Union soldiers found diaries, the keeping of which was a common hobby of elite white girls, an especially amusing spoil of war. Enemy soldiers frequently stole, and sometimes published, Confederate girls' journals and letters. Consequently, many elite girls took pains to hide their journals from prying enemy eyes. As the enemy advanced, LeConte "destroyed most of my papers, but have a lot of letters still that I do not wish to burn." She did, however, want to protect them. "I do not care to have them share the fate of Aunt Jane's and Cousin Ada's in Liberty Co., which were read and scattered along the roads. I will try to hide them." Keeping their innermost thoughts out of the hands of soldiers became a priority for many girls that often required that they destroy written memories of childhood.[18]

Soldiers also destroyed feminine items like sheet music and pianos, dresses and dolls, and various girlish trinkets. All along the march Confederate girls faced similar situations. The young daughter of the postmaster in Winnsboro, South Carolina, found it infuriating that the soldiers "stole much that was useless to them, for even Bibles were taken." Her resentment, as well as her assumption that Yankee soldiers were godless, was not unusual. The actions of Union men reaffirmed for many Southern girls that the enemy was so different from southerners as to constitute a different "race." By routinely transcending gendered rules of behavior, Yankees became seen as inherently and unnaturally different. Even Union soldiers noticed the nonmilitary reasons for the actions of "'bummers'—stragglers under nobody's charge" who, as Harvey Reid of the 22nd Wisconsin noted, "ransack the houses, taking every knife and fork, spoon or anything else they take a fancy to, break open trunks and bureaus, take women or children's clothing, or tearing them to pieces trampling upon them &c. besides taking everything eatable that can be found." Although this soldier had "never heard . . . of personal violence . . . they are insulted in every other way possible." Union commanders similarly noticed the pillaging of Southern homes. Oliver O. Howard wrote that strag-glers "have been guilty of the vilest conduct entering houses where there were women & little children & utterly destroying everything stealing knives fork, & spoons opening trunks &c&c." Reports that some of the personal belongings were being shipped back to Northern cities infuriated Confeder-ate girls. North Carolinian Janie Smith raged that "they got all my stockings and some of our collars & handkerchiefs." She hoped that she would have the chance to return the favor. "If I ever see a Yankee woman I intend to whip her and take her clothes off of her very back.[19]

The destruction of homes and personal items became commonplace along the march. William Wettleson, a Wisconsin soldier, repeatedly reported the scene to his family. In November, he observed that as a result of Sherman's campaign, "the land has been ruined down here. The houses have been torn down and burned up and the fences are all burned too." However, it was not just the landscape that had suffered. In addition, "women and children have neither food nor clothes." More than a month later, he still marveled at "the distress and misery caused by the War." Again he noted that "there are women and children by the thousands who have neither food nor clothing." Further-more, "everything has been destroyed—all fences burned, houses wrecked." In February, as he prepared to leave the Deep South, he emphasized that "children are nearly naked and women the same, and both are on the point of starving to death. They are so ragged that one cannot see what their clothes are made of." In Georgia, a Union soldier observed that "everyone is poorly clothed. At every station there are so many girls selling pies, and corn cakes, potatoes, etc. that one can scarcely turn around." The lack of clothing represented more than loss of property. In many cases it demonstrated the upheaval of the Southern social system as invading soldiers primarily destroyed the property of elite families and redistributed much of it among the slaves. Reverend G. S. Bradley observed that "little daughters can at some places be seen without shoes and stockings, while the negro children at their sides are comfortably clad."[20]

As much as Confederate civilians recognized that Sherman's march oper-ated with new rules of war, many of them hoped that some antebellum con-ventions would remain and shield them from the worst that war could bring. Some rules remained, making the murder, rape, and physical assault of white girls (and women) a rarity on the march. Confederates extended hope to the presumed sanctity of churches, hospitals, and public institutions. As one Union soldier recounted in a letter to his parents, because Confederate civilians feared that "we made a practice *a la Pharoah* of killing the male children," many fami-lies looked for safety as troops arrived. Some Confederate civilians took comfort in the region's institutional buildings. After the arrival of Sherman's troops in Columbia, for example, many girls fled with their mothers to the South Carolina Lunatic Asylum in hopes that it would live up to its name. The Female College was "uninjured and is now occupied by houseless women and children."[21]

In many cases, their searches for safe refuge inside the besieged towns and cities were unsuccessful. Eyewitness Mary Maxcy Leverett noticed that the burning of Columbia, South Carolina, thrust children into the streets. "As the houses burnt down one after another the terrified women & children rushed into the Asylum for safety surrounded by these yelling devils." However, the Asylum was not necessarily a safe place that night. Leverett decried the actions of the enemy soldiers and their treatment of the civilians, especially children. Despite the presence of "500 ladies & children" in the Asylum, "the fiends raged curseing [sic], screaming up and down in front of the Asylum swearing they were going to blow [it] up." A Union soldier similarly commented on the presence of children as the city of Columbia burned: "The streets were full of drunken Soldiers, guards, firemen, women, and children, &c&c. All was Confusion & excitement." Janie Smith and her family left their house during the Battle of Averasboro. Even though they followed military commands to a "safe" place, at "about five in the evening the Enemy flanked our right, where we were sent for protection, and the firing was right over us. We could hear the commands and the groans & shrieks of the wounded." No places could be guaranteed safe for youngsters during the campaign.[22]

Children and families not only sought protection in institutions but also hoped for safety in their own homes. In many cases, mothers and daughters expected and received protection by virtue of their sex and age. The protections afforded to children often manifested themselves in Union guards being posted outside many of the homes in occupied areas. Even in these instances, some Confederate girls suffered in privileged ways suited to their race, gender, and age. After North Carolinian Elizabeth Collier and her family—a group of "helpless women"—had a gun pointed at them by an invading soldier as he plundered her parents' Everettsville house, they "succeeded in getting a 'safe guard.'" Although the guard protected their house, "everything outdoors was destroyed—all provisions taken—fences knocked down—horses, cows, carriages, and buggies stole, and everything else the witches could lay their hands on—even to the servants[sic] clothes." Guards prevented sexual and physical assaults, but they permitted other insults.[23]

Union troops did not heed all pleas for protection. North Carolina teenager Janie Smith did not have the good fortune of a guard. Although she "had heard that the officers would protect ladies," she discovered that "it is not so. Sis Susan was sick in bed, and they searched the very pillows that she was lying on and keeping such a noise tearing up and breaking to pieces that the Gens could not hear themselves talk, but not a time did they try to prevent it." Many Union soldiers deemed that the civilians, regardless of age or sex, were unworthy of protection; as one wrote, "the women and children of the south must suffer." In Columbia, one soldier took blankets away from Southern children: "let the d——d little rebels suffer as we have had to do for the past four years." Charles Brown reported to his family that men in his regiment had no sympathy for civilians. He saw "one old woman…with prehaps [sic] 1/2 a peck of potatoes the last morsel of food in the world, & which she was trying to save for her children be ordered by a man to hand them over & be forced with a cocked revolver to do the same." Once they had determined civilians of all ages and sexes to be enemies of the United States, Union soldiers treated them as such.[24]

The sights, sounds, and smells of Sherman's march made a great impression on young Southerners and permanently transformed their familiar surroundings. This was especially true for homes that became makeshift hospitals. One girl from North Carolina explained that the "house is ruined with the blood of the Yankee wounded." She could not get past the fact that everything was destroyed except "our Piano, [but they] used cousin Sallies['] for an amputation table." Other scenes made similarly lasting impressions on the minds of Confederate girls. Eight-year-old Sally Hawthorne of Fayetteville, North Carolina, would "never forget that scene" of the evacuation of Confederate troops. As Southern soldiers left the town, she and her sisters handed out sandwiches. They watched unknowingly as Sherman's men arrived, even pointing out their own home to the enemy soldiers who ultimately used her house as a headquarters. She and her siblings were terrified, and her mother would not leave her room. Sally not only remembered the terror of occupation and the sounds of battle but also asserted that "the most gruesome sound" was that of "the scream of a mortally wounded horse." It was a sound that stayed with her for the rest of her life.[25]

Teenager Janie Smith witnessed the Battle of Averasboro, and its smells, sights, and sounds ambushed her senses. The smell of unwashed Union soldiers repulsed her. After enemy soldiers ransacked her home she judged that "of all the horrible smelling things in the world the Yankees beat." Even "the battlefield dont [sic] compare with them in point of stench. I dont [sic] believe they have been washed since they were born." Later, when her home was serving as a hospital for Confederate wounded, she wrote, "It makes me shudder when I think of the awful sights I witnessed that morning . . .

every barn & out house was filled and under every shed & tree the tables were carried for amputating the limbs." The aftermath of battle also assaulted her senses. "The blood lay in puddles in the grove, the groans of the dying & the complaints of those undergoing amputation was horrible, the painful impression has seared my very heart. I can never forget it."[26]

Several scholars have explained that Confederates began to script many elements of the Lost Cause in the midst of the fighting. Girls who lived through Sherman's march did not have to look far to find confirmation of their belief that Confederates fought honorably while Union soldiers did not. Emma LeConte gave voice to the anger that outlived the war and highlighted Sherman's treatment of children. "This is civilized warfare!" she marveled. "This is the way in which the 'cultured' Yankee nation wars upon women and children! Failing with our men in the field, *this* is the way they must conquer!" She ridiculed the enemy's dishonorable tactics: "It is so easy to burn the homes over the heads of the helpless women and children, and turn them with insults and sneers into the streets." Reconciliation with the Yankees "who practise such wanton and useless cruelty" would be unthinkable. "Think of the degradation of being conquered and ruled by such a people! It seems to me now as if we would choose extermination." Similarly outraged by Sherman's tactics, many girls hoped, like Janie Smith, that as the war continued Confederates could repay the "kindnesses" of Union soldiers. "When our army invades the North I want them to carry a torch in one hand and the sword in the other. I want desolation carried to the heart of their Country, the widows & orphans left naked & starving just as ours were left." General Robert E. Lee may have surrendered his army three days later, but Smith and other girls did not. They instead threw their energies into crafting a glory- and honor-filled interpretation of the Confederate war effort.[27]

During Sherman's march, Union soldiers disregarded and ultimately destroyed the presumed separation between childhood and warfare. Although girls received some protection due to their age and sex, they learned that war "means something more than a holiday parade." During their home front invasion of Georgia and the Carolinas, Union troops directly invaded the world of elite girls by engaging in tactics that targeted the markers of girlhood and adolescence. Consequently, girls had to deal with the burning of homes, theft of food, and plundering of valuables. They also dealt with the destruction or loss of mattresses, dolls, diapers, books, and sheet music. The children of the march found themselves forever altered by the scenes and experiences of invasion.[28]

1. Emma LeConte, January 28, 1865, Diary, Southern Historical Collection, University of North Carolina, Chapel Hill.

2. See Lee Ann Whites and Alecia P. Long, eds., *Occupied Women: Gender, Military Occupation, and the American Civil War* (Baton Rouge: Louisiana State University Press, 2009); James Marten, *The Children's Civil War* (Chapel Hill: University of North Carolina Press, 1998); Anya Jabour, *Scarlett's Sisters: Young Women in the Old South* (Chapel Hill: University of North Carolina Press, 2007); Victoria E. Ott, *Confederate Daughters: Coming of Age during the Civil War* (Carbondale: Southern Illinois University Press, 2008); Edmund L. Drago, *Confederate Phoenix: Rebel Children and Their Families in South Carolina* (New York: Fordham University Press, 2008).

3. William T. Sherman to Edwin M. Stanton, June 21, 1864, *Official Records*, Ser. 1, Vol. 39, Pt. 2, 132.

4. G. Moxley Sorrell, *Recollections of a Confederate Staff Officer* (New York: Neale, 1905), 287.

5. Mark Grimsley, *The Hard Hand of War: Union Military Policy toward Southern Civilians, 1861–1865* (New York: Cambridge University Press, 1995); Scott Reynolds Nelson and Carol Sheriff, *A People at War: Civilians and Soldiers in America's Civil War, 1854–1877* (New York: Oxford University Press, 2001), 157.

6. Henry Halleck to William T. Sherman, September 28, 1864, *Official Records*, Ser. 1, Vol. 39, Pt. 2, 503.

7. William T. Sherman to Maria Boyle Ewing Sherman, August 6, 1862, in *Sherman's Civil War: Selected Correspondence of William T. Sherman, 1860–1865*, ed. Brooks D. Simpson and Jean V. Berlin (Chapel Hill: University of North Carolina Press, 1999), 262.

8. Emma LeConte, February 5, 1865, Diary.

9. William T. Sherman to Henry W. Halleck, September 9, 1864, *Official Records*, Ser. 1, Vol. 38, Pt. 5, 839; Rev. G. S. Bradley, *The Star Corps; or, Notes of an Army Chaplain, during Sherman's Famous "March to the Sea"* (Milwaukee: Jermain and Brightman, 1865), 156.

10. John Bell Hood to William T. Sherman, September 9, 1864, *Official Records*, Ser. 1, Vol. 39, Pt. 2, 415; Sylvester Daniels, September 16, 1864, Sylvester Daniels Diary, Huntington Library, San Marino, California; Horatio Dana Chapman, September 20, 1864, *Civil War Diary: Diary of a Forty-Niner* (Hartford, CT: Allis, 1929), 95.

11. Louisa Warren Patch Fletcher, October 12, 1864, Louisa Warren Patch (Mrs. Dix) Fletcher Journal, Georgia Department of Archives and History, Atlanta; J. S. Pearson to Annie, March 23, 1865, J. S. Pearson Letter, South Carolina Historical Society, Charleston.

12. James M. Calhoun, E. E. Rawson, and S.C. Wells to William T. Sherman, September 11, 1864, *Official Records*, Ser. 1, Vol. 39, Pt. 2, 417; William T. Sherman to James M. Calhoun, Mayor, E. E. Rawson and S. C. Wells, representing the City Council of Atlanta, September 12, 1864, in *Memoirs of General W. T. Sherman*, ed. Michael Fellman (New York: Penguin Books, 2000), 494; William T. Sherman to John Bell Hood, September 10, 1864, *Official Records*, Ser. 1, Vol. 39, Pt. 2, 416.

13. Edward W. Allen to James and Emily Allen, September 25, 1864, Edward W. Allen Papers, Southern Historical Collection.

14. Carrie Berry, September 10, 1864, Diary, August 1864–January 1866, Atlanta History Center, Georgia.

15. Emma LeConte, February 5, 1865, February 14, 1865, February 15, 1865, Diary.

16. S. McCain to Daughter, March 5, 1865, Mary Amarinthia Snowden Papers, South Caroliniana Library, University of South Carolina, Columbia; Janie Smith to Janie N. Robeson, April 12, 1865, Mrs. Thomas H. Webb Collection, North Carolina Division of Archives and History, Raleigh.

17. Janie Smith to Janie N. Robeson, April 12, 1865; Emma LeConte, February 18, 1865, Diary.

18. Emma LeConte, February 15, 1865, Diary.

19. As quoted in Emmy E. Werner, *Reluctant Witnesses: Children's Voices from the Civil War* (Boulder, CO: Westview Press, 1998), 130; Harvey Reid to Homefolk, December 14, 1864, Bell Irvin Wiley Files, Special Collections Department, Emory University, Atlanta, Georgia; O. O. Howard, August 29, 1864, David I. Carson Civil War Papers, Georgia Department of Archives and History; Janie Smith to Janie N. Robeson, April 12, 1865.

20. William O. Wettleson to Father and Sisters, November 27, 1864, January 3, 1865, February 1, 1865, Wiley Files; Bradley, *Star Corps*, 158.

21. Edward W. Allen to James and Emily Allen, February 27, 1865, Edward W. Allen Papers; *Providence Daily Journal*, May 8, 1865.

22. Mary Maxcy Leverett to Milton Maxcy Leverett, February 24, 1864, in *The Leverett Letters: Correspondence of a South Carolina Family, 1851–1868*, ed. Frances Wallace Taylor, Catherine Taylor Matthews, and J. Tracy Power (Columbia: University of South Carolina Press, 2000), 386; C. C. Platter, February 17, 1865, C.C. Platter Journal, South Caroliniana Library; Janie Smith to Janie N. Robeson, April 12, 1865.

23. Elizabeth Collier, April 20, 1865, Elizabeth Collier Diary, 1862–1865, Southern Historical Collection.

24. Janie Smith to Janie N. Robeson, April 12, 1865; Bradley, *Star Corps*, 222; Jeremiah W. Jenkins as cited in Charles Royster, *The Destructive War: William Tecumseh Sherman, Stonewall Jackson, and the Americans* (New York: Vintage Books, 1993), 23; Charles S. Brown to Etta, April 26, 1865, Charles S. Brown Papers, Rare Book, Manuscript, and Special Collections Library, Duke University, Durham, North Carolina.

25. Janie Smith to Janie N. Robeson, April 12, 1865; Sally Hawthorne, "What Did General Sherman Say?" in *When Sherman Came: Southern Women and the "Great March,"* ed. Katharine Jones (New York: Bobbs-Merrill, 1964), 276, 284.

26. Janie Smith to Janie N. Robeson, April 12, 1865.

27. Emma LeConte, February 18, 1865, Diary; Janie Smith to Janie N. Robeson, April 12, 1865.

28. Bradley, *Star Corps*, 225.

8

Love in Battle

*The Meaning of Courtships in
the Civil War and Lost Cause*

VICTORIA E. OTT

In 1911, Emma Riely Macon published her remembrances of life in the Union-occupied town of Winchester, Virginia. Born in 1847, young Macon experienced the Civil War as a teenage youth coming of age in a secessionist, slaveholding household. Her narrative, an ardent defense of the Confederate South in the postwar years, retold accounts of her interaction with Union soldiers. She depicted an internal struggle between remaining loyal to the Confederate cause and the desire to pursue romantic relations amid a dearth of southern gentlemen. Her notion of patriotic duty meant making the needed sacrifices, even declining social activities so common to young women her age. This was a difficult feat for someone in her stage of life, as she recalled. One evening a Union officer, a man of similar socioeconomic status and respectable reputation, approached her with an invitation for a sleigh ride through the city. The request, one of many invitations she received from Union soldiers, tested her sense of loyalty. "It was oftentimes hard to resist," she wrote, "and required all the loyalty I could bring to bear to do so." When the officer suggested that she conceal her identity behind a veil, she responded that "her conscience would be behind that veil" and declined his invitation. She reminded readers that a true Confederate daughter struggled with such temptations on a daily basis: "What a severe test it was to my loyalty and devotion to my country to be able to resist my enemies when I might have enjoyed so many privileges dear to a young girl's heart."[1]

Understandably, Macon's attempts to reject potential courtship activities in the grim environment of the Civil War South emerged from her devotion to the Confederate cause. Southern daughters who came of age in the Confederacy held tight to the gender ideals and racial ordering of the slaveholding culture. As young children reared in the Old South, they learned from their parents, teachers, and ministers to accept the feminine ideal that heralded domesticity and maternity as the epitome of womanhood. And, from their earliest recollections, these daughters identified with the privileged class and delighted in the trappings of an elite, youth culture, including embellished fashion, private education, and participating in an array of social engagements. They had come to anticipate that they would one day assume their positions as wives, mothers, and slave mistresses, allowing them to retain their elite identity with all its trappings. Courtships as the process of finding a potential mate and maintaining elite kinship ties served as a means for young women to secure this cultural script.[2]

Unfortunately for these youths, the sectional conflict, wrapped, as it were, in the institution at the center of their way of life, threatened to eclipse their efforts to pursue a life course of privilege. The movement to abolish slavery challenged the continuation of the economic and social status of their families. The secession of the southern states and the formation of the Confederacy did, however, provide hope for the preservation of their life course and ultimately their sense of self. For this age-group in the formative stages of development, the Confederate cause meant nothing short of preserving their class and racial privilege. In demonstrating their allegiance to the Confederate cause, southern daughters turned to the primary feature of their youth culture: courtships. They transformed their romantic relationships into political expressions that were unique from those of their older, married female kin. Their courtship activities, moreover, helped sustain patriotic sentiment toward the southern cause in the face of growing economic, political, and social dissent. The effort to find continuity with the Old South past remained in the years following Confederate defeat. Young women, now adults, remained devoted to the traditional values and offered up their own version of the southern experience in hopes of venerating the region but also to advocate a return to the gender ordering of the antebellum period. Courtship stories likewise became the basis on which this group of southern youths constructed their own image, separate from that of older women of the war years, in the language and symbols of the postwar narrative that touted the Confederate mission as a noble cause. Concentrating on the lives of young women from slaveholding, secessionist families coming of age in a time of great regional strife over slavery's expansion into the new western territories, this essay demonstrates the relevancy of age in determining the gendered experience of those living through the tumultuous years of 1861 to 1865 and the creation of public memory in the decades following the Civil War. These young women were born between 1843 and 1849, placing them between the ages of twelve and eighteen when the war commenced, and

Figure 8.1. A romanticized vision of Civil War–era courtship. *The Four Seasons of Life: Youth*, from *The Season of Love*. Lithograph by Currier and Ives, 1868. Prints and Photographs Division, Library of Congress.

came from middling and elite households with financial ties to the slave-holding South. Members of this age group, who would later be called adolescents, were immersed in their emotional, social, and physical development, and thus in a formative period of their lives. What emerges from their diaries, letters, and reminiscences is a story of how female youths transformed what it meant to be southern and female.[3]

Courtships played a crucial role in the youth culture of slaveholding daughters. The expectation of romantic affection and notions of companionate marriage had replaced ideas about patriarchal authority so common in the relationships between men and women prior to the nineteenth century. But affection was not the only criterion by which young women chose a potential mate; a successful suitor had to meet the standards set by a young woman's parents. Mothers and fathers would only approve men who came from their same class group and who embodied the ideal of respectability. A young man's blood ties as well as economic aspirations, education, and manners all helped determine whether parents would give their blessing for a union.[4]

Educators also warned of the dangers of allowing a young woman to engage in social relations with the opposite sex, which, without proper guidance, could tarnish their reputations. James Garnett, a southern educator, conducted a series of lectures at the Elm-Wood School in Virginia on the proper conduct of young women. He noted that marriage "should never be precipitately entered" and that potential beaux should be chosen with "parental approbations on both sides." Male lecturer and educational expert J. Burton also trumpeted the need for parental consent when choosing a proper suitor. Burton spoke before students in Maryland, but his work was subsequently published and widely circulated among educators in other southern states. He warned his female charges that they "may be disposed to make an improper and imprudent choice" and should thus turn to the judgment of their parents when choosing a proper suitor. A daughter who disregarded her parents' wishes, he asserted, acted "unwisely as well as undutifully."[5]

Teachers prescribed the proper conduct for a female youth. Foremost on their minds was discouraging the practice of coquetry, a type of flirtation that appeared to cross the boundaries of respectability. "Your influence, at this period of life," Burton implored, "may . . . be injurious to the young part of the other sex, by enticing them from those pursuits which might be profitable to their country, and glorious to themselves." Garnett also emphasized the importance of preserving reputation when he warned that "stripped of all disguise, it [coquetry] is neither more, nor less, than an artful mixture of hypocrisy, fraud, treachery, and falsehood."[6]

Courtship rituals provided a period of freedom for many young women that they attempted to extend as long as possible. Their activities ranged from family-arranged social engagements to parties, dances, and church functions where young women had an opportunity to meet and interact with potential suitors. Some avoided accepting marriage proposals in an attempt to assert their freedom from the female prescription of southern slaveholding culture. Sarah Wadley, for example, wrote in her diary that she was happy "to pass a single life." Wadley's privilege allowed her such freedom as her family was among the well-to-do households in Monroe, Louisiana. Born in 1844, Wadley was taught to laud the maternal and domestic ideal yet recognized the hardships that it brought. She wrote that her "health, or more properly my constitution," she elaborated, "is too feeble to sustain the burden which a wife and mother must bear." In 1860, at the young age of seventeen, Catherine Louisa McLaurin, of Sumter County, South Carolina, echoed Wadley's sentiments after she spent time with a recently married friend. "If getting married has such a bad effect upon all girls as it has on her," she confided to her diary, "then all should hold fast their hands." Myra Inman from Cleveland, Tennessee, also relished the freedom of her youth. At the tender age of fourteen on the eve of the Civil War, she began the process of socializing with male counterparts. Myra Inman, whose father passed away before the war, lived with her mother in their family residence, which counted nine slaves among it. On the eve of the Civil War, she was in the throes of developing her reputation as a pious, educated young woman as she attended the Cleveland Masonic Female Institute and was active in the local Baptist church. Yet courtships could at times challenge the constrictive nature of her education. This aspect of her youthful development was a time of freedom for Inman and her peers. She expressed joy in the social opportunities and potential courtship, intimating little desire for marriage even in the distant future.[7]

The Civil War, however, called into question typical courtship practices and raised questions concerning attitudes governing conduct. Despite the absence of their potential suitors for service in the army or with the Confederate government, most young women held fast to the notion of marrying someday in the future. The disruptions on the home front precipitated by war, separation, and economic misfortune made social interactions with the opposite sex even more significant. In areas where young men were absent for long periods, young women reoriented their courtship pursuits to accommodate the dearth of potential suitors. In particular, letter writing became the means by which young courting couples continued relationships and explored whether a potential engagement was possible. In areas with a greater presence of Confederate soldiers, moreover, young women found patriotic functions a new venue for social interaction with men from outside their community. Such accommodation provided a sense of normalcy and a connection to the Old South slaveholding culture. It allowed them to pursue the path to finding a future mate while giving them the freedom to explore romantic relationships away from the watchful eyes of parents.[8]

Social activities continued and, at times, increased during the war, allowing young women to find avenues to romantic relationships. The presence of Confederate soldiers in southern communities increased a young woman's chances of meeting a potential suitor. Richmond, Virginia, for example, witnessed a constant presence of eligible young men either preparing to leave for or returning from the battlefront. As a result, there were always social engagements to attend. Margaretta Ellen Wise, a young woman living in Richmond during the war, recalled in her memoirs that she and several female peers attended a host of dances and parties throughout the course of the war. These engagements allowed young men and women to meet and exchange information to begin writing to each other. Pauline de Caradeuc, of Aiken, South Carolina, bragged that while visiting relatives in Augusta, Georgia, she was offered several invitations to social functions. Born in 1843, de Caradeuc was in her early twenties when she confided to her diary, "I really didn't recognize Pauline de Caradeuc in the character of a belle. She has been so long in quiet and retirement, that I had almost forgotten her in society." De Caradeuc relished this period of romantic interaction until she married Guerard Heyward after the war in 1865. In the more rural areas of the Confederate South, young women had to become creative in their efforts to continue their pursuit of courtships. Sarah Wadley of Monroe, Louisiana, along with other young women her age, organized dances and parties for officers and soldiers when they moved through the community.[9]

Parents grew increasingly concerned with the added freedoms their daughters had in the pursuit of romantic relations. Adding to their anxieties was the frequent separation of family members during the war. Mothers often left for extended visits to family members or to nurse male relatives recovering from injury or illness as a result of Confederate service. Fathers, too, found their service to the military or government called them away from home for long periods. As a result, parents' control over their daughters' behavior weakened. Younger women, however, found that despite the liberalization of courtship practices, their parents attempted to guide their social interaction. The concern that worried mothers and fathers the most was their daughters' conduct with Confederate soldiers. Hearing about instances of women rushing to marry soldiers, parents grew concerned that their daughters would place themselves in danger of impropriety. For those parents separated from their daughters, their fears about possible impropriety were heightened. Jane Sivley, who spent the war away at the Judson Institute in Marion, Alabama, received several letters from her mother imploring her to avoid any inappropriate associations. Rumors of young women marrying soldiers only to be abandoned by their husbands, who were never seen again, exacerbated Mrs. Sivley's anxieties about her daughter's conduct. In 1864, she warned Jane that "some of the Raymond [Mississippi] girls are causing a good deal of talk . . . some of the Shurbuta [Mississippi] girls are going to have *babies*, the girls are acting disgracefully the men will soon have no respect for them." Mrs. Sivley worried that her daughter, away from her mother's watchful eyes, would follow the same path and urged Jane to avoid hasty courtships with a soldier. "It really looks like the girls will marry anybody these days," she wrote. "My dear daughter keep a strict watch over your affections and don't be deceived, men are very deceiving." She urged Jane to stay clear of "strange soldiers."[10]

ous occasions discussed her engagement to a "Yankee beau." In an 1863 diary entry, she noted that the friend "carried on shamefully and...any girl that had one particle of modesty would not have talked as she did." This sentiment was further entrenched as the death toll of Confederate soldiers increased during the course of the war. Ellen Renshaw House also questioned "how a southern girl can marry a Yankee." Maria Smith Peek grew embarrassed when she heard that her cousin had married a minister from Vermont. She believed that her relative acted disgracefully and that her association with the enemy would subsequently harm the reputation of the family. Although community members already ostracized her cousin for her actions, Maria pronounced to her family that they need not be concerned as her remaining kin were "as true to the South and to her sacred memory of precious dead as ever."[19]

Even as the economic and emotional consequences of war took their toll on southern families, young women continued to endorse the cause of Confederate nationalism. They remained committed to an independent nation, seeing separation from the Union as the only means by which to secure their futures as privileged women. Yet, inevitably, the war began to affect the lifestyle of southern daughters. In Charleston, by late 1863, according to Pauline de Caradeuc, "a cheap calico or homespun dress costs $100.00, and one bushel of corn $4.50 and $5.00." Emma LeConte noted that after the burning of Columbia in 1865, her family relied on rations distributed by the town government. Despite the economic hardships of diminishing supplies and rising inflation, southern daughters hoped that the war would continue on. By 1865, the hope for Confederate victory appeared to fade as the armies suffered losses on the battlefront and internal dissent challenged home front morale.[20]

Despite home front deprivations and looming defeat, southern daughters remained loyal to the Confederate cause. As the news of Appomattox began to reach the countryside, they admonished political and military leaders for the possible surrender of the South. Of course, they relished the thought of their brothers, fathers, and beaux returning home but anguished over the idea of the demise of the Confederate nation. For many young women, the responsibility of defeat rested squarely on the shoulders of male leaders; their own male friends and family members were merely following orders. They conceptualized the Confederate nation as a family with leaders such as Robert E. Lee and Jefferson Davis as its metaphorical paternal figures, owing responsibility to the care and security of its people. When the Confederacy finally surrendered, female youths of the region criticized leaders for shirking their masculine duty to the home and community. Although they remained loyal to patriarchal notions of female dependence to southern men, they openly expressed their mixed emotions over defeat, and courtship activities served as an age-appropriate means of articulating their sentiment.[21]

Pauline de Caradeuc expected Confederate officers to remain faithful to the cause. Throughout the war, she attended many social events during which she interacted with Confederate soldiers. She changed her attitude at the end of the war, however, regarding activities honoring the return of soldiers. On one occasion, she rejected an invitation to attend a picnic, noting that "I . . . never thought of going, now, that the country for which I have worked, suffered, and prayed for . . . has met with the greatest of all trials." De Caradeuc punctuated her sentiment when she rejected an appeal by Confederate soldiers to attend the community event. She intimated that the soldiers had denied their masculine duty to protect the nation and was shocked at their willingness to "dance and be merry over the death of their country." When the young men sent a carriage to deliver her to the event, she sent it back to them empty. Yet the loyalty of Confederate daughters failed to sustain the cause. As southern soldiers returned home in defeat, young women turned their attention to reconciling the loss of the Confederate nation with their continued reverence of its mission.[22]

In the decades following the war, southern daughters who had come of age during the conflict situated themselves within the emerging cultural narrative of the Lost Cause. Women of all ages played a central role in portraying the Confederate cause as a noble effort intended to defend southerners' constitutional right to secede. White southerners created a "metanarrative" of the Confederate experience that emphasized the divine righteousness of secession, the honorable nature of southern military and political leaders, and the unanimity of support for the war. They likewise romanticized the Old South as an ideal culture separate from the materialistic North bent on destroying a traditional and honorable culture. Confederate defeat came not from the immorality of mission but rather from the South's inability to withstand the overwhelming resources of the Union. Southern females from all generational perspectives promoted this public view of the Confederacy. From memorial movements to the re-internment of Confederate soldiers to the formation of the United Daughters of the Confederacy (UDC) in the 1890s, women lauded the bravery and honor of the southern mission and its men. Hoping to concede a victory in the battle over public memory, many women wrote memoirs of the war that were subsequently published. What emerged was a dominant maternal imagery of southern women that overshadowed the significance of age in understanding differences of female wartime memories. The southern females were touted as "mothers" of the Confederacy, emphasizing their nurturing duties as wives, mothers, and nurses on the home front. Louise Wigfall's reminiscence of the war trumpeted southern women as a prime example of female fortitude during the conflict. "I have in my mind, as I write," she expressed, "a picture that comes before me whenever I hear of the suffering of women of the South." She recalled that while traveling she sat across from a mother on a train who "had journeyed from her far-away home in Alabama to the hospital in Richmond to find her boy and bring him back with her." Wigfall believed that it was the "spirit of motherly love" that would allow the soldier to survive and return to his family.[23]

Southern daughters, now mothers and wives, offered their own defense of the Confederacy in their personal and published recollections of the war unique from that of their mothers and older female kin. They constructed a romantic narrative that focused on the relationships between young men and women during the war, transforming their flirtations and courtships into public acts of support for the southern cause. They lauded the bravery and honor of southern soldiers while impugning the reputation of those who refused service. Gone was the ambivalence of losing potential suitors to the battlefield. Rather, they appeared in their writing to make the needed female sacrifices to sustain the Confederate nation, in their estimation, divinely ordained to achieve victory. These romantic narratives therefore were often gross exaggerations of courtship relations, sometimes teetering on the margins of fiction. These constructions of wartime memories raise the larger question of what purpose they served in the postwar decades. Southern men returning from the front, as historian LeeAnn Whites demonstrates in her study of gender in postwar Augusta, Georgia, suffered from social emasculation in the wake of defeat. Moreover, the demise of slavery coupled with the destruction of the southern economy and their loss of political hegemony in the Reconstruction era, left white men searching for a means of resurrecting the social ordering that existed before the war. White women, in hopes of returning to a life of normalcy and to reclaim their class status, willingly promoted white, elite males as "the best men" to govern community affairs. Trumpeting their experiences in the war as brave and honorable, women contributed to the re-creation of the gender and subsequently racial ordering of the South that emerged by the beginning of the 1900s.[24]

While Lost Cause advocates emphasized the maternal female role, southern daughters created a representation that mirrored their youth in wartime and in doing so contributed to the public effort to promote the Confederate memory. Free from the burdens of motherhood and marriage during the war, they concentrated their narrative of the female supportive role on courtships stereotypical of a southern belle. They legitimized the continuation of courtship activities during the conflict—activities that some deemed frivolous in the face of such a grim environment—by demonstrating the political nature of such engagements. They wrote about their relationships with Confederate soldiers as morale-sustaining diversions from the brutality of war. Many of these writings became a matter of public record when they were published as books and series in newspapers. Other women of this study wrote to leave what they considered a "true" account of events to pass on to subsequent generations of their family, never intending them for publication. Using a romantic motif in her remembrances, Caroline Joachimson, writing her memoirs for a South Carolina newspaper in the 1880s, emphasized the idealization of a southern soldier, noting that "the privates of the beloved army were as dear to the female hearts as the most gaudily decorated officer, and each all wished to dance, and to make love, and even flirt, never once being appalled by the fear of quick coming danger." Esther Alden, of Plantersville, South Carolina, extolled the masculinity of Confederate soldiers in her memoir. While participating in a dance at Fort Sumter with several soldiers, she exclaimed that they all "seemed to me a hero," noting that the young men changed in her estimation when she realized that they "could be killed to-morrow." These men, she concluded, were worthy of her romantic affections because they were fulfilling their duty to home and country.[25]

Another prominent theme in defending the bravery of Confederate soldiers was the story of separated lovers. While mothers offered up their sons and husbands to the war, their daughters reminded readers that they made similar sacrifices with their potential suitors. Florida Saxon's narrative of Katie Weston addresses a sad scene of a female youth conflicted over her suitor's choice to serve in the army. He offered to marry Katie and hire a substitute to fight for him. Saxon, however, argued that Katie would hear nothing of it, noting that she would never "forget the cause that is so dear to her heart," and encouraged her betrothed to "bravely do your duty." The reader is unsure if Weston was a pseudonym for Saxon or merely a fictional character. Nonetheless, her point is clear: the noble nature of the southern cause was enough to overcome the sadness of a separated couple. The extreme examples of female sacrifice came with the death of a young woman's beau. Joachimson recalled that Cecil, her sister, lost her suitor to the battlefield, but despite her sister's sadness, both resolved that it was "the price they paid for peace."[26]

Female youths, conversely, used the imagery of exempted men as the opposite of the dutiful Confederate male. Florida Saxon, for example, decried men who avoided service as "skulkers" not deserving of female attention. Through the fictional character Katie Weston, Saxon reminisced how young women refused to interact with such civilian men. One particular target was Henry Johnson, who invoked an exemption clause to avoid service. Saxon wrote that he was a "handsome fellow" who was "captivated by the charms of our fair Katie." But her female protagonist refused to acknowledge his attentions and "repeatedly taunted" him for "his want of bravery." On one occasion, as a group of youths sat around singing patriotic songs, Katie turned to Johnson and sang to him, "If you would with the fair, go to the field, where honor dwells, and win your lady there. Remember that our brightest smiles are for the true and brave, and that our tears shall fall for those who fill a soldier's grave." The young Johnson subsequently left the party in shame, according to Saxon's account.[27]

When Emma Riley Macon penned her reminiscences of her wartime experience, the romantic narrative had already become etched in the narrative of the Lost Cause. But for teenage daughters of the Confederacy, their courtships served more than to situate themselves in the center of the public movement to venerate the South in the aftermath of war. Rooted in the culture of slaveholding youths, courtships helped southern daughters to separate themselves from the activities of their mothers and older female kin in expressing their allegiance to the Confederate nation. The venue of romantic relationships and social engagements also afforded these young women the freedom to brazenly proclaim their loyalty to Confederate nationalism even in the face of Union occupation. Southern society deemed the world of courtships as age-appropriate for white female youths. Calling on this social acceptance of their relationships with their male counterparts, they situated themselves within the public world of wartime patriotism. Resonating from a conservative movement to preserve the social order of the Old South, they stepped into the world of civic involvement, and their presence there continued long after the war ended.

NOTES

1. Emma Cassandra Riely Macon, *Reminiscences of the Civil War* (Cedar Rapids, IA: Torch Press, 1911), 115–16.

2. For studies that examine the role of parents, clergy, and educators in teaching notions of proper womanhood and female duty, see Anya Jabour, *Scarlett's Sisters: Young Women in the Old South* (Chapel Hill: University of North Carolina Press, 2007), and Victoria E. Ott, *Confederate Daughters: Coming of Age during the Civil War* (Carbondale: Southern Illinois University Press, 2008). For primary documents concerning the education of southern women in gender expectations, see James Garnett, *Lectures on Female Education and Manners, Comprising the First and Second Series of a Course Delivered to Mrs. Garnett's Pupils, at Elm-Wood, Essex County, Virginia* (Richmond, VA: Thomas W. White, 1825), and J. Burton, *Lectures on Female Education and Manners* (Baltimore: Samuel Jefferies, 1811).

3. The sample for this study comes from my larger work on the lives of eighty-five female youths of the slaveholding class. Ott, *Confederate Daughters*.

4. Ibid., 26–28; Anya Jabour, *Marriage in the Early Republic: Elizabeth and William Wirt and the Companionate Ideal* (Baltimore: Johns Hopkins University Press, 1998), 1–7. For additional studies of female youth culture and the centrality of courtships, see also Jabour, *Scarlett's Sisters*.

5. Garnett, *Lectures on Female Education and Manners*, 57–59; Burton, *Lectures on Female Education and Manners*, 55–56.

6. Burton, *Lectures on Female Education and Manners*, 56; Garnett, *Lectures on Female Education*, 221.

7. Sarah Lois Wadley Diary, October 2, 1860, Sarah Lois Wadley Papers, Southern Historical Collection, University of North Carolina, Chapel Hill (hereafter cited as SHC); Catherine Louisa McLaurin Diary, November 6, 1860, Catherine Louisa McLaurin Collection, South Caroliniana Library, University of South Carolina, Columbia; William R. Snell, ed., *Myra Inman: A Diary of the Civil War in East Tennessee* (Macon, GA: Mercer University Press, 2000), 6, 10.

8. Ott, *Confederate Daughters*, 101–2.

9. Margaretta Ellen Wise Mayo Reminiscences, Virginia Historical Society, Richmond, Virginia (hereafter cited as VHS); Mary D. Robertson, ed., *A Confederate Lady Comes of Age: The Journal of Pauline De Caradeuc, 1863–1888* (Columbia: University of South Carolina Press, 1994), 72–73; Sarah Lois Wadley Diary, April 8, May 16, 1863.

10. George Rable, *Civil Wars: Women and the Crisis of Southern Nationalism* (Urbana: University of Illinois Press, 1989), 51–52; Mother to Jane Sivley, January 21, December 5, 1864, Sivley Family Papers, SHC.

11. Ott, *Confederate Daughters*, 36; Drew Gilpin Faust, *Mothers of Invention: Women of the Slaveholding South in the American Civil War* (Chapel Hill: University of North Carolina Press, 1996), 207–12; Annie Jeter Caramouche Memoirs, Annie Jeter Caramouche Papers, Louisiana and Lower Mississippi Valley Collections, Louisiana State University; Daniel E. Sutherland, ed., *A Very Violent Rebel: The Diary of Ellen Renshaw House* (Knoxville: University of Tennessee Press, 1996), 21, 36, 48–50, 127–29, 165–63.

12. Nettie Fondren to Robert Mitchell, May 14, October 9, 1862, Mitchell-Fondren Family Civil War Letters, Georgia Department of Archives and History, Atlanta, Georgia; Cordelia Lewis Scales to Loulie, August 17, 1861, Cordelia Lewis Scales Collection, Mississippi Department of Archives and History, Jackson, Mississippi (hereafter cited as MDAH).

13. James M. McPherson, *For Cause and Comrades: Why Men Fought in the Civil War* (New York: Oxford University Press, 1997), 22–29; James Hankins to Virginia Hankins, November 21, 1860, Hankins Family Papers, VHS.

14. Robert Scott Davis, ed., *Requiem for a Lost City: A Memoir of Civil War Atlanta and the Old South* (Macon: Mercer University Press, 1999), 44–45; Mary Fries Patterson Diary, September 9, 1863, SHC; Sarah Lowe Journal, May 1, 4, 5, 14, 1861, Alabama Department of Archives and History, Montgomery, Alabama.

15. Annie Jeter Caramouche Memoirs; Mrs. D. Giraud Wright, *Southern Girl in '61: The Wartime Memoirs of a Confederate Senator's Daughter* (New York: Doubleday, 1905), 57–59; Amanda Worthington Diary, April 13, 1862, MDAH; Kate D. Foster Diary, June 25, 1863, Perkins Library, Duke University, Durham, North Carolina; Virginia Hankins to Louisiana (Wilson) Hankins, undated 1862, Hankins Family Papers, VHS.

16. *Charleston Mercury*, February 8, 1862; May 29, 1861; March 3, 1864.

17. Snell, *Myra Inman*, 261; Kate D. Foster Diary, September 20, 1863.

18. Henry C. Blackiston, ed., *Refugees in Richmond: Civil War Letters of a Virginia Family* (Princeton: Princeton University Press, 1989), 60–61, 68–69.

19. Nannie Haskins Journal, July 24, 1863, Nannie Haskins Williams Papers, Tennessee State Library and Archives, Nashville, Tennessee; Sutherland, *Very Violent Rebel*, 145; Blackiston, *Refugees in Richmond*, 38.

20. Robertson, *Confederate Lady Comes of Age*, 28; Earl Schenck Miers, ed., *When the World Ended: The Diary of Emma LeConte* (New York: Oxford University Press, 1957), 47.

21. Ott, *Confederate Daughters*, 67, 70.

22. Robertson, *Confederate Lady Comes of Age*, 74–75, 76.

23. Ott, *Confederate Daughters*, 130–35; Wright, *Southern Girl in '61*, 216–17. For studies of the maternal image in Civil War memory, see Sarah Gardner, *Blood and Irony: Southern White Women's Narratives of the Civil War, 1861–1937* (Chapel Hill: University of North Carolina Press, 2004); Karen Cox, *Dixie's Daughters: The United Daughters of the Confederacy and the Preservation of Confederate Culture* (Gainesville: University Press of Florida, 2003); and Caroline E. Janney, *Burying the Dead but Not the Past: Ladies' Memorial Associations and the Lost Cause* (Chapel Hill: University of North Carolina Press, 2008).

24. Ott, *Confederate Daughters*, 135–36, 142; LeeAnn Whites, *The Civil War as a Crisis in Gender: Augusta, Georgia, 1860–1890* (Athens: University of Georgia Press, 1995), 200–209. Laura Edwards, *Gendered Strife and Confusion: The Political Culture of Reconstruction* (Urbana: University of Illinois Press, 1997), also examines postwar efforts to reconstruct southern white masculinity.

25. Ott, *Confederate Daughters*, 142–44; Caroline Joachimson, "Just One Family," in *Our Women in the War: The Lives They Lived; the Deaths They Died* (Charleston, SC: News and Courier Book Presses, 1885), 31–32; Esther Alden, "Fun in the Fort," ibid., 355.

26. Florida Saxon, "Unto the Bitter End," ibid., 71; Joachimson, "Just One Family," 41.

27. Saxon, "Unto the Bitter End," 71.

PART III

Aftermaths

I think Abraham Lincoln didn't do just right, 'cause he threw all the negroes on the world without any way of getting along.
—William Pratt, *The American Slave*[1]

Elizabeth Ware Pearson, who had gone to the Sea Islands of South Carolina in 1862 to teach the newly freed "contraband" children, was in the middle of scolding a small group of black students chattering in the back of the church sanctuary she used as a classroom. When she asked crossly why they even came to school if they were not going to take it seriously, the naughtiest of the little girls immediately grew somber and declared, "If we are educated, they can't make slaves of us again." Unfortunately, and inevitably, it was never that straightforward. The war may have resolved, at least in the short term, a number of political issues, but as the quotation from former slave William Pratt indicates, it also exacerbated old problems and created new ones for Civil War children and youth. Humanitarian motives clashed with political reality and, once again, children became characters in politicized parables about race relations, the nature of gratitude, and the role of public and private institutions in the lives of children.[2]

A major theme linking children to these and other major issues during Reconstruction and its aftermath was race. Just as slave children during the antebellum period had provided object lessons for abolitionists and proslavery advocates alike, so, too, did African American children's transition from commodity to personhood clash with the inability of white Americans to see them as truly free people. Education and economics became two of the biggest challenges facing southern blacks and whites and northern policy makers in the first several years after the war. In both cases the Freedmen's Bureau played an important role in the lives of the first generation of free African American children. Troy Kickler explores the ways in which the Freedmen's Bureau, northern missionaries, and southern whites attempted to shape the course of postwar race relations by manipulating the organization and content of educational opportunities for freedchildren. Although most former slave children and youth did manage to obtain at least some schooling, like their parents they also had to work. The transition from slave to free labor was difficult for everyone involved, and Mary Niall Mitchell suggests that plantation owners and the Freedmen's Bureau rarely acted in the best interests of either black children or their parents in organizing the labor of former slaves immediately after the war.

Perhaps the most obvious direct impact of the war on children and youth was the ultimate sacrifice of tens of thousands of fathers. Most orphans or, in the parlance of the day, "half-orphans," were absorbed into families and communities. But local and state authorities in the North and South made at least tentative efforts to take on the responsibility of caring for these child victims of war. Catherine Jones explores the ways in which the war affected Richmond orphanages—and, no doubt, orphanages in other southern and northern states—not only by creating more need but also by changing the terms on which the children were accepted. As in so many other facets of life in the South, war and defeat caused southerners to look at children and at institutions designed to care for children, in different ways, and to seek to differentiate themselves from their Yankee counterparts. Judith Geisberg's study of the rise and fall of the Pennsylvania Soldiers' Orphans School system demonstrates the clash between patriotism and profit making, as children and youth once again became object lessons in the possibilities and pitfalls in expressions of public gratitude.

NOTES

1. George P. Rawick, *The American Slave: A Composite Autobiography*, 19 vols. (Westport, CT: Greenwood Press, 1972–74), 3 (1): 279.

2. Elizabeth Ware Pearson, ed., *Letters from Port Royal, 1862–1868* (Boston: W. B. Clarke, 1906; New York: Arno Press, 1969), 65.

9

Caught in the Crossfire

African American Children and the Ideological
Battle for Education in Reconstruction Tennessee

TROY L. KICKLER

"The Yankee teacher entered the South on the heels of the soldier," writes historian Henry Swint. "Whenever a foothold had been secured by the Federal Army . . . philanthropic organizations sent out schoolmasters." Considering education the cornerstone of Reconstruction, Freedmen's Bureau agents and Northern missionaries established schools across Tennessee to prepare young former slaves for freedom. Many white Tennesseans, on the other hand, opposed the education of black children and worked to undermine an intellectual and ideological reconstruction.[1]

In Sabbath schools, Bureau and missionary day schools, and the public schools (also known as free schools), black and white instructors worked to mold the first free generation of African Americans in the image of Northern Protestantism. Children listened to lectures and completed assignments addressing such Christian doctrines and values as church attendance, stewardship, and obedience. Other lessons, for instance, labeled secession as unchristian. These lessons were many times coupled with Victorian values, including punctuality, diligence, cleanliness, and temperance. These Christian and Victorian values (and sometimes their conflation) were supposedly essential not only to national progress but also to helping freedchildren adapt and live successfully in Victorian society and in a free-labor economy.

At the end of the Civil War, Freedmen's Bureau agents and Northern missionaries considered educating freedmen their primary task in the South. Without schooling to prepare freedmen for freedom, many Northerners believed, the war would have been fought in vain. Oliver O. Howard, national superintendent of the Freedmen's Bureau, considered it his Christian duty to educate the black children of the South. He and many other Northerners hoped to overcome the negative effects of slavery by preparing freedmen for their lives as independent and prosperous citizens. John Eaton, the superintendent of public education in Tennessee from 1867 to 1869, worked to ensure that the schools under his supervision taught the kinds of lessons that would enable African American Tennesseans to lead good lives. He hoped that black children would grow to be patriotic Americans who practiced "Pure Protestant Christianity—the basis of American religion." The behavior and attitudes of the Northern middle class would therefore be the standard by which the freedmen's progress would be measured.[2]

More than a few freedpeople willingly adopted Northern middle-class attitudes and wholeheartedly agreed with the missionaries' beliefs regarding education's importance. Time and again, visitors to Tennessee noticed that many African Americans wanted an education above all else. J. T. Trowbridge, for one, observed that black residents of Chattanooga were "far more zealous" than whites about education. Even during tough economic times, the freedmen did more than just dream about establishing schools or asking for financial aid from the Freedmen's Bureau or Northern missionaries. To the astonishment of agent J. E. Jacobs, blacks in Chattanooga operated highly respected schools with only the aid of three African American benevolent organizations. Some freedmen, such as John Tate of Clinton, bought land and a school building for fellow African Americans and then assumed most of the school's operating expenses. All across Tennessee, black parents pooled their capital to build schoolhouses; some even saved enough to start private schools and compensate teachers.[3]

Missionary and Bureau aid, however, remained substantial, and throughout 1865 and 1866, the cooperation between religious and government agencies in starting schools across the state influenced many white and black Tennesseans to believe that the work of the national government and the work of Northern missionaries were virtually the same. With the approval of Congress, Bureau superintendent Clinton Fisk ordered his agents in Tennessee to work closely with religious and benevolent agencies in aiding the freedmen: the Bureau would help build and protect schoolhouses while the agencies provided teachers and paid their moving costs and salaries. Historian Joe Richardson claims that "almost every association college, normal, and secondary school was partially built with Bureau funds." He further concludes that the federal agency gave the American Missionary Association (AMA) approximately $300,000 for its work, and if "transportation, rentals, salaries paid to those who were employed jointly by the Bureau and the AMA, and property deeded to the association are added to construction costs, the total probably exceeds a half million dollars."[4]

The Bureau contributed greatly to freedmen's education before the state finally created a public school system in 1867. All of Tennessee's Bureau superintendents emphasized the importance of freedmen's education; Superintendent J. R. Lewis, like Fisk, considered it his "most important work." Congress allotted $25,000 annually to the Tennessee branch for building and repairing schools and authorized its agents to use seized Confederate property to help fund schools. As early as July 1865, black children attended Bureau schools in Chattanooga and Memphis and learned from teachers who were on the agency's payroll. Although former slaves supported schools as much as they could, at times the Bureau was the only thing keeping freedmen schools open. African Americans may have saved enough money to construct a schoolhouse, but many could not afford to rebuild it if it was burned to the ground. Agents did their best to protect the freedmen schools from vengeful whites and came to the rescue in other ways, too, such as buying lumber and glass to repair storm-damaged schoolhouses.[5]

The Bureau's financial assistance came with strings attached. Students and parents had to prove themselves trustworthy and promise that federal funding would be well spent. Agents of benevolent and religious associations were also closely supervised. The Bureau demanded proof that donated funds supported viable projects. For instance, in 1867 Superintendent W. P. Carlin withheld money from an orphanage desiring to start an industrial school until he learned that there would be at least ten to fifteen pupils. On another occasion, Carlin sent subordinates to meet with Methodist bishop C. P. Gunland to determine what materials were actually necessary for the construction of freedmen schools and to ensure that the work was done efficiently.[6]

Some missionaries were infuriated over what they perceived as the Bureau's parsimony in dealing with a population in great need of relief and reform. Ewing O. Tade considered the local Bureau office "a poor miserable broken reed—worse than nothing," for it had "not furnished a cord of wood for the schools under the immediate care of its own appointed government." What is more, Tade's Memphis schools suffered at the hands of federal soldiers. Twice during the winter of 1866, soldiers stormed in, stealing stoves and benches and vandalizing other property.[7]

Freedmen also turned to Northern religious agencies for financial aid. By 1870 the American Baptist Home Mission Society (ABHMS) had dispatched twelve missionaries to Tennessee; they formed sixteen churches and ten schools in towns ranging from Bristol to Memphis. Attendance at Sabbath and day schools approached 2,600. Old and New School Presbyterians were also heavily involved in education, establishing church-affiliated schools in East and Middle Tennessee. Many of these Northern missionary associations continued their charitable work even after the establishment of public schools. In Clinton, for instance, black children attended a school in 1869 sponsored entirely by the New York Presbyterian Committee for Home Missions.[8]

African American churches also played an important role in educating black children. In many cases, children from families unable to afford tuition or without access to a school learned how to read and write at church. Throughout Tennessee, African American denominations established Sabbath schools for the young and old. By 1869 African American Baptists in Middle Tennessee alone had started thirty-seven Sabbath schools with a staff of 275 teachers, serving 2,602 students. By 1870, a total of 1,067 students were being taught by 75 teachers sponsored by the Brownsville Baptist Association of West Tennessee.[9]

According to missionaries and Bureau agents, black children needed a proper Sabbath school education. Many children, in the opinion of the devout, not only distracted worshipers by playing all day on Sunday but also desecrated the Sabbath. These irreverent little ones should be in Sunday school, missionaries announced in newspaper advertisements for their outreach ministry. Sunday school students would learn not only the three Rs but also correct religious interpretations, not the "secesh doctrine" that formerly had trampled down "the promising scions and tender plants" of the South. The situation in the countryside of Tennessee was deemed even more troublesome, for black children there were considered even less civilized and more superstitious.[10]

In urban and rural areas, a typical Sunday for young churchgoers started with morning Sunday school devoted to Christian doctrine. Congregating outside the church around 9:30 a.m., youngsters heard teachers calling them to worship by singing hymns such as "Sweet Hour of Prayer" and "Rock of Ages." Once assembled in the sanctuary, the children and teachers repeated verse by verse the scripture reading of the day. They then departed to their respective fifty-minute classes. In large churches, children attended classes with peers of the same age and scholastic ability. At E. O. Tade's Lincoln Chapel in Memphis, forty to fifty toddlers were enrolled in the "Busy Bee" class, where they mostly recited and memorized catechisms and verses. A much smaller class, the "Stewards," ranging from three to ten students on any given Sunday, was capable of following advanced instruction. Teenage boys and girls at Lincoln Chapel attended sexually segregated classes. The girls in Mrs. Tade's "Ladies class" attended Sunday school more regularly on the whole than any other class. The boys' class regularly discussed such matters as the need for workers to witness to others in their communities.[11]

Many other churches held similar Sabbath schools between the morning and evening services. Young attendees spent practically all of Sunday at church, attending classes, worshiping, and eating. Children followed a typical schedule at Mount Zion Missionary Baptist Church in Knoxville, where they started with morning worship at 10:50 a.m., followed by dinner and then Sabbath school at 2:00 p.m. After a short break, they came back for evening services. Some churches, such as the Logan Chapel American Methodist Zion Church of Knoxville, had two Sabbath school sessions, one in the morning and one after dinner.[12]

Regular church attendance, many children believed, provided the best means to an education. After the morning reading and writing lessons, many adults with "no particular interest" in the sermon commonly left before the worship service. To encourage church attendance, teachers included reading and writing lessons in their evening services. The young Sunday-night worshipers in one Tennessee community demonstrated not only a higher level of literacy but also a bit of arrogance. They called morning-only worshipers "visiting friends" and treated them as second-rate students and Christians.[13]

In Sunday school, freedchildren heard a recurring lesson: although they and their parents needed spiritual reform, they must live up to their status as beacons in a world of spiritual darkness. To begin with, students were to abstain from tobacco and alcohol. They heard countless lessons describing how liquor and tobacco use led to abuse, which undermined wisdom, decency, and "the finer feelings of [blacks'] nature." That was only the beginning of personal reformation. The young were also admonished to shun exuberant worship. Missionaries deemed ardent worship uncontrolled and unseemly and therefore displeasing to God. Many children also learned that they were the great hope for the future of genuine Christianity and patriotism and that they should shine the light of their Christian faith everywhere. They could start by upholding doctrinal truths in the home even when their parents did not.[14]

Children studied from texts carefully chosen for them. The Baptists of West Tennessee, in particular, were concerned that students learn only the "true" faith and reject such heresies as baptismal regeneration and infant baptism and sprinkling. In Germantown, some criticized the language of the catechisms. Baptists were not alone in their concern. Students of every denomination learned scriptural and doctrinal lessons while learning to read and write. Alphabetic lessons, for instance, included stories of Bible characters. One went, "B was a Chaldee, who made a feast," which was followed by a reading of Daniel 5:1–4, which revealed that "B" referred to "Belshazzar." Other ABC lessons focused on good manners: "I [Ishmael] was a mocker, a very bad boy—Gen. xvi. 24." In some Sunday schools, children received a "Pocket Etiquette of the Ten Commandments" that included such lessons as "Always say, Yes, sir, No sir; use no slang terms; never enter a private place with your cap on; always offer a seat to a lady or an old gentleman."[15]

In the morning worship service, black children heard the same Victorian and scriptural values reinforced. Young members of the six churches constituting the Pleasant Grove Missionary Baptist Association listened to many sermons admonishing them to "be temperate in all things: eating, sleeping, drinking, and all other exercise and enjoyment." In the churches of the General Missionary Baptist Association, young black Tennesseans learned that the Freedmen's Bank was a valuable and trustworthy enterprise and that they should save their money and become productive citizens.[16]

Not surprisingly, the Bureau and missionary day schools (both met on weekdays and were conducted mainly by missionaries) stressed the same moral and economic philosophies. Bureau superintendents across the South regarded schools as the cornerstone of Reconstruction and the means by which the negative effects of slavery could be undone. For many educators, academic success was secondary to properly socializing black children. As a result, the Bureau and missionary day schools were agents of "white, bourgeois American standards." Among the eleven goals delineated by Freedmen's Bureau general superintendent of education, John Alvord, in his semi-annual reports were several that blended religious and Victorian values: schools were to ensure that black children became a "moral, virtuous, and Christian people," to eradicate every "mean, low passion" from the hearts of little ones, and to teach young freedmen that they were not only responsible to their neighbors but also to "Him who is their Creator, Redeemer, and final judge." The educators of Tennessee's Bureau schools were expected also to teach young blacks "cleanliness, dress, home habits, social proprieties, use of furniture, preparation of food, and tasteful construction of dwellings."[17]

Although public school proponents had advocated a state-supported system as early as 1863, the common school system of Tennessee was not established until 1867 and lasted statewide for only three years. In that short time, however, public school students were exposed to free-labor values. Students who embraced those lessons—one taught them the importance of "doubling their efficiency"—received recognition and praise. John Eaton delivered speeches to students across the state, reminding them of the importance of time management: "Punctuality and regularity of habits will save you much in the future life. . . . Take care of the minutes, and the hours will take care of themselves." Bureau teachers kept copious attendance records that noted punctuality: of the 6,810 black students, almost 4,500 usually attended school; and of those, 2,501 were considered "always punctual." The consistently punctual were applauded, but the tardy were punished. In the Memphis school district, children who were "repeatedly tardy, without excuse" were suspended and could return to school only with the local superintendent's approval. Unless absences were excused, public grammar and high school students missing more than three days and primary students missing more than four lost their seat to another child. Those at school were reminded that hard work not only helped them climb out of poverty but also allowed them to assist the less fortunate. From the first day, children were taught that literacy and numeracy guaranteed a better future. But to excel one must put forth great effort, as Eaton reminded public school students: "There is no royal road to learning. Do not expect to ascend to the hill of science without climbing. . . . Seek perfection in each practice. . . . Do no duty by halves." What cost them little as children, Eaton believed, would profit them much as adults.[18]

Students of the public and missionary day schools were immersed in religious teaching, too. Pupils learned about the value of prayer and of the certainty of Christ's personal intervention in human lives. Children also read lessons that combined husbandry and Christianity; one lesson stated that the abuse of animals was a sin against God. Their McGuffey readers reminded students that individual and national prosperity resulted from obeying the scriptures. A "permanently prosperous man" did not break the Sabbath, and regular churchgoers were never found in a state of decadence.[19]

Committing themselves to moral lives redeemed individuals and mended a broken nation, or so many believed. According to educators across Tennessee, enlightening the masses was "the primary hope of the country," and thus a large part of schooling was devoted to civic education. The right choice of textbooks, suggested E. O. Tade, could inculcate "patriotic . . . character" and enable students to "serve the purposes of truth and progress." Black students were taught that patriots were heroes and that being patriotic required one to perform good civic works and evince a devotion to the nation.[20]

Not surprisingly, some students were not receptive to all of these well-intentioned lessons. Many, especially the older ones, defied their teachers, resisted instruction, and thereby threatened to undermine the entrenchment of Victorian values in the South. The continued use of alcohol, tobacco, and profanity particularly troubled Northern teachers. Tennessee was infamous in the eyes of some Northerners for its "universal custom . . . of smoking, drinking, and dipping" and proved to be a difficult place to instill the value of temperance. Everywhere children went in Chattanooga, observed John Alvord, they saw "colored customers" patronizing "low drinking saloons." Teachers and missionaries encouraged youths to join temperance societies, the two most prominent being the Band of Hope and the Vanguard of Freedom. Male and female members not only pledged to abstain from alcohol but also vowed not to touch tobacco or utter a profane word. Members also abjured the use of what teachers regarded as vulgar language, including such words as "fool," "liar," and "nigger." But in some schools, alcohol use, and even abuse, remained a problem. James Byers of Tipton County was troubled by the "prematurely developed vice of liquor drinking" among his older students. Before and after school, and even during breaks, they purchased whiskey from a nearby store.[21]

But teachers remained focused on the larger picture. A typical school day included much more than hearing numerous value-filled lessons, however. Students memorized speeches, facts, and more facts. And black children heard many of the same lessons again and again, for as teachers read in the *McGuffey Eclectic Primer*, "Repetition is necessary in instructing young children." Teachers also employed music to teach many subjects, for they believed that blacks were a peculiarly musical race. But children learned that their preferred music was often regarded as too expressive and emotional; they were encouraged to adopt a more sedate and seemly style. After students had mastered the alphabet, they read short stories, which taught syntax and semantics. Meanwhile, like students in schools all over the United States, they learned how to properly inflect their voices in order to be expressive and articulate. As children moved beyond elementary instruction in English and mathematics, they accepted the challenge of more advanced classes, including geography, physiology, elementary algebra and geometry, composition and speaking, botany, mental and moral philosophy, chemistry, and U.S. history.[22]

The absence of a single, universal textbook, however, was believed to confuse freedmen and thwart the advancement of free-labor and Victorian values. From 1867 to 1869, Freedmen's Bureau and the Department of Public Instruction superintendents worried that young freedmen were reading conflicting interpretations of history, Christianity, and government; only the standardization of texts guaranteed that the correct values would be taught and that children would march toward progress. Although benevolent and denominational societies chose the texts for their schools from 1865 to 1867, the Bureau encouraged all to cooperate in creating a unified curriculum. The associational texts should not have worried Bureau officials, however. *The Freedmen's Book* by L. Maria Child, to use one example, described in great detail the negative effects of slavery and the positive influence of abolitionists while including biographies of successful and hardworking African Americans and lessons on the importance of good morality and hygiene. Nor was anything particularly disturbing about the content of McGuffey's readers. Superintendent of public schools John Eaton nevertheless asked several local superintendents to review texts and recommend specific ones for statewide adoption. Many teachers in East Tennessee, however, resisted efforts to standardize texts, preferring and continuing to use McGuffey's readers rather than Eaton's choice, Hillard's readers.[23]

It was, perhaps, easier to ensure a standard set of values among teachers. All, no matter their race, sex, or age, were supposed to be testifying Christians capable of teaching the proper values that would heal a wounded nation. Clinton Fisk demanded that teachers be "able Christian ones . . . with malice toward none, with charity for all. Yet with firmness for the right, marching on 'in the word.'" Presbyterians wanted teachers who possessed the "peculiar spirit, and qualifications necessary to success in the field" and expressed disappointment in not finding many. AMA leaders also prized energetic yet practical teachers of any race or sex. Some Tennessee communities preferred white Christians, however. The presence of black teachers in Greeneville, some feared, would slow educational reconstruction because many whites there would rather have no schools than to allow blacks to assume respected positions—even if they taught only black students. Prejudice appeared even among the ranks of what were considered humanitarian circles; the prejudice of some white instructors undoubtedly concerned John Eaton, whose thinking was influenced by essayists claiming that racists denied the revolutionary and egalitarian teaching of Christ.[24]

Many young black Tennesseans were under the tutelage of genuinely humanitarian and hardworking white teachers, who Eaton believed laid the educational foundation on which national progress and national reconciliation would rest. In Chattanooga E. O. Tade worked hard to ensure that his pupils studied in remodeled buildings. They saw him working at all hours, going without sleep and meals, and performing his tasks to the point of exhaustion. Tade's exertions were not unusual. Children of the Cumberland School in Nashville appreciated their two schoolmarms for showing "energy and excellent, practical judgment," and for being "true, earnest, and consistent friend[s]." Older students in particular realized the sacrifices some teachers made on their behalf. In her last hour, a dying sixteen-year-old student in Nashville called for her teacher, expressed to him her love for Jesus and Sabbath school, and thanked him for laboring among freedmen. When sincere and dedicated teachers died, the young eulogized them. Before J. G. McKee, a well-known and respected teacher in Nashville, was put into the ground, hundreds of sobbing black students attended a chapel service in his honor and then marched through Nashville in an impressive funeral procession.[25]

From the beginning of Reconstruction, Bureau officials and denominational leaders had encouraged the hiring of black teachers, for the profession not only provided employment to educated blacks but also gave young blacks models of good citizenship and scholarship among their race. Superintendent Clinton Fisk and Tennessee Bureau superintendent of education John Ogden also promoted the employment of black teachers out of expediency: African Americans helped meet the high demand for educators and worked for less than Northern whites. To satisfy the great need for teachers, especially in the rural areas, agents and missionaries selected advanced black students with "good moral character" and offered training that prepared them to take over their own schools. Many graduates from normal schools, such as Fisk University in Nashville, did indeed return to rural Tennessee, for schools outside the towns were unattractive to most Northern teachers. Black children particularly admired teachers of their own race and seemed to respond better to their instruction. According to John Alvord, children respected most of all the "former common field boys" who went back to their communities to teach.[26]

Not all school experiences would become fond memories, however. Many white Tennesseans remained hostile to the idea of freedmen schools, and in an effort to counter the Northern teachers' efforts, some made life miserable for educators and their students. One missionary in Chattanooga complained that missionaries lived a "dog's life," in which they were "hated, shunned, and despised" for their work among African Americans. White or black, male or female, teachers faced trials, but men in particular worked amid physical threats. Some children witnessed teachers being dragged away from their homes or schools, beaten, and choked. In front of his students, William Newton of Somerville was stoned by white boys, whose threats and disruptions eventually provoked the deployment of Federal troops. At his home in Lebanon, a white teacher was threatened by twenty-five night riders, but he bravely continued his work, thanks in great part to sympathetic neighbors who protected him.[27] At a Springfield school, children stopped studying to take shelter from young thugs pelting the schoolhouse with rocks. On other days, pupils trying to concentrate on their studies were interrupted by obscenities shouted from outside the school. Only after the posting of sentinels at the front door and on the grounds could the teacher resume his work.[28]

They might not have endorsed Northern educators' curricula, but not every white Tennessean was an enemy of public education and freedmen schools. Addressing aspiring black educators at Fisk University, former Unionist and Republican governor William G. Brownlow approved using Federal troops and declaring martial law to protect freedmen's schools. He advised blacks to be avid learners but, for their safety, not to provoke whites intentionally. Over time, some white opponents of black education had a change of heart. Agents reported that perceptive planters realized that slavery was truly dead and that an educated workforce was useful in a free-labor society. The "better classes," observed John Alvord, endorsed black education once they had seen its benefits. Risking retaliation from neighbors, some whites boarded missionary teachers, and some helped construct or rebuild schoolhouses. For example, when the Clinton school was burned down in January 1869, children saw whites and blacks working side by side to reconstruct it.[29]

In many cases educators and students worried about more than whether whites approved of their educational efforts; for one thing, money was essential to ensure Reconstruction's success. In many places schools were closed in midterm because administrators were unable to pay maintenance costs, even after extensive fund-raising efforts. Educators sometimes managed to find free accommodations, such as a church building, but because they were subject to the whim of the owner, they could not always depend on remaining in them. Children and their teachers who were turned out of their building by the owner sometimes wound up in a state of vagabondage, searching for a permanent location. As J. G. McKee, a Presbyterian missionary teacher in Nashville, recalled, "We were tossed from place to place, sometimes our school was thrown out without a day's notice." Financial problems continued even with the creation of public schools. All across the state, a lack of money hindered educational efforts. The shortage of funds hurt black Tennesseans the most. Many young blacks of Rutherford County, for example, waited longer than whites to begin the 1869–70 school year; in a segregated school system, there just was not enough money, civil authorities claimed, to rent or build all the necessary schoolhouses for the large number of black students.[30]

Rural life presented children with distinct problems and fewer opportunities to learn patriotic and Victorian lessons. Northern missionaries and teachers were less willing to serve their Lord and their nation in the rustic country-side of Tennessee, and Bureau agent C. B. Davis of Lawrence County in 1866 reported that a teacher shortage delayed the first day of school. Furthermore, school buildings were few and far between in rural areas; missionaries and agents had given towns first priority, and rural blacks had to wait their turn. In 1868, John Alvord encouraged educational efforts in the countryside, where black parents resented the broken promises of the Bureau and missionaries, and the children anxiously awaited an education. By 1869 many rural blacks were, in the words of local superintendent W. H. Stillwell, "importunate . . . impatient, and bitter." With the arrival of teachers and schools, new problems arose: hostility toward teachers and crimes against schools were more pro-nounced in the rural areas, where there was less Bureau protection. In May 1868 alone, black children in Somerville, Saulsbury, and Pocahontas saw their teachers insulted by whites. The fierce prejudice and violence in such places as Obion and Tipton Counties forced missionaries and agents there to aban-don all educational work. Black farmers also expected administrators to adjust schedules to meet their needs. In Blount and Johnson Counties, for instance, parents requested that the beginning of the school term be delayed until mid-October so children could help with the harvest.[31]

Problems in the public school system affected many black students, in urban as well as rural areas. In September 1869 some Nashville children were unable to attend school because the city school system had insufficient funds to meet the demands of increased enrollment; the city was forced to close selected schools—many of them freedmen schools. Another serious and recurring problem was a lack of money to build schoolhouses, buy furniture and texts, and pay teachers. Across the state black schools (and white ones, too) lacked money not only to provide good education but even, in many cases, to stay open at all. Struggling to solve his schools' financial problems, Superintendent M. C. Wilcox of Knox County eventually declared bankruptcy but was con-vinced nevertheless that in God's ledger he was "morally solvent."[32]

However, it was the political triumph of the Democrats (representing the combined forces of Conservative Unionists and ex-Confederates) that ulti-mately led to the death of the statewide public school system. After the elec-tion of Governor DeWitt Senter in 1869, educators and Bureau agents feared that all of their work had been in vain. They were right: the Democrat-domi-nated legislature repealed the common-school law and delegated the respon-sibility of public education to the counties (of which only twenty-three had organized schools two years later).

• • •

In Reconstruction Tennessee freedchildren were taught not only the three Rs but also religious and Victorian values and civic duties in the Sabbath schools, Bureau and missionary day schools, and public schools. In all three black children were taught what educators believed were correct interpretations of Christianity and citizenship and learned how to live independent and industrious lives—essentially how to be free. To get along in these schools, students had to conform their thoughts and actions to Northern middle-class standards. As a result, many black children, as part of the first free generation of African Americans, matured into Protestant Christians who exhibited a fervent and particular American nationalism and a belief in free labor.

NOTES

1. Henry L. Swint, *The Northern Teacher in the South, 1862–1870* (Nashville, TN: Vanderbilt University Press, 1941). Although there were some publicly funded city schools, a statewide free-school system did not exist in Tennessee before 1867, but Sabbath and Bureau and missionary day schools continued after the passage of the common school law. In Sabbath schools, missionaries and clergymen—and in some cases laypeople—taught children and adults basic literacy and Christian doctrine. Sponsored by a benevolent association or their denomination, missionaries also started day schools, where students paid tuition to receive more advanced instruction. In many instances, missionaries and African Americans appealed to the Bureau for financial help; whether or not it met those requests, the agency monitored and endeavored to protect all schools in which blacks were taught. Public schools operated similarly to Bureau and missionary day schools; their teachers still taught moral and scriptural lessons, and Bureau agents were involved in advising and supervising many aspects of the schools. Bureau and missionary day schools and public schools reinforced what was taught on Sunday. Therefore, the educational experiences of black children in Sabbath, Bureau, missionary day, and public schools are presented here as one story.

2. Swint, *Northern Teacher*, 36, 58; Robert C. Morris, *Reading, 'Riting, and Reconstruction: The Education of Freedmen in the South, 1861–1870* (Chicago: University of Chicago Press, 1981), 173; O. O. Howard, *Autobiography of Oliver Otis Howard: Major General United States Army*, 2 vols. (New York: Baker and Taylor, 1908), 1:329–30; John Eaton Notebook, John Eaton Papers, Special Collections, University of Tennessee, Knoxville (hereafter cited as JEP).

3. C. Stuart McGehee, "E. O. Tade, Freedmen's Education, and the Failure of Reconstruction in Tennessee," *Tennessee Historical Quarterly* 43 (1984): 381; J. E. Jacobs to Clinton B. Fisk, March 12, 1866, Selected Records of the Tennessee Field Office of the Bureau of Refugees, Freedmen, and Abandoned Lands, 1865–1872, r. 38, National Archives, Washington, DC (microfilm) (hereafter cited as SRTH); John Tate to John Ogden, December 1, 1865, American Missionary Manuscripts, Tennessee, r. 1, Amistad Research Center, Dillard University, New Orleans (microfilm) (hereafter cited as AMATN).

4. Special Order no. 134½, Office of Clinton B. Fisk, August 30, 1866, Records of the Assistant Commissioner for the State of Tennessee, Bureau of Refugees, Freedmen, and Abandoned Lands, r. 16, National Archives, Washington, DC (microfilm) (hereafter cited as RACTN); Joe M. Richardson, *Christian Reconstruction: The American Missionary Association and Southern Blacks, 1861–1890* (Athens: University of Georgia Press, 1986), 83–84.

5. J. R. Lewis to O. O. Howard, October 10, 1868, Special Order no. 6, Chattanooga Office, 7 July 1865, O. O. Howard to J. R. Lewis, November 26, 1866, RACTN, r. 10; Special Order no. 161, Office of J. R. Lewis, October 18, 1866, RACTN, r. 16; John Ogden to C. B. Fisk, December 31, 1865, RACTN, r. 11.

6. [?] to Nashville Office, February 1, 1867, C. P. Gunland to Nashville Office, February 21, 1867, RACTN, r. 5.

7. E. O. Tade to M. E. Strieby, February 6, 1866, AMATN, r. 2.

8. *Thirty-Eighth Annual Report of the American Baptist Home Mission Society Convened in the City of Philadelphia May 26th, 1870* (New York, 1870), 38–39 (hereafter cited as *Thirty-Eighth ABHMS*); Report, John Ogden to Clinton Fisk, December 31, 1865, RACTN, r. 11; Charles D. McGuffey to John Eaton, July 29, 1869, JEP.

9. *Minutes of the Second Annual Session of the General Missionary Baptist Convention of Tennessee Held at the First Colored Baptist Church, Memphis, August 19, 20, 21, 23, 24, 1869*, 16 (hereafter cited as *Second GMBC*); *Minutes of the Third Annual Session of the General Missionary Baptist Convention of Tennessee Held at the First Colored Missionary Baptist Church, Clarksville, September 8, 9, 10, 11, & 12, 1870*, 14 (hereafter cited as *Third GMBC*).

10. E. H. Truman to Samuel Hunt, June 28, 1866, AMATN, r. 2; *Knoxville Whig*, 28 May 1866.

11. *Third GMBC*, 14; *Second GMBC*, 16.

12. E. O. Tade to M. E. Strieby, February 6, 1866, AMATN, r. 2.

13. Ibid.

14. C. A. Crosby to C. S. Crosby, May 1, 1866, AMATN, r. 2; *Thirty-Eighth ABHMS*, 15.

15. *Tennessee Baptist*, November 16, 1867, and April 17, 1869.

16. *Minutes of the Pleasant Grove Missionary Association*, 3; *Second GMBA*, 10–11.

17. John W. Alvord, *Seventh Semi-Annual Report on Schools for Freedmen, January 1, 1869* (Washington, DC, 1869), 60–62, 82–83 (hereafter cited as *Seventh SAR*); Ronald E. Butchardt, *Northern Schools, Southern Blacks, and Reconstruction: Freedmen's Education, 1862–1875* (Westport, CT: Greenwood Press, 1980), 168.

18. John Ogden to John Eaton, October 24, 1868, Horace Andrews to John Eaton, n.d., JEP; John Eaton Jr., *First Report of the Superintendent of Public Instruction of the State of Tennessee, Ending Thursday, October 7, 1869* (Nashville, 1869) (hereafter cited as *First Report*), xxxi; L. Maria Child, *The Freedmen's Book* (Boston, 1865; New York: Arno Press, 1968), 37; Paul David Phillips, "Education of Blacks in Tennessee during Reconstruction, 1865–1870," in *Trials and Triumph: Essays in Tennessee's African American History*, ed. Carroll Van West (Knoxville: University of Tennessee Press, 2002), 149, 152.

19. Child, *Freedmen's Book*, 97–100, 123; William H. McGuffey, *McGuffey's New Sixth Eclectic Reader: Exercises in Rhetorical Readings with Introductory Rules and Examples*, 22–23 (hereafter cited as *Sixth Reader*).

20. Samuel Thomas to John Eaton, March 5, 1870; E. O. Tade to Barnard and Barnum, November 29, 1867, JEP.

21. Alvord, *Letters from the South Related to the Condition of the Freedmen Addressed to Major General O. O. Howard*, 29; *Seventh SAR*, 42; A. S. Mitchell to John Eaton, November 18, 1867, JEP.

22. William H. McGuffey, *McGuffey's Newly Revised Eclectic Primer*; John W. Alvord, *Eighth Semi-Annual Report on Schools for Freedmen, July 1, 1869*, 85 (hereafter cited as *Eighth SAR*); *First Report*, xxv–vi.

23. John Ogden to J. M. Walden, August 26, 1865, AMATN, r. 1; John W. Alvord, *Third Semi-Annual Report on Schools for Freedmen, January 1, 1867*, 38; M. C. Wilcox to John Eaton, October 3, 1867, A. E. Plume to Barnard and Barnum, November 1, 1867, JEP.

24. Clinton B. Fisk to George Whipple, October 21, 1865, AMATN, r. 1; *Third PCUSA*, 23; Anna Hagar to Rev. Whipple, August 18, 1866, AMATN, r. 2; Morris, *Reading*, 89–90.

25. E. O. Tade to E. M. Strieby, February 6, 1866, E. H. Truman to Samuel Hunt, 28 June 1866, AMATN, r. 2; Jason S. Travelli to John Eaton, Jr., October 7, 1867, JEP; James McNeal, "Biographical Sketch of Rev. Joseph G. McKee, the Pioneer Missionary to Freedmen in Nashville, Tennessee," in *Historical Sketches of the Freedmen's Missions of the United Presbyterian Church, 1862–1904*, ed. Ralph Wilson McGranahan (Knoxville, TN: Knoxville College Printing Department, 1905), 11, 13.

26. Clinton B. Fisk to John Ogden, June 4, 1866, AMATN, r. 2; *Second Annual Report on the General Assembly's Committee on Freedmen of the Presbyterian Church in the United States of America*, 7, 12; *Third SAR*, 36; John W. Alvord, *Ninth Semi-Annual Report on Schools for Freedmen, January 1, 1870*, 48.

27. McGehee, "E. O. Tade," 384, 386, 388; Phillips, "Education of Blacks," 161–62; J. R. Lewis to O. O. Howard, October 10, 1868, RACTN, r. 16; *Memphis Evening Post*, August 25, 1869.

28. Howard, *Autobiography*, 378–79; "W. F. Carter to John Eaton, March 29, 1869," JEP.

29. Fred Palmer, Summary of Reports, r. 11, RACTN, N-S; *Fifth SAR*, 8; *Eighth SAR*, 64.

30. E. O. Tade to Samuel Hunt, June 28, 1866, AMATN, r. 2; John Ogden to Clinton Fisk,. 1865, RACTN, r. 16; McNeal, "Biographical Sketch" 11, 13; N. H. Pearne to John Eaton, December 31, 1868, and January 26, 1869, JEP; McNeal, "Biographical Sketch of Rev. Joseph G. McKee."

31. C. B. Davis to C. B. Fisk, February 28, 1866, RACTN, r. 17; *Seventh SAR*, 60; *Sixth SAR*, 46–47; T. J. Lamar to John Eaton, April 15, 1868; George Grace to John Eaton, January 23, 1869; and W. H. Stillwell to John Eaton, April 19, 1869, JEP.

32. McNeal, "Biographical Sketch," 11, 13; H. Clay Griffith to John Eaton, July 28, 1869; M. C. Wilcox to John Eaton, August 7, 1869, JEP; *First Report*, cxvii–cliv.

10

"Free Ourselves, but Deprived of Our Children"

Freedchildren and Their Labor after the Civil War

MARY NIALL MITCHELL

"I am the mother of a woman Dina who is now dead. My Daughter Dina had a child by the name of Porter."

This is how Cyntha Nickols began her appeal, in 1867, to the assistant commissioner of the Freedmen's Bureau in Louisiana, hoping that he might help her retrieve her grandson from the man who had once owned her. "I am a Colored woman former slave of a Mr Sandy Spears of the parish of East Feliciana La.," she explained. Porter, "now about Eleven years of age," had been bound to Spears under an apprenticeship, a labor contract that would leave the boy under Spears's control until he became an adult, without her consent. Apparently unable to convince the local Bureau agent to help her, she directed her plea to his superiors, choosing her words carefully. "I do not wish to wrongfully interfere with the arrangement of those who are endeavoring to properly control us black people," Nickols explained with pointed deference to the Bureau's authority. "I feel confident that they are doing the best they can for us and our present condition—but I am the Grandmother of Porter—his father Andrew is now and has been for sometime a soldier in the army of the U.S. he is I am told some where in California I do not know only that he is not here to see to the interest of his child I am not by any means satisfied with the present arrangement made for my Grand Child Porter." She had known Mr. Spears "for many years" and would write "nothing of his faults but I have the means of educating my Grand Child of doing good part by him." Porter's uncle, "lately discharged from the army of the U.S.," would be able to help care for Porter. "We want him we do not think Mr. Spears a suitable person to control this boy."

Nickols placed before the Bureau every available qualification for her guardianship of Porter: her blood kinship, her ability to provide for his education, and the military service of his father and uncle. She also argued that Spears was unfit: Spears was "very old and infirm" and "for many years addicted to the use of ardent spirits. This fact I do not like to mention but truth requires me to speak now is there no chance to get my little boy the agent of this place will not listen to me," she explained, "and I am required to call [on] you or I must let my Grand-Child go, which greatly grieves me." Nickols closed with another plea, signing her letter: "Truly yours a poor old black woman."[1]

In addition to facing down her former owner over the right to raise her grandchild, however, Cyntha Nickols also had to appeal to the federal government, in the form of the Freedmen's Bureau, which was charged with promoting the successful transition to free labor in the South. The Bureau of Refugees, Freedmen, and Abandoned Lands, or "Freedmen's Bureau," founded in early 1865, was charged with the management of abandoned lands, the facilitation of labor contracts, the distribution of food and clothing, and the establishment of schools for freedpeople, among other duties.[2] Often the Bureau's most contentious role, as James DeGrey's position between Cyntha Nickols and Mr. Spears illustrates, was as an intermediary between former slaveholders and freedpeople. The Bureau's overarching concern in governing these disputes was to keep agricultural production in the South from faltering by encouraging the signing of labor contracts. But as many a Bureau agent discovered, the signing of a labor contract in the postbellum South was not a purely economic transaction.

The most pressing problem in the South after emancipation, as many historians have noted, was what kind of labor system would replace chattel slavery. The process of slave emancipation throughout the Americas in the nineteenth century was fueled by arguments, both ideological and material, about who would define the "free" in free labor and how that would translate into profit and loss, wages and shares, sustenance and want. The problem of freedom, in the largest sense, was how to reconcile the conflicting visions of the future that slave emancipation engendered.

Struggles over the labor of black children such as Porter were attempts to spell out what the end of slavery would mean in practice, to articulate what *should* be. As a member of the first generation of African Americans to grow up in a former slaveholding republic, the black child—freedom's child—represented the possibility of a future dramatically different from the past, a future in which black Americans might have access to the same privileges as whites: landownership, equality, autonomy. Through debates over the labor of the black child, in turn, nineteenth-century Americans anticipated and articulated the social, political, and economic consequences of slave emancipation.[3]

Yet these debates were also disputes about the economic autonomy of black households and the authority of black adults to control their own off-spring. Under slavery, black parents and relatives often had to watch as slaveholders directed, punished, and otherwise controlled the fate of their children. After emancipation, freedpeople demanded the legal right to raise their own children and, in so doing, also demanded the right to sustain their own households.[4] Deprived of the labor of children, freed black households suffered. As a white Unionist in Maryland named Joseph Hall observed in a letter to the Bureau, freedpeople "Can and would do very well if they Can have what they ought to have. that is to get there children un bound. or restored to them and have the privilege of hireing them or working them themselves. in order that they can help now to surport there parents in order that they may not be come a burthen opon the government."[5]

The greatest point of conflict regarding freedchildren's labor after the Civil War was the apprenticeship system, a form of labor contract written into state laws since the colonial period. Until the mid-nineteenth century, craft apprenticeship as it was practiced in the early republic was most widely used as a system of labor by which a male apprentice lived in a master's household and trained in a trade or skill until he came of age and established himself in business. Girls also could be bound out to work in other people's homes, assisting with household chores and learning skills such as weaving and seamstress work, but the majority of skilled trades depended largely upon the apprenticed labor of boys. As cities grew, apprenticeships also served as a means of supervising and training potentially wayward working-class children—boys and girls—by teaching them to earn a livelihood and keeping them off the streets. But with the rise of factories in the 1830s, these apprenticeship arrangements increasingly resembled those of wage labor. Although the apprentice still trained with a master or mistress, he or she earned a wage and no longer lived in the master's household. Eventually, particularly in urban areas of the North, apprenticeship was replaced almost entirely by wage labor.[6]

In the South, too, apprenticeship had been an early form of social welfare particularly for orphaned or "half-orphaned" children and had served, ostensibly, to train children in a skill or trade—from farming and housekeeping to carpentry and bricklaying. But in the antebellum South, apprenticeship also became a means of social and racial control. Southern judges apprenticed the illegitimate children of poor white women and those of free black parentage, typically on the grounds that such arrangements would keep them from becoming public charges.[7]

It was into this history of apprenticeship in the South that former slaveholders tapped at the close of the Civil War. Southern courts and legislatures continued to use apprenticeship as a form of racial control and forced labor, but in the service of postbellum realities—that is, as an extension of unfree labor and black people's dependence upon the planter class after emancipation. Southern legislatures issued new apprenticeship clauses aimed at the freed population at the close of the war, through the notorious Black Codes. Under Presidential Reconstruction in 1865, before Congress derailed President Andrew Johnson's lenient policies toward the South, southern legislatures passed codes that set forth the legal rights and limitations of the freed population, including vagrancy laws designed to keep every able-bodied freedperson working for southern landowners.[8]

The apprenticeship system was perhaps the most egregious of these codes. Black children could be bound to employers as apprentices through the state district courts, but the Freedmen's Bureau also governed and administered apprenticeships. According to Bureau regulations, agents could not bind out children if their parents opposed the apprenticeship. Girls, typically, were apprenticed to the age of fifteen and boys to eighteen, with their contracts stipulating they should receive clothing, medical attention, and "a reasonable amount of schooling" in return for their labor.[9] (The latter part of such agreements made it imperative for freedpeople like Cyntha Nickols, contesting such arrangements, to prove that they could provide for the children's education.) The "trade" or "skill" usually listed on the forms of indenture was "housekeeping" (for girls) and "planter" or "farmer" (for boys.) Some children, girls and boys, were contracted to receive "training" in both. In 1866, for instance, ten-year-old Thomas Boultt Johnson was bound to William Payne until the age of eighteen, "to learn the occupation of farming and also that of House Servant."[10]

Former slaveholders like Spears seized upon apprenticeship just after the Civil War as a way to hold onto the children of their freed slaves, often regardless of whether the parents were living or dead, and with little consideration for extended family members like Cyntha Nickols. This practice had the effect not only of depriving freedpeople of their children and the labor they could contribute to black households but also of limiting the mobility of both freedchildren and their parents and relatives, who wanted to remain near their bound children.[11]

In 1867, Congress demanded that all southern states rewrite their constitutions, ratifying the Fourteenth Amendment on civil rights and establishing voting rights for all male citizens. In the process, the Black Codes met their demise. (Apprenticeship remained a legal avenue of child welfare, so long as it made no distinction between black and white children.)[12] In 1865, however, neither freedpeople nor former slaveholders knew that apprenticeship would fail as a system of compulsory free labor. As one Bureau agent very crudely observed about southern planters after the war, "They *hate* to give up the *little niggers* in hopes that something will turn up. If Mac [George McClellan] had been elected [instead of Abraham Lincoln] they expected the little nigs would be good property and now they hope for something else to happen.")[13]

One of the first tasks facing local Bureau agents after the Confederate surrender was to situate freedchildren who appeared to them to be orphans, or as one agent put it, "the disposal of children practically orphans."[14] Another agent asked cautiously whether he might apprentice children in his parish who seemed to him to be "without proper protection." Several planters had petitioned him either to bind children to them or to remove them from their property. "In worse instances," the agent explained to his superior, "the fathers of such children are dead and the mothers have left them on plantations without making provisions for them." He was concerned that the children's parents were still living and might object but was told abruptly by headquarters to "bind these children out," that the parents could claim the children later if necessary.[15]

The Bureau's desire to bind children out often worked to the disadvantage of freedpeople whose families had been separated by slavery or the war. When parents or extended family did come to retrieve children, they found the children bound to former slave owners unwilling to relinquish their claims to them.[16] But even when relatives were present and able to care for children, former slaveholders and others wishing to apprentice children lied to the Bureau, often representing the children as orphans.

In some cases, the former slaveholders may not have known the whereabouts of the children's parents. In others, they seem to have been purposefully dishonest. An agent in Madisonville, Louisiana, explained to his superiors, for instance, that he had indentured "the two Grandchildren of Simon Bookster to Thos Zachary last September, Zachary misrepresented the case by stating the children, Edward and Eliza, were total orphans, and were living with him, and had no friends or relatives to care or provide for them." But upon investigation, the agent discovered that Zachary had "abducted the children in the absence of the Grandparents." Zachary had also lied about the ages of the children, stating that Edward was eight and Eliza five, when Edward was, in fact, ten and his sister eight. (Lying about the age of children was a tactic used to prolong the period of indenture. According to a chaplain serving as a local Bureau agent in Mississippi, "children are almost invariably bound out from two to 12 years younger than they are").[17] The agent investigating Edward and Eliza's case also learned that their grandfather had "supported and schooled them since their Freedom and is willing and able to do so."[18]

Although disputes over the custody and apprenticeship of freedchildren involved children of all ages, those perhaps most often at the center of custody complaints brought before the Bureau were at least ten years of age. Pointing to struggles between freedpeople and former owners, a Bureau agent in Virginia wrote snidely, "Blood don't seem to thicken until children get to be about ten years of age."[19] He might have added that most slaveholders, too, marked the age of ten as the point at which a child became valuable as a worker and less in need of caretaking by an adult. Antebellum Alabama law, for instance, prohibited the sale of children under the age of ten.[20] It seems that in agricultural labor, children aged ten or older were the most able to contribute to the daily workload. When Diana Jackson lodged a complaint against her husband, Joseph Jackson, for abandonment and lack of support for his child, for instance, the agent initially ordered Joseph to pay eight dollars per month to support the child. But on the advice of a superior, he "modified this decision to $4.00 per month until the child is ten years old at that age she will be able to take care of herself."[21]

The economic value of freedchildren's labor was undeniable. But disputes over which party laid the largest claim on that labor were often shaped by old master-slave relationships. Offering his opinion in the case of Porter, in an endorsement to Nickols's letter, the local agent, James DeGrey, reported that Sandy Spears was indeed "Old.—but not infirm," and "addicted to ardent Spirits, but not more so than the most of men in the Parish." "The boy Porter is ten (10) years of age," DeGrey wrote, putting a finer point on the age Porter's grandmother had given, seeming to undermine her claim to the boy. Spears had "raised him from a child," the agent reported. "My belief is that the old lady wants the boy because he is now able to do Some work."

While DeGrey accused Porter's grandmother of pure economic interest in the boy, he painted Spears—the former slaveholder—as the parental figure in Porter's life. It was Spears, he wrote, who had "raised" Porter, a point Spears must have made to DeGrey when the agent investigated the case. The characterization of Spears as the boy's true guardian and caretaker was in the interest not only of the former slaveholder but of the Bureau as well, since leaving the boy with Spears would keep him in a labor contract for the next eight years. Despite his support of Spears, however, DeGrey also understood the strength of freedpeople's suspicions regarding apprenticeship and the active role of extended family in the lives of freedchildren. At the close of his endorsement he wrote, "The binding out of children Seems to the freedmen like putting them back into Slavery—In every case where I have bound out children thus far Some Grandmother or fortieth cousin has come to have them released."[22]

Thousands of freedchildren like Porter became caught in this tangle of emotional, economic, and bureaucratic demands. Efforts to free them started a fierce pull and tug—backward to the dependencies and false kinship of the slaveholder (although some masters had fathered their slaves) or forward toward a wage system and the rights of black families. Complaints and hearings before agents of the Freedmen's Bureau about the custody of freedchildren seem to appear in nearly every monthly report from local agents to their superiors between 1865 and 1867, in addition to longer correspondences related to the custody of freedchildren. This fails to include, of course, the incidents that never appeared before the Bureau at all. In the simplest terms, battles over the custody of freedchildren were often uneven negotiations between Bureau agents, freedpeople, and former slaveholders. But the question of *who* would raise freedom's child was fundamentally a question about who would determine the economic future of black people after slavery.[23]

Apprenticeship arrangements were, first and foremost, contracts. As such, they were pieces of paper invested with conflicting economic and social meanings by former slaveholders, former slaves, and Bureau agents. In the nineteenth century, labor contracts in general were documents through which groups voiced different visions of slavery and freedom. Abolitionists, northern workers, slaveholders, and freedpeople all defined free labor and slavery in light of one another, and they often did so while debating the positive and negative aspects of the wage contract. Although antislavery advocates framed the labor contract as the very negation of slavery and the demonstration of self-ownership, for instance, freedpeople and other wage workers often viewed contracts more ambivalently. Though apprenticeship agreements took the *form* of contracts—agreements between free laborers and employers—freedpeople recognized the ambiguities within apprenticeship agreements, proliferating as they did on the still slippery ground between slavery and freedom.[24] In the eyes of many freedpeople like Cyntha Nickols, the conditions of apprenticeship left black children in a relation of servitude to their former owners.

DeGrey's criticism of Cyntha Nickols for wanting Porter's labor, therefore, had truth in it. Children's economic value as workers was an understood part of their role as members of freed households. As contributors to the family economy, children often made it possible for freed families to separate themselves from the claims of former owners and sustain independent households. A child's labor and the money he or she could bring in were necessities in freed families, as they were among working-class families in the urban North and agricultural families in the West. Strictly in terms of labor, the rural childhoods of most freedchildren were comparable to those of poor children in other rural areas of the United States, especially white children on the western frontier and Chicano children in California.[25]

After emancipation, most freedpeople remained in rural areas of the South, working parcels of plantation land for a share of the crop or for wages and rations. But they also grew their own food for sustenance and marketing. The labor of freedchildren, both for the plantation owner and for their families, was critical to the survival of most freedpeople's households. They often labored within a family, under the direction of parents or relatives, and attended school for a few months out of the year. Whether the family was sharecropping, working the task system (predominant in coastal plantation areas of Georgia and South Carolina), or cultivating their own land, the agricultural labor of children was critical to the household's survival. Freedchildren also performed domestic labor, and like most working-class children in the nineteenth century (black, white, and Hispanic, urban and rural), many were "hired out" by their parents for periods of time, to work in other households.[26] In addition to bringing in earnings as field hands or house servants (a labor contract frequently carried the name of a child with his or her X as a signature), they fed the family's livestock, sold produce at the market, tended younger children, hunted game, sewed clothes, and cleaned house.[27]

It is not clear where Porter lived before Nickols approached the Bureau, but DeGrey's assessment that "the old lady wants the boy because he is now able to do Some work" suggests that Porter may have been living with Spears. If so, then Porter's predicament also may document a strategy used by many freedpeople, particularly freedwomen: they left their children in the household of former owners (where they would receive food and shelter in exchange for small household duties) until the women could support them themselves. In Porter's case, Nickols might have been able to support her grandson once he was able to contribute economically to the household. At the very least, Nickols did not want Porter to be bound over to Spears until he was grown—an arrangement that would deprive her of her grandson and his labor. She would not be able to take him from Spears's place, nor would she be able to hire him out, as the white Unionist from Maryland astutely pointed out.

Family members much preferred freedchildren to be hired rather than apprenticed. Freedpeople negotiated the contracts of their children and protested when employers failed to pay them. Freed parents and relatives made hundreds of complaints to the Freedmen's Bureau concerning wages that had not been paid to their children.[28] Freedchildren themselves also complained when they had not received the pay that was due to them. (In 1865, the going rate for boys under fourteen was three dollars per month and for girls, two dollars.)[29] Other children made complaint to the Bureau against employers for abuse or for refusing to let them board with their parents.[30]

But the dependent status of the freedchild made the contract between freedpeople and employers always a matter of interpretation. A boy named William, for instance, charged that a Mrs. Crawford had refused to pay him for one month and two weeks labor at three dollars a month. Crawford protested that William was "not worth anything more than his rations" and had sent word to that effect to his mother. Crawford did not see William as a wage laborer. Rather, she wanted to have him as a child-servant, fed but not paid, "raised" but not otherwise compensated for his work. The agent in the case decided in favor of William and awarded him a month's wages.[31]

Despite freed families' dependence on freedchildren's labor, however, the economic value of children like Porter did not cancel their emotional value and may have even strengthened bonds between family members.[32] Particularly in single-parent families, children had to contribute to the household income as soon as they could. Ex-slave John Moore explained that after his father died of cholera, "my mudder hire me 'n' some 'r' d' uder chillen out t'wuk 'n' she draw us money." After Millie Randall's mother retrieved her children from their former owner—the reluctant former slaveholder drove the children "'roun an' 'roun" in a wagon to keep them from her—she had the job of supporting herself and her children. Randall recalled, "Maw tuk ober de care of de chillen an' done de bes' she could. Dey put me in a fiel' of co'n to hoe."[33] The words of Cyntha Nickols, too, suggest that her relationship with Porter was far from detached. "I am the Grandmother of Porter," she wrote. And "I am required to call [on] you or I must let my Grand-Child go, which greatly grieves me."

Former slaveholders, however, were not so ready to relinquish power over the raising of freedchildren precisely because it meant the erosion of their control over their own households—households that, until the war, had structured the lives and labors of black as well as white.[34] It is not surprising, then, that former slaveholders' arguments to retain control over freedchildren were often voiced in the seemingly intimate, but easily appropriated language of family. The ideology of slaveholder paternalism—based on the notion that southern slaveholders were good to their slaves because their slaves depended on them in the same way that children depended on a father—became part of a testimonial to their concern for the freedchild's best interest.

Indeed, very often the justification offered by former slaveholders for retaining freedchildren was that the children had grown up in their master's household. Their most common refrain in this regard was one that DeGrey seemed to accept without critique, that is, that they had "raised" the children themselves. Mary Golbert, demanding the return of a "servant girl" named Sarah, was typical in her pleading with federal authorities. In 1863, Sarah had sought refuge from her mistress in a New Orleans hospital, and in efforts to have her returned, Golbert declared: "She is a girl I have raised and I am good to my servants."[35] And when several freedpeople complained to the Bureau, for instance, that a woman named Woodward "has repeatedly abused a child in her possession," Woodward responded that the child's parents were dead and "that she had raised the child from infancy and was anxious to keep him and do well by him." Just as before the war, however, this was an ideology that failed to conceal former slaveholders' economic interest in the people they once owned. Mr. Spears *"raised"* the child Porter, but he *contracted* for his labor until he was grown. In fact, Spears seems to have bound Porter to him in 1867, when he was ten or eleven, not in 1865, at the close of the war. He opted to legally support the child, through contract, only after he reached working age.

Porter's case, and those of other freedchildren at the center of such disputes, was further complicated by ideas about the welfare of poor children that governed the thinking of many Bureau agents, ideas that combined poor children's domestic arrangements with the expectation that they would be put to work. "Placing out" poor orphans with individual families—where they would receive supervision and shelter in exchange for their labor—was increasingly common in the plans of northern reformers, as an alternative to orphanages. The idea behind such arrangements was not just to find homes for poor children but also to place them in an environment that would teach them hard work and, in the words of one reformer, "improve their intellects."[36] This attitude toward the welfare of poor children could work against freed families (and in favor of former slaveholders) as often as it aided freedpeople in the retrieval of their children. DeGrey, for instance, was making the assumption that Porter would be better off working under Spears as an apprentice than for Nickols, his grandmother.

Freedpeople made it clear, as agent James DeGrey found out, that they viewed apprenticeship as it was practiced during and after the war, "like putting them back into slavery." As an angry freedman from Alabama wrote: "I think very hard of the former oners for Trying to keep My blood when I kno that Slavery is dead." Based upon Bureau records, it is uncertain whether or not Cyntha Nickols succeeded in retrieving her grandson from his former owner. But with fortitude, thousands of freedpeople like her managed to reconstitute their families, against heavy odds. The right to control their children was, it seems, as sacred to them as their freedom. Indeed, they made little separation between the two. As a freedwoman in Maryland, whose child was bound as an apprentice against her wishes, told the Freedmen's Bureau: "We were delighted when we heard that the Constitution set us all free, but God help us, our condition is bettered but little; free ourselves, but deprived of our children....It was on their account we desired to be free."[37]

NOTES

1. Cyntha Nickols to the Chief Agent of the FB at N Orleans, January 10, 1867, N-1 1867, Letters Received, ser. 1303, East Feliciana, LA, Asst Comr., RG 105, Bureau of Refugees, Freedmen, and Abandoned Lands, National Archives and Records Administration (hereafter BRFAL), Freedmen and Southern Society Project Archives (hereafter cited as FSSP) [A8620].

2. Eric Foner, *Reconstruction: America's Unfinished Revolution, 1863–1877* (New York: Harper and Row, 1988), 68–70.

3. Disputes over freedchildren's labor were just one struggle among many in which the black child became both muse and metaphor for the future of the postbellum South. See Mary Niall Mitchell, *Raising Freedom's Child: Black Children and Visions of the Future after Slavery* (New York: NYU Press, 2008).

4. Marie Jenkins Schwartz, *Born in Bondage: Growing Up Enslaved in the Antebellum South* (Cambridge: Harvard University Press, 2001), passim.

5. Joseph Hall to General Howard or those having charge of freedmen at Washington D.C., September 14, 1865, no. 16, 1865, Letters Received, ser. 456, DC Asst Comr., RG 105, BRFAL, FSSP [A-9720], in *Freedom: A Documentary History of Emancipation, 1861–1867,* ed. Ira Berlin, Steven F. Miller, Joseph P. Reidy, and Leslie Rowland, ser. 1, vol. 1, *The Wartime Genesis of Free Labor: The Upper South* (Cambridge: Cambridge University Press, 1993), 545. On the economic struggles of black households, see Sharon Ann Holt, "Making Freedom Pay: Freedpeople Working for Themselves in North Carolina, 1865–1900," *Journal of Southern History* 60 (May 1994): 229–62.

6. W. J. Rorabaugh, *The Craft Apprentice: From Franklin to the Machine Age in America* (New York: Oxford University Press, 1986), vii, passim; Karin L. Zipf, *Labor of Innocents: Forced Apprenticeship in North Carolina, 1715–1919* (Baton Rouge: Louisiana State University Press, 2005), chap. 1; Steven Mintz, *Huck's Raft: A History of American Childhood* (Cambridge: Belknap Press of Harvard University Press, 2004), esp. 113–15, 137–40.

7. Victoria E. Bynum, *Unruly Women: The Politics of Social and Sexual Control in the Old South* (Chapel Hill: University of North Carolina Press, 1992), esp. chap. 4.

8. William Cohen, *At Freedom's Edge: Black Mobility and the Southern White Quest for Racial Control, 1861–1915* (Baton Rouge: Louisiana State University Press, 1991), 29–37; Foner, *Reconstruction,* 200–201.

9. The first circular concerning apprenticeships stated the ages of majority for girls and boys to be eighteen and twenty-one, respectively. See Circular no. 25, War Dept., Washington, DC, October 4, 1865, BRFAL. But a random survey of indentures signed in Louisiana state the ages of majority to be eighteen and fifteen.

10. Indentures, Parishes of Sabine and Natchitoches, ser. 1776, box. 23, Natchitoches, LA Agent & Asst Subasst Comr, RG 105, BRFAL.

11. Berlin et al., *Freedom,* ser. 1, vol. 2, *The Wartime Genesis of Free Labor: The Upper South,* 495; Barbara Jeanne Fields, *Slavery and Freedom on the Middle Ground: Maryland during the Nineteenth Century* (New Haven: Yale University Press, 1984), 142; Rebecca J. Scott, "The Battle over the Child: Child Apprenticeship and the Freedmen's Bureau in North Carolina," *Prologue* (Summer 1978): 100–113.

12. Foner, *Reconstruction,* 372. It was not until 1909, for instance, that North Carolina eliminated apprenticeship laws in favor of the Child Welfare Act with broadened state powers and responsibilities regarding children. Zipf, *Labor of Innocents,* chap. 6.

13. Capt N. G. Gill to Capt & Provost Marshal, February 19, 1865, Provost Marshal Letters Received, ser. 1488, Lafourche Parish, LA, RG 393, pt. 4, BRFAL.

14. Thomas Calahan Asst Supt to Thomas W. Conway, Asst Comr., September 6, 1865, Unregistered Letters Received, ser. 1304, Shreveport, LA, Asst Comr, RG 105, BRFAL, FSSP [A-8549].

15. Capt J. W. Keller to Lt. Hayden, July 2, 1866, Unregistered Letters Received, ser. 1602, Franklin, LA, Asst. Subasst Comr, RG 105, BRFAL, FSSP [A-8523].

16. Scott, "Battle over the Child," 102; Noralee Frankel, *Freedom's Women: Black Woman and Families in Civil War Era Mississippi* (Bloomington: Indiana University Press, 1999), 138–43; Barry A. Crouch, "'To Enslave the Rising Generation': The Freedmen's Bureau and the Texas Black Code," in *The Freedmen's Bureau and Reconstruction: Reconsiderations,* ed. Paul A. Cimbala and Randall M. Miller (New York: Fordham University Press, 1999), 269.

17. Chaplain L. S. Livermore to Lt. Col. R. S. Donaldson, January 10, 1866, "L" 1866, Registered Letters Received, ser. 2188, Jackson MS Acting Asst Comr of the Northern District of Mississippi, BRFAL, FSSP [A-9328], printed in *Families and Freedom: A Documentary History of African-American Kinship in the Civil War Era,* ed. Ira Berlin and Leslie S. Rowland (New York: New Press, 1997), 221.

18. W. H. R. Hangen, Asst Subasst Comr to 1st Lt. J. M. Lee, October 3, 1867, Madisonville, LA, Letters Received, Asst Comr, RG 105, BRFAL, microfilm, M-1027, reel 16 [999].

19. William F. Mugleston, "The Freedmen's Bureau and Reconstruction in Virginia: The Diary of Marcus Sterling Hopkins, a Union Officer," *Virginia Magazine of History and Biography* 86, no. 1 (1978): 55; quoted in Dylan C. Penningroth, *The Claims of Kinfolk: African American Property and Community in the Nineteenth-Century South* (Chapel Hill: University of North Carolina Press, 2003), 168.

20. Wilma King, *Stolen Childhood: Slave Youth in Nineteenth-Century America* (Bloomington: Indiana University Press, 1995), 102.

21. Register of Complaints, May 13, 1867, ser. 1807, v. 404, p. 2, New Orleans, L.B. [Left Bank] Asst Subasst Commissioner and Register of Complaints, May 10, 1867, ser. 1807, v. 404, p. 8, New Orleans, L.B., Asst Subasst Comr, BRFAL.

22. Cyntha Nickols to the Chief Agent of the FB at New Orleans, January 10, 1867, N-1 1867, Letters Received, ser. 1303, East Feliciana LA, Asst Comr. Endorsement Lt. James DeGrey, FB agent, to Capt Wm H. Sterling Act Asst Adjt Genl, Parish of East Feliciana La, Clinton, La, January 29, 1867, RG 105, BRFAL, FSSP [A8620].

23. Julie Saville, *The Work of Reconstruction: From Slave to Wage Laborer in South Carolina, 1860–1870* (Cambridge: Cambridge University Press, 1994), 4. Michele Mitchell has studied the importance of black children to African American ideas about racial destiny in a later period. Michele Mitchell, *Righteous Propagation: African Americans and the Politics of Racial Destiny after Reconstruction* (Chapel Hill: University of North Carolina Press, 2004).

24. Amy Dru Stanley, *From Bondage to Contract: Wage Labor, Marriage, and the Market in the Age of Slave Emancipation* (Cambridge: Cambridge University Press, 1998), x and passim.

25. King, *Stolen Childhood*, 160; Jacqueline Jones, *Labor of Love, Labor of Sorrow: Black Women, Work, and the Family from Slavery to the Present* (New York: Basic Books, 1985), 61–62, 87–88, 91, 94; Priscilla Ferguson Clement, *Growing Pains: Children in the Industrial Age, 1850–1890* (New York: Twayne, 1997), 129–31.

26. See Mintz, *Huck's Raft,* chap. 7.

27. Penningroth, *Claims of Kinfolk,* 166; King, *Stolen Childhood,* 154–58.

28. See, for instance, L. Jolissant to Assistant Commissioner, October 31, 1867, Letters Received, New Orleans, LA, Asst Comr, RG 105, BRFAL, microfilm, M-1027, reel 17 [0155].

29. "Labor Regulations," May 25, 1865, Undated Daily Picayune (?) Letters Received, Assistant Comr, RG 105, BRFAL, microfilm, M-1027, reel 11 [0042].

30. Lt. James DeGrey to Capt. William H. Sterling, April 30, 1867, Letters Received, Clinton, LA, Asst Comr, RG 105, BRFAL, microfilm, M-1027, reel 14 [861].

31. Bvt. Capt. Richard Folles to Assistant Commissioner, July 20, 1867, Trimonthly Report, Letters Received, Algiers, LA, Asst Comr, RG 105, BRFAL, microfilm, M-1027, reel 15 [0342].

32. As E. P. Thompson suggested, "feeling might be more, rather than less, tender or intense because relations are 'economic' and critical to mutual survival." E. P. Thompson, "Happy Families" (review of Lawrence Stone, *The Family, Sex, and Marriage in England, 1500–1800*), *New Society* 41 (September 1977): 501.

33. Interview with Millie Randall, n.d., George P. Rawick, ed., *American Slave: A Composite Autobiography* (Westport, CT: Greenwood Press, 1972), suppl. ser. 2, vol. 8 (Texas), pt. 7.

34. Peter W. Bardaglio, *Reconstructing the Household: Families, Sex, and the Law in the Nineteenth-Century South* (Chapel Hill: University of North Carolina Press, 1995), 116–19.

35. Mrs. Mary Golbert to Maj Genl Banks, January 26, 1863, Letters Received, ser. 1920, Civil Affairs, Dept of the Gulf, [box 2], RG 393, Pt. 1, BRFAL.

36. Mintz, *Huck's Raft,* 158; Laura Smith Haviland, *A Woman's Life-Work* (New York: Arno Press, 1969 [1881]), 377.

37. Lucy Lee to Lt. Col. W. E. W. Ross, January 10, 1865, in "Communication from Major Gen'l Lew. Wallace, in Relation to the Freedmen's Bureau, to the General Assembly of Maryland," *Maryland House Journal and Documents* (Annapolis, 1865), document J, pp. 68–69, printed in Berlin et al., *Freedom,* ser. 1, vol. 2, *The Wartime Genesis of Free Labor: The Upper South,* 498; Charles M. Hooper to Wager Swayne, April 20, 1867, Wager Swayne Papers, Alabama State Department of Archives and History, quoted in Foner, *Reconstruction,* 201.

11

Reconstructing Social Obligation

White Orphan Asylums in
Post-emancipation Richmond

CATHERINE A. JONES

Writing in her diary in May 1865, Emma Mordecai noted the arrival of "Annie," a white orphan girl from the Richmond Female Humane Association. For Mordecai, the Confederate defeat had unleashed a crisis in domestic labor organization at her farm on the outskirts of Richmond—a crisis she hoped a needy orphan might alleviate. In the month leading up to Annie's arrival, Mordecai recorded the intense negotiations among freedpeople in the household about the future of their relationships to each other, and to her. After composing a careful record of her former slaves' refusal to obey her commands, Mordecai wrote, "To have to submit to the Yankees is bad enough, but to submit to negro children is a little worse."[1]

Mordecai's decision to take on Anna Lewery arose less out of a desire to aid a vulnerable orphan than from the hope that the girl might prove more biddable than the freedpeople around her. Lewery, however, had other ideas. She made it clear that she was unhappy with the arrangement and began planning her return to the city almost from the moment of her arrival. Having lived in the orphan asylum since her admission at age eleven in 1860, Lewery apparently found submitting to the labor demands of Mordecai, and living away from the city neighborhoods she had known, unbearable. She soon fled the farm and, it seems likely, returned to the heart of the city that had long been her home.

Although the conflicting expectations that doomed the arrangement—Mordecai's desire for obedience, Lewery's commitment to maintaining connections to home—could have arisen at any juncture, the specific circumstances of spring 1865 resonated within the encounter. Mordecai's attempt to substitute a white orphan for freedpeople in her household intersected with pressing anxieties about the future of labor organization in the wake of emancipation and its implications for social order in the state. Throughout Virginia, the disposition of orphans in the postwar context became an ethically charged problem that sheds light on how white Virginians used race to shape understandings of ethical obligation among the state's citizens. The Richmond Female Humane Association (RFHA) and the Richmond Male Orphan Asylum (RMOA), expanded their missions to serve more children, reduced the length of children's stays in the asylum through placing out, and confronted disagreement about what constituted appropriate care for white orphans in the wake of the Civil War. The nineteenth-century definition of orphans as fatherless children tightened the association between orphaned white children and fallen Confederate soldiers, which in turn helped the advocates of Richmond's orphan asylums recast the bonds of Confederate loyalty into an explicitly racialized and historicized understanding of social obligation.[2]

As the Civil War raged in Virginia, both the RFHA and the RMOA charted a steady decline. Although the need for the asylums' services grew with each battle, their resources shrank, charges ran away in ever-larger numbers, and relatives came forward to claim children earlier relinquished. The high demand for children's labor on the home front and the battlefront during the war, along with the asylums' deteriorating financial positions, produced a sharp drop in admissions for both institutions and shorter asylum stays for many children. By 1864, the RMOA's insolvency led the directors to close their doors to new admissions, despite their perception of mounting demand. As the directors explained, "It is obvious that these claims [on asylum resources] must increase more rapidly than usual, whether the present cruel war continue, or, as we would fair hope, cease during the present year [but] . . . the Board must continue to shut the doors of the asylum to any beyond the present number until it can enlarge its resources." The RFHA supporters complained of having to resort to labor-intensive and largely unsuccessful fund-raising strategies like targeted canvassing. In 1877, William W. Parker, the president of the Richmond Male Orphan Asylum, recalled that the managers had felt so pressed to find alternate homes for their charges during the war that upon discovering the father of two asylum residents, presumably a Union soldier, living in a Confederate prison in the city, they queried him regarding his willingness to take his sons north if a prisoner exchange could be arranged.[3]

Beyond the asylums' walls, the war intensified demand for children's labor. As the conflict dragged on, the erosion of slavery and the steady stream of men entering military service disrupted home front labor supply and temporarily increased the value of children's labor. As early as 1862, the

RMOA's board of managers reported twenty-two departures, including four runaways, and the remainder "having been placed in positions more advantageous under the circumstances, or having been returned to their mothers, who needed their aid, and could find them employment in these trying times." The relatively large number of wartime runaways (fifteen, compared with twenty-six children admitted during the war) suggests that sometimes children themselves sought alternatives to continued asylum residency, including service in the Confederate army.[4]

In the decade following Union victory, both institutions experienced a reversal of wartime trends and saw their populations grow rapidly. During 1866, the RMOA admitted the highest number of children in a single year since its founding—seventeen. The RFHA was somewhat slower in building up its numbers, but between 1865 and 1875, it admitted sixty-two girls. The correlation between an increase in the number of orphans resident in the asylum and the war's creation of a large number of orphans at first seems so clear as to require no further explanation. Yet, the existence of need did not automatically generate the will or ability to assuage it; the expansion of the number of children in the city's asylums depended upon the willing participation of the institutions as well as of the children and their guardians. In practice, conflict, as often as cooperation, characterized asylum operations.[5]

In adapting their institutional missions to postdefeat circumstances, the RFHA and RMOA adopted a more expansive view of their missions. Before the Civil War, both asylums had carefully demarcated their spheres of responsibility through geographic restrictions (serving only Richmond residents) and bodily ones (refusing children with physical or mental disabilities). Instead of developing additional exclusions to winnow the large postwar population of Richmond orphans to a reasonable number of worthy charges, both institutions loosened their admissions policies but retained a categorical exclusion of black children. In 1871, the RFHA explicitly overturned its Richmond residency requirement in favor of an experiential and historical qualification by passing a resolution that gave asylum directors authority "to admit such Orphan Children of Confederate Soldiers residing in the State of Virginia as may demand admittance by reason of peculiar destitution." In the same year, the published annual report of the Male Orphan Asylum proclaimed itself "more of a State than a City Institution" and claimed to reject no worthy boy, regardless of residency. With increasing frequency, both asylums invoked the recent history of Confederate sacrifice as the impetus behind their institutional missions and a compelling source of binding ethical obligation among white Virginians.[6]

In addition to expanding their sphere of responsibility to include potentially all Confederate orphans in the state, the Richmond asylums also
extended their reach into the city's population by granting entry to indi-
gent white children with no apparent family or community connections. In
the antebellum era, children entered the asylums primarily through private
social networks, and in the case of the RFHA, only upon the approval of the
asylum's advisory board. After the war, the asylums regularly accepted children from the overseers of the poor. In 1875, the Virginia legislature gave
the RMOS legal authority to hold boys who were simply vagrants, as well as
known orphans. By 1877, both asylums had agreed to accept children from
the city almshouse in return for appropriations from the city to support the
asylum. Postwar changes in the laws governing the two asylums and their
practices reconfigured the balance of their hybrid public private character, in
regard to both whom they served and where they sought financial support.[7]

The postwar shift to assuming responsibility for vagrant children pro-
ceeded uneasily and unevenly. In contrast to northern child savers like
Charles Loring Brace, whose missions were predicated on the stark difference between the purveyors of benevolence and the children of the "dangerous classes," the Richmond asylums generally cast their charges as community insiders in need of assistance to weather a reversal of fortune, not an
alien presence in need of acculturation. The frequency of asylum directors'
expressions of doubt about the feasibility of rehabilitating vagrant children
after the war highlights the extent to which the new policies constituted a
challenging departure. For example, in 1874, the Richmond Male Orphan
Asylum board of managers turned out one child because it determined he
was insane, and another because he was so "vicious" that he threatened
to "endanger the whole school." In the same year, the school described an
uneasy relationship with a small group of vagrant children it admitted to its
care. "The three boys that I received last year," the president explained, "were
recommended to me by friends who said they were well disposed, and this
would be their only chance for an education as they had neither father nor
mother, and were indeed utterly homeless. Unfortunately, one ran away, and
one was sent away. The third still remains, and promises well, but we have
our fears." The concerns that emerged alongside the asylums' expanded missions revealed conflicting expectations regarding institutional responsibilities to their charges.[8]

The expansion of placing-out practices, both in numbers and in geographic reach, created additional opportunities and challenges. In contrast to
the antebellum practice of apprenticing orphans to tradesmen within Rich-

mond, boys admitted after the Civil War were much more likely to be sent to households in surrounding counties with no specific promise of training in a trade. Available records for the RFHA also indicate that after the war, girls were most frequently placed in Virginia counties beyond Richmond's city limits, primarily in the Piedmont and Tidewater regions. Pragmatism, much more than a condemnation of asylums or critiques of the city (both prominent rationales for northern placing-out practices), pushed asylum managers to look beyond burgeoning Richmond for homes for their child charges. While the asylums' modified placing-out policies gave weight to their claims to being state institutions, the rhetoric of their appeals for support explicitly asserted that the history of the war bound all former Confederates to support the state's white orphans.[9]

As advocates for both asylums invoked the legacy of Confederate loss in their appeals for support from fellow citizens, they developed a new accounting of the ethical obligations white Virginians bore each other. "Loyal," the author of "An Appeal to the Young Ladies of Richmond," published in the *Richmond Daily Dispatch*, closed her request for donations with this reproach: "Remember your homes were defended in time of trouble by them that have sacrificed their lives upon the battle-field, and now you are enjoying that home, while the widows and orphans are forgotten." In a public address on the occasion of the twenty-second anniversary of the Richmond Male Orphan Asylum in 1869, Major Robert Stiles queried the audience: "*Whose* are the little ones pressing to come in? Where are their fathers? Some of them lie in shallow graves, the saddest ever dug in the bosom of the earth;—fallen in an unsuccessful war—a struggle in which a nation was still born. . . . Against these remorseless decrees of history I have nothing to say now;—but, oh! if the pale faces of the dead must fade from our sight, what of their living mementos left helpless among us?" By casting the audience's responsibility to orphans as a debt that honor demanded be paid, Stiles implicitly offered his audience a chance to demonstrate that the failure of the Confederate cause had not destroyed a sense of mutual obligation among Confederates. Embracing responsibility for the state's orphans was a way to contain defeat.[10]

Stiles's appeal implied that Confederate identity could have political value in war's aftermath by unifying white citizens in a way that proposed race and history, not just kinship and city limits, as the foundation of postwar communities of support. The menace in his appeal came not from vagabond children but from the failure of adults to embrace an opportunity to shore up community ties battered by defeat and emancipation. Stiles used specifically proprietary language in calling for financial support of the asylum, saying, "It is *ours*, and the orphans who fill it, or ought to fill it are *ours*, and not sufferers of some other community. It is our business, therefore, to support it and them, more than it is the business of any other community." This appeal to duty emphasized commonality between those in need and those in a position to provide assistance. While the collective "ours" was initially directed at the audience of asylum supporters assembled to hear Stiles's speech, the subsequent distribution of the address suggests that the asylum hoped that the "ours" was elastic enough to draw support from across the state. In 1872, Dr. Wall concluded his address on behalf of the asylum by explicitly making race the boundary of a community that generated ethical obligations. He exhorted his audience "that no one shall regard" the asylum's "mission as fully accomplished whilst there is one single little orphan brother of our race to be found uncared for in the lanes and alleys of our city." While race had always been a criterion for excluding children from the city's asylums, in the postwar context asylums began testing whether whiteness was a viable basis for asserting a vision of social obligation that was at once more geographically expansive and more pointedly racially exclusive.[11]

In calling on Virginians to rise to the challenge of assisting orphans, Stiles attempted to describe a regionally distinct form of philanthropy that emphasized associative duties arising from community membership rather than humanitarian sentiment. Although the Richmond asylums' repertoire of strategies for helping orphans resembled that of their northern counterparts, Stiles and other asylum advocates were anxious to explain how charity would help Virginia retain its own distinctive moral order. He savaged the "self-deifying mind of man" that suggested that benevolence was a practical response to need. Within the careful construction of governing documents and appeals for support, asylum advocates revealed their belief that children should not expect that knowledge of their need would be a sufficient goad to public action. Rather than making an appeal to benevolence, Stiles tied the obligations arising from the Confederate past to Christian duty in a way that yielded an utterly unsentimental account of orphans. In a rhetorical question directed at an imagined orphan, he asked, "You are such a very little thing, how could any one love you; how could you even love yourself as much as you do Jesus? [Were] we to work for you, only for our love to you, and not for love we bear our blessed Jesus. Why[,] you wouldn't expect to have much done for you, would you?" According to Stiles's formulation, duty created by sacrifice—Jesus' or Confederates'—was the surest foundation on which to build a hope of mutual support.

The centrality of Confederate sacrifice to the asylums' postwar public appeals seems unsurprising, given its prominence in public discourse that emerged around the Lost Cause and the certainty that soldiers' deaths had indeed left orphans in their wake. Nevertheless, it is important to recognize that it was a choice on the part of the asylum directors, which invites consideration of its appeal. Rather than calling on potential donors to consider the future harm that might befall the public at the hands of inadequately tended children, as they had in the antebellum era, the asylums' advocates appealed to ideas of duty and moral obligation arising from the recent war. While the appeals themselves promoted the welfare of white orphans, the form they took contributed to a larger political goal of adapting Confederate identity to serve new purposes in the postwar context.[12]

In practice, appeals to a common Confederate past did not produce consensus regarding the treatment of white orphans. From some angles the orphan asylums appeared to serve as labor brokerages connecting farmers in the country to excess children in the city. In October 1866, W.W. Parker, the president of the Richmond Male Orphan Asylum, placed a small announcement in the *Richmond Daily Dispatch*, soliciting children between the ages of eight and fourteen to be brought to his office. He explained that he had "been applied to by worthy people in the Valley, and also in southwestern Virginia, for orphan boys and girls. He can at once get good situations for ten or a dozen of the former, and four or five of the latter." While such schemes held appeal in the most desperate days of 1865 and 1866, asylum directors found that treating white children as part of a fungible labor supply in the state sat uneasily with their vision of mutual obligation arising from a shared Confederate past. In the fifteen years following the end of the Civil War, Virginia's orphan asylums revised their postwar missions, first in response to the acute need for their services and later in response to concerns about preserving racial difference.[13]

In order to serve an expanded population of orphan charges, the RMOA and the RFHA limited the length of children's residency in the asylums more aggressively, frequently through indenture arrangements. Asylum directors saw a happy coincidence between their need to place children outside the asylum and emancipation's expanded demand for child labor. In December 1877, the RFHA's board of directors reported, "Owing to the change of labor in the South we find that we have more demands made on us for children to go out into service than we have ever had before. For some time past we have taken in children at a more tender age than has been usual with us & we have put out more than we have ever done before in the same space of time."

The increased reliance on binding out necessitated clarifying the institutions' legal authority to do so. As a consequence, in the mid-1870s, both asylums amended their charters to require parents and guardians to relinquish all legal claims to a child as a condition of admission. While asylum appeals for support emphasized shared community values among white Virginians, the practice of binding out revealed conflicting understandings of what constituted an acceptable arrangement.[14]

Despite attempts to strengthen the legal authority of orphan asylums, it is clear that binding out, like admissions, depended on consent from children and surviving parents who regularly influenced orphans' relationships to the asylums. Children themselves took advantage of openings in the institutional management of their lives to exercise a measure of independence, sometimes to the frustration of asylum officials. In 1872, the board of managers of the RMOA blamed the boys' frequent escapes from the asylum on the freedom they were given to attend church without supervision. The scene the records paint of "small squads" of boys rambling through the city to church and Sunday schools suggests that children enjoyed a degree of liberty within the institution. Such actions hinted at broader problems that arose from ignoring orphans' capacity to act in their own perceived interests.[15]

Parents of orphans, mostly mothers, also challenged the institutions' assertions of authority over their charges by remaining engaged in their children's lives by monitoring their treatment and sometimes demanding their return. Upon learning that the asylum superintendent had severely whipped her son, one mother had the man arrested by the police. She successfully negotiated the return of her child in exchange for dropping the charges, leading the asylum president to admonish the superintendent to be less severe in his punishment of the boys. Some mothers appear to have used the institutions strategically to mitigate the burden of caring for young children. For example, in 1876 a Mrs. Hicks succeeded in convincing the RFHA's board of visitors to allow her to substitute a younger child for her seven-year-old, then living at the asylum.[16]

Despite these instances of successful interventions, mothers who placed children in the asylums with the expectation that it would be a short-term disruption in a long-term plan for familial unity took a gamble. While many mothers were able to recover their children, particularly if they had remarried, others were less successful. In a particularly protracted exchange, the RMOS denied a Mrs. McNamee's request to retrieve her son Robert from the asylum in June 1870. The asylum's refusal did not deter McNamee; two years later the asylum ledger recorded that she had succeeded in "stealing away" young Robert. In another instance, the asylum went so far as to call in the police to force the return of a child who had gone to visit his mother. While the records are too limited to discern whether the directors' determinations regarding parents' rights to their children might best be characterized as attempts to protect their charges from dangerous parents, or concerted efforts to defend the primacy of the contractual obligations that established the asylums as legal guardians over the prerogatives of kinship, it is clear that many actors shaped children's careers within Richmond's orphan asylums. Ultimately, it was the web of relationships children did or did not figure in that determined their experiences both within institutions and in the long-term placements made on their behalf. The negotiation, and even open conflict, that attended institutions' efforts to exercise authority over dependent children underscores that Richmond's asylums were accountable to multiple constituencies as they adapted their missions to postwar circumstances. The power of legal authority was of little value without consent from the children and their guardians, which in turn appears to have been contingent upon the institutions' meeting evolving ideas of guardianship and benevolence, not assertions of their devotion to a shared Confederate past.[17]

Virginia orphan asylums' reliance on indenture for the long-term care of children made the question of what constituted an acceptable placement crucial, particularly given the importance of work in maintaining racial distinctions. During Reconstruction, binding out retained legal and social legitimacy as a practice for addressing the needs of children, although its application was frequently contentious and marked by racial discrimination. In the absence of kinship guiding understandings of mutual obligation between adults and children, contract ideally provided a measure of protection for children and an incentive for adults to accept the burden of caring for them. By fixing terms of exchange of care and labor, contract created a relationship, if asymmetrical and often exploitative, that promised a level of mutual care. In practice, the character of such arrangements varied widely, with some serving as little more than legal sanction for the reenslavement of black children, while others succeeded in providing needed support for orphaned children. It seems clear that racial ideology, when it separated the children being bound from the adults who would be their new guardians, sanctioned exploitative arrangements. The question of how it shaped the character of placing-out arrangements when the orphans and their new guardians shared a common racial identification is less clear. The placements of white orphans suggest that asylum managers struggled to balance the use of apprenticeship to manage a large number of child charges with evolving expectations regarding appropriate care for white children.[18]

Although glimpses into the experiences of children who were placed out are elusive, applications for children give some insight into expectations regarding orphans' privileges and responsibilities in their new homes. For example, a testimonial on behalf of Mr. and Mrs. George Collins, who sought a child from the Jackson Orphan Asylum in Norfolk, expressed confidence that they would be responsible caregivers, even as it frankly acknowledged that the child would be a servant: "They wish a child under 12 years of age, one that has been brought up in the church, to play with and wait upon their children. They will bind themselves to keep her until she is twenty one—longer if she is capable and gives satisfaction. They promise to do a good part by the child." The coexistence of expressions of concern for the child with an explicit commitment to inequality among children within a household reveals that distinctions among bound, adopted, and "blood" children were real, despite a common racial identification. In most households, blood children enjoyed particular privileges, while children united with the family via the formal mechanism of contract had a lower threshold of acceptable care and faced heavier work burdens. Under the pressure of expanded need, contractual binding-out became even more prominent in asylums' approaches to managing the high numbers of children admitted to their institutions after the war. To the managers of orphan asylums as well as the children and parents involved, the legitimacy of such arrangements ultimately depended upon their lived quality.[19]

While some children may have settled into stable household relations, others seem to have eventually rejected the capacity of the indenture contract to bind them into adulthood. In 1877, the president of the Richmond Male Orphan Asylum complained that children themselves were undermining the practice of apprenticeship by unilaterally nullifying contracts: "So soon as they learn enough to make their labor worth fifty or seventy-five cents a day they take the cars and are heard of no more. . . . The want of good faith in the boys makes it much more difficult to get them good trades." The president called for greater fidelity on the part of both the boys and their employers. He went on to assert that this represented a change: "This was not the case twenty-five years ago. An apprenticeship then meant something." It is tempting to reject the assertion of change over time as a matter of nostalgia and frustration, yet it is clear that circumstances *had* changed dramatically between 1850 and 1877. The training supplied in indenture arrangements had less value as Virginia's economy continued to change, as railroad track proliferated and alternatives to farming became more attractive. Harder to capture, but perhaps even more important, was the influence of emancipation on the viability of such arrangements. It seems plausible that the deference to authority that had underlain apprenticeship in the antebellum era was less compelling in the wake of war and emancipation. Anna Lewery was not alone in deciding that hazarding life on her own was better than being a substitute for emancipated slaves. For many orphans, black and white, it appears that apprenticeship lost appeal after emancipation made self-possession a universal expectation. Appeals to the vitality of Confederate ties could not obscure emancipation's profound impact on labor markets and the importance of work in policing racial difference in the absence of slavery.[20]

Children were not alone in challenging the practice of placing out. As the war receded into the past, the asylums' increasingly vocal preference for adoption suggests that they had become more skeptical of the desirability of such arrangements. They expressed concern that, at best, apprenticeship left children poorly poised for success in life and, at worst, it threatened to undermine social distinctions between black and white children. When Mrs. Johnson of the RFHA proposed at the 1876 annual meeting that girls not be placed out before the age of fifteen, she made an exception for adoption. Although the amendment did not carry, it suggests that some of the women engaged in the work of the asylum questioned the desirability of children's departure from the institution simply to become workers in private homes. The RMOA also began to draw a sharper distinction between adoption and binding out, revealing a preference for adoption, particularly for younger children. On June 10, 1874, the RMOA declared, "No boy will be put out except to learn a trade unless those applying are willing to adopt him." In their 1879 annual report, the asylum managers announced that in order to respond to the board's directive to reduce the population of the asylum, it hoped to have as many young charges adopted as possible. The RMOS identified childless couples as particularly desirable adoptive placements for children, perhaps because there was greater confidence that the absence of blood children improved the likelihood of full familial integration. The distinction between binding out and adoption became increasingly meaningful to the directors of Virginia's orphan asylums in the 1870s as a predictor of the kind of care a child would receive.[21]

Throughout the United States at midcentury, adoption was gaining legal ground as state legislatures passed laws that provided for the permanent displacement of parents' birth claims to children through legal adoption. In turn, adoption integrated children into new families permanently, significantly giving them inheritance rights. The distinction regarding inheritance seems to have been of particular concern to Norfolk's Jackson Orphan Asylum in making determinations regarding placements. In 1867, the asylum minutes noted that the board's acceptance of Mrs. Sally Spence's petition to adopt a girl from the asylum depended upon her verbal promise that she would immediately "deed some portion of her property upon Priscilla Ann Chadwick so as to be secure to Priscilla in case of her death." Spence apparently failed to do so but defended her actions by providing testimonials to her good character and offering evidence of the excellent care she had taken of the child. Despite Spence's insistence that she would treat the girl as her own, the asylum continued to press her to make an official legal transfer of property to the girl in case of her death. The asylum managers' attention to the promise of inheritance reflected concerns about the long-term provision for their charges but also, perhaps, its importance as a marker of a child's full familial integration and an indication of the kind of care a child would receive within her new household.[22]

Race, as constitutive of ethical obligation among white Virginians and the basis of suspicion toward black Virginians, explicitly informed the asylum directors' accounting of their responsibilities for children in their charge. The leaders of the asylums reported rescuing white children from black families with a sense of great urgency. In the asylum's 1873 annual report, President W. W. Parker reported that he at first refused to take in the three-year-old son of an eighteen-year-old woman who appeared at the asylum door, claiming to have been abandoned by her husband. He objected to the age of both the child and the mother, but "finding afterwards that she had given him to a negro woman, and was about to leave the city, I got her relinquishment and took the boy." In 1884, Parker sought the support of the police to get possession of a white boy whose mother had left him in the care of a black woman. He proudly reported that he succeeded in removing the boy from this dangerous situation and placing him in the safekeeping of the asylum. Although such events were rare, their prominence in the records suggests that they were meaningful to asylum leaders.[23]

The institutions' commitments to policing racial difference contributed to a retreat from placing out. The male orphan asylum's 1877 annual report explained that it would no longer place children with farmers who already had children of their own, making reference both to the limited long-term benefits to the child and to the short-term violation of racial separation. "If a farmer, well-to-do and of good character, without children, will take one of our boys at his table and in his house and promise to make him a farmer, we see no objection," remarked the asylum's managers. "But the chances for the average boy, who spends several years in minding cows, living in an out-house with negroes, and doomed to dig the balance of his life at ten dollars a month, are not very promising." The fungibility of postwar labor raised the specter of blurred racial difference and pushed the asylums to revise poli-cies. The expectation that adoption, unlike placing out, would ensure that white children would not be treated like black children contributed to its increasing prominence. The role of race in the asylums' appeals for public support suggests that its leaders understood the object of its work to be not only orphaned children in need but also the meaning of race and the failed Confederacy.[24]

The work of Richmond's orphan asylums sheds light on how Confeder-ate identity was repurposed after defeat to elide differences among whites and to provide a racially exclusive accounting of ethical obligation among whites. Their policies also demonstrate that a wide gulf often separated talk and practice. Like women's societies dedicated to maintaining the graves of soldiers, orphan asylums simultaneously contributed to a positive, popular memorializing of the Confederacy and depended upon appeals to its legacy for their survival. The experiences of the asylums suggest that the persistence of the Confederacy's value in public discourse depended on its attachment to immediate needs and concerns, particularly those of women and chil-dren left vulnerable by the colossal failure of Confederate ambitions. Further, making the Confederate past the guide to mutual obligation in the present had important implications for postwar understanding of public responsibil-ity to children in the state.[25]

Charging private institutions like orphan asylums with responsibilities for public welfare helped naturalize racial segregation in the public sphere. In contrast to the state's poorhouses, which had been racially mixed during the antebellum era, private orphan asylums had from their beginnings been racially exclusive institutions. The antebellum exclusion of black children from these institutions appeared to be of a piece with the range of restric-tions in place to differentiate asylums from poorhouses by making them a refuge from outside dangers, including racial mixing. In the postwar con-text, this racial exclusion was expressly paired with invocations of the war's legacy of expanded mutual obligation among white Virginians. The vision of racially exclusive social welfare provision for children within the state was a precedent that would shape the character of southern progressivism in the decades to come.[26]

1. April 19, 1865, undated May 1865 entry, *Diary of Emma Mordecai*, reel 22, *American Women's Diaries: Southern Women* [microform].

2. Discussion of the Richmond Female Humane Association relies on the Memorial Foundation for Children Records at the Library of Virginia (LVA) (hereafter cited as RFHA Records). Discussion of the Richmond Male Orphan Asylum relies on the Richmond Male Orphan Society Records at the Virginia Historical Society (VHS) (hereafter cited as RMOA Records).

3. "Female Humane Association," *Richmond Daily Dispatch*, March 18, 1864; "Church Intelligence," *Southern Churchman*, December 14, 1865; quotation from "Report of the Board of Directors of the M. Orphan Society at the City of Richmond for April 1864," Philip Francis Howard Papers, LVA; Elna C. Green, *This Business of Relief: Confronting Poverty in a Southern City, 1740–1940* (Athens: University of Georgia Press, 2003), 82; E. Susan Barber, "The Female Humane Association and Richmond's White Civil War Orphans," in *Before the New Deal: Social Welfare in the South, 1830–1930*, ed. Elna C. Green (Athens: University of Georgia Press, 1999), 127; clipping, "Male Orphan Asylum," May 31, 1877, Minute Book, 1870–1901, 72, RMOA Records.

4. "Report of Board of Managers, Presented to Annual Meeting, Spring of 1862," Philip Francis Howard Papers, LVA.

5. Admittance Books, box 22, folder 11, RFHA Records; Boys Home Registry, 1846–1925, box 6, RMOA Records.

6. First quotation, loose minutes sheets, December 4, 1871, RFHA Records; second quotation, Clipping, "Male Orphan Asylum—What One of Our Charitable Institutions Has Done and Is Doing," Minute Book, 1870–1901, p. 17, RMOA Records.

7. 1875 Annual Report, Minute Book, 1870–1901, 59, RMOA Records; Clipping, "Male Orphan Asylum," May 31, 1877, Minute Book, 1870–1901, 72, RMOA Records; "An Act to Amend the Charter of the Female Humane Association of the City of Richmond," approved February 28, 1874, box 24, folder 14, RFHA Records.

8. Clipping, "Male Orphan Society," June 10, 1874, Minute Book, 1870–1901, 52, RMOA Records.

9. Admittance Books, box 22, folder 11, RFHA Records; Boys Home Registry, 1846–1925, box 6, RMOA Records; Barber, 128.

10. "An Appeal to the Young Ladies of Richmond," *Richmond Daily Dispatch*, February 15, 1866; Robert Stiles, *Address Delivered at the Twenty-Second Anniversary of the Richmond Male Orphan Asylum, April 19th, 1869* (Richmond: Gary, Clemmitt and Jones, Printers, 1869), LVA.

11. First quotation, Stiles, "An Appeal"; second quotation, clipping, "Male Orphan Asylum Annual Meeting and Address," June 25, 1872, Minute Book, 1870–1901, 25, RMOA Records.

12. Amy R. Minton, "Defining Respectability: Morality, Patriotism, and Confederate Identity in Richmond's Civil War Public Press," in *Crucible of the Civil War: Virginia from Secession to Commemoration*, ed. Edward L. Ayers, Gary Gallagher, and Andrew Torget (Charlottesville: University of Virginia Press, 2006), 80–105.

13. "Our Orphan Children," *Richmond Daily Dispatch*, October 19, 1866.

14. Quotation from report of the Board of Directors, December 1, 1877; "An Act to Amend the Charter of the Female Humane Association of the City of Richmond" Approved February 28, 1874, RFHA Records; Asylum Minutes, April 10, 1876, 65–66, Minute Book, 1870–1901, RMOA Records.

15. Minutes, September 17, 1872, Minute Book, 1870–1901, 28, RMOA Records.

16. Minutes, November 21, 1877, Minute Book, 1870–1901, 69, RMOA Records; Minutes, June 5, 1876, RFHA Records.

17. On McNamee, see Minutes, June 13, 1870; for other examples, see, e.g., February 19, 1872; October 21, 1872, Minute Book, 1870–1901, RMOS Records; Minutes on Annual Meeting, December 3, 1877, RFHA Records.

18. June Purcell Guild, *Black Laws of Virginia: A Summary of the Legislative Acts of Virginia Concerning Negroes from Earliest Times to the Present* (Richmond, VA: Whittet and Shepperson, 1936), 179, 218. For more on the apprenticeship of black children, see, e.g., Barbara J. Fields, *Slavery and Freedom on the Middle Ground* (New Haven: Yale University Press, 1985), and Karin L. Zipf, *Labor of Innocents: Forced Apprenticeship in North Carolina, 1715–1919* (Baton Rouge: Louisiana State University Press, 2005).

19. Quotation from minutes, November 16, 1867, Jackson Orphan Asylum Records, LVA.

20. Quotations from clipping, "Male Orphan Asylum," May 31, 1877, Minute Book, 1870–1901, 72; see also Minutes of Annual Meeting, June 17, 146–47, RMOA Records; Annual Report, 1882–1883, RFHA Records.

21. Minutes of annual meeting, December 4, 1876, RFHA Records; first quotation, clipping, "Male Orphan Society Annual Meeting," June 10, 1874, Minute Book, 1870–1901, 52, RMOA Records; clipping, "Annual Meeting of the Male Orphan Society," 1879, Minute Book, 1870–1901, 94, RMOA Records.

22. Michael Grossberg, *Governing the Hearth: Law and Family in Nineteenth-Century America* (Chapel Hill: University of North Carolina Press, 1985), 268–73; quotation from minutes, July 29, 1867, Jackson Orphan Asylum Records, LVA; Letter read into minutes, August 29, 1867, Minutes, Jackson Orphan Asylum Records, LVA.

23. First quotation, loose clipping, "Male Orphan Asylum: Annual Meeting—Election of Officers—Addresses, &c." [1873]; Minutes, June 15, 1884, Minute Book, 1870–1901, RMOA Records.

24. Quotation from clipping, "Male Orphan Asylum, Anniversary Celebration" [1877], Minute Book, 1870–1901, RMOA Records.

25. Ann Sarah Rubin, *A Shattered Nation: The Rise and Fall of the Confederacy* (Chapel Hill: University of North Carolina Press, 2005), 7; William A. Blair, *Cities of the Dead: Contesting the Memory of the Civil War in the South, 1865–1914* (Chapel Hill: University of North Carolina Press, 2004), 127–43.

26. See, for instance, Timothy James Lockley, *Welfare and Charity in the Antebellum South* (Gainesville: University Press of Florida, 2007), 37–54; Shelley Sallee, *The Whiteness of Child Labor Reform in the New South* (Athens: University of Georgia Press, 2004).

12

Orphans and Indians

Pennsylvania's Soldiers' Orphan Schools and
the Landscape of Postwar Childhood

JUDITH GEISBERG

In her 1885 annual report on the status of Pennsylvania's Soldiers' Orphan Schools, inspector Elizabeth Hutter strayed from her usual bland descriptions of contented children and smoothly run schools to wax eloquent about the larger meaning of this grand experiment in public welfare begun during the Civil War. Describing the cannons at the Gettysburg National Cemetery, guns that had stood silent for more than twenty years beside the graves of dead soldiers, Hutter spoke of birds making nests inside the barrels. "No longer these great guns belch forth fire, smoke, and death," Hutter declared, "but they now serve as the peaceful home of the sweet songsters that now fill the beautiful herbage and trees which mark the growth of twenty years of peace." Grown, too, were the children of the brave men who died in that war. Yet the orphan schools lived on, serving the children of veterans who died years after the war and those who became incapacitated or incapable of supporting their families. Hutter found "a wonderful resemblance between the nests of defenceless little birds" and the soldiers' orphan schools, which she called "the larger nests." Like the songbirds that made their homes inside the dormant cannons, Pennsylvania orphans were cared for in peaceful homes, protected from the tragedies of the past and the dangers of the contemporary world.[1]

Full of sentimentality and self-congratulation, the annual report gave no inkling of the controversy that was about to wash over Pennsylvania's Solders' Orphan Schools, a controversy over which both Elizabeth Hutter and her fellow inspector John Sayers would lose their jobs and one that would resonate throughout the country. And in the eye of the storm stood the children of Pennsylvania soldiers, along with questions about how best—and who best—to care for them. In the twenty years since the war, communities that housed the schools changed considerably, and a generation of children grew up with none of their own memories of the war. The schools, though, stayed the same, frozen in time, like the cannons on the quieted Pennsylvania battlefield. Boys were still issued uniforms and received military training, and members of the Grand Army of the Republic periodically dropped in to watch them drill. Meanwhile, outside the schools, scientific reformers and experts raised new questions about how best to prepare children for adulthood, how to assimilate immigrants and others, and how education might help contain the disorder of modern life.[2] Within a few months of Hutter's report, Pennsylvania's Solders' Orphan Schools became subjects of intense scrutiny, much of it centered on finding solutions to industrial labor problems. And in only four years, all but one of the schools would be closed.

For two decades, the schools had been celebrated as institutions through which a grateful nation repaid the sacrifices of a generation. Then, rather suddenly, Pennsylvanians came to see the schools not as a solution to the problem of wartime displacement but rather as a source of a number of modern problems. Elizabeth Hutter's "peaceful homes" became battlegrounds, where children were buffeted by crusading reformers, conspiring politicians, muckraking journalists, and aging veterans all claiming to have the orphans' best interests in mind. This essay tells the story of the end of Pennsylvania's Solders' Orphan Schools—the first and the most ambitious attempt to care for Civil War orphans—placing the closures within the context of contemporary debates about the assimilation of immigrants and Indians and growing fears of labor radicalism. Some participants in the debate complained that the orphans were as mistreated as the Indians; others feared they were potentially as dangerous as labor radicals. The Civil War had raised questions about class and race: What would distinguish American class relations from those of Europe, for example, and what sort of citizenship would be extended to people of color? When the schools closed twenty years later, they represented an outdated ideal of class relations among reformers and legislators who equated the problems of poverty with race. Schools could no more save the children of poor white men than they could solve the problem of racial diversity—but they might aggravate both problems.

Controversy and Investigation

The *Philadelphia Record* broke the news in a dramatic front-page article on February 22, 1886. The stacked headline told much of the story: "Soldiers' Orphans: A Syndicate's Traffic upon Humanity. Official Corruption, Neglect, Discrimination—Bathing Orphans in Pickle Barrels—A Furnace Cellar for a Playroom—Crowded Three and Four Children into One Bed—Forcing Them to Wear the Same Clothing in Winter and Summer." The operators of Pennsylvania's network of privately owned soldiers' orphan schools had conspired to deprive 1,600 children of the most basic care, pocketing the annual per child allowance given them by the state while they crowded children into close quarters and denied them an education. The once "grand purpose" of Pennsylvania, the article explained, was being "prostituted" as owners profited from exploiting the orphans entrusted to their care. Spending most of their time "scrubbing floors and peeling potatoes," the children received little schooling and were left to fend for themselves when they became ill. The exposé left little doubt that something had gone terribly wrong at institutions that had long stood as stalwart reminders of the state's generosity to the poor children of veterans. But in case any doubt remained, the author John Norris made pointed and deliberate comparisons between the soldiers' orphan schools and Dotheboys Hall, the infamous English boarding school portrayed in Charles Dickens's *Nicholas Nickleby*. In vivid and sensational prose, Norris described the thin potato soup afforded hundreds of orphans who were forced to watch as school officials "breakfasted on chops and delicious etcetera." Like "the unfortunate pupils" in the care of Dotheboys' "Wackford Squeers, Esq., the mere sight of the officer's plate" piled high with delicacies agitated Pennsylvania's hungry little orphans.[2]

The Dickens comparison stuck as the story was repeated in papers around the country. Weeks later, the *New York Times* referred to the "so-called Soldiers' Orphan School" in Mercer, Pennsylvania, as "[a]nother Do-the-Boys Hall." In March, Pennsylvania's young crusading governor Robert Pattison—an American Nicholas Nickleby—launched a personal investigation of the schools. Pattison brought along Attorney General Lewis Cassidy and the reporter from the *Philadelphia Record* who had authored the damning exposé. For several weeks, the three visited schools and took testimony from school principals, inspectors, and students, and Pattison kept the papers informed of what he found. Follow-up news stories corroborated the *Record*'s account of grievous crimes committed against the children of the state's veterans.[3]

Frank Leslie's Illustrated Newspaper ran a story on Pattison's investigation, complete with a full page of illustrations inspired by testimony taken from orphans at the Mount Joy School in Lancaster. Nine frames summed up problems found in several schools, including, counterclockwise from the top, the use of dirty and inadequate dormitories and lavatories; failure to provide the children with adequate clothing; use of older orphans in place of medical professionals; crowding of multiple children into narrow beds; inadequate play rooms (the *Record* referred to the basement at Mount Joy as a "foul dungeon"); boys working instead of learning marketable skills; bathing multiple children together in pickle barrels ("Pickling Orphans," read the *Record* headline); and, finally, the death of an ill child left alone in his room. Whereas the original story singled out so-called syndicate schools run by joint-stock owners who profited by overcrowding and understaffing— Mount Joy, Mercer, Chester Springs, and McAlisterville—out-of-state papers picked up and repeated one or more of the charges, leaving the impression that neglect was endemic and that the entire network of schools was kept in operation only to line the pockets of Keystone State Republicans. As Democrats in a state controlled by Republicans, Pattison and Cassidy might have ignored counterevidence, but, in any case, testimony taken by Pattison left little doubt that children were not being adequately cared for.[4]

Much of the testimony focused on determining who was profiting from the schools, but the scope of the questions was expansive. Pattison and Cassidy asked repeatedly about how much food and clothing was provided the children, the kind of health problems the children suffered, how much time they spent in instruction, and if they prayed at night. And the governor vigorously pursued local rumors about abuse and sexual misconduct at the schools, pushing teachers and students to come forth with names of children and adults involved. With an eye toward the public's interest in the story, the investigation became a spectacle of its own, as the governor and his attorney general asked children to remove their shoes to reveal the holes in their socks and to undress so that the men could examine the children's bodies for evidence of neglect and abuse. Thirteen-year-old James Ginley, for instance, was at first reluctant to talk about his skin ailments, but the governor persisted, until the boy "expose[d] his loins" for the three men so that they could satisfy their curiosity that the boy was suffering from "camp itch." One line of questioning that ran through the entire investigation focused on establishing the details of how, when, and by whom the children were bathed; another had to do with the intimate sleeping arrangements that resulted from overcrowding at the syndicate schools. Once the governor established that schools provided inadequate arrangements for sleeping and bathing the children, questions posed repeatedly to young children about bathing practices and what clothes they wore to bed were gratuitous and seemed to be aimed at making good newspaper copy rather than turning up any new details. Indeed, *Leslie's* illustration of the three young boys crowded into bed and the suggestively empty pickle barrel invited readers to see for themselves what their crusading governor had witnessed.[5]

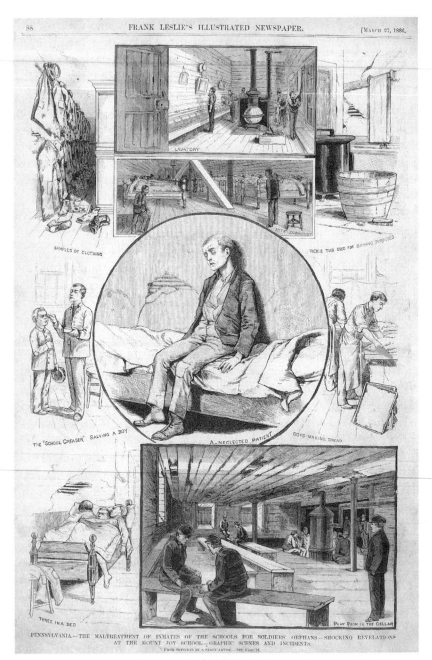

Figure 12.1. *Maltreatment of Inmates of the Schools for Soldiers' Orphans, Frank Leslie's Illustrated Newspaper*, March 27, 1886. Library Company of Philadelphia.

The self-righteous tone and the sometimes prurient details of the depositions served political aspirations; indeed, the orphan schools had always served humanitarian and political purposes simultaneously. The nascent Republican Party had come to power promising to steer clear of the labor problems and class divisions that plagued Europe at midcentury. The orphan schools were supposed to give poor children of soldiers the education and preparation for adulthood denied children of their class—boys were to acquire training in skilled labor, and girls were to be prepared for domesticity. Two decades later, Pennsylvania's young, inexperienced governor was in search of an issue to raise his political profile in the last year of his term when he decided on the orphans. Preceded and succeeded as governor by men with distinguished military careers and impeccable Republican credentials, Pattison had neither when he ran for office in 1882 and again in 1890. Although the investigation had all the qualities of a rescue operation, Pattison left office in the fall of 1886 having done little to effect a change in the soldiers' orphan schools and leaving the fate of 1,600 children in the hands of his Republican successor, James Beaver. Under Beaver, the state legislature took over the schools and began closing them down. In 1895, when the state opened up a new State Industrial School, only three schools remained in operation, and Robert Pattison was completing his second term as governor. The upstart Pattison might have been out to score some short-term political points against an entrenched Republican Party, as his critics charged, but the public applauded the closing of the schools and sought to put the matter behind them. Schools that had stood for twenty years as a model of child welfare and as reminders of a generation that had sought to ameliorate class relations had outlived their usefulness.[6]

Beyond the politics, the governor's investigation resonated with the public because it reflected changes in social anxieties since the Civil War. Americans who still hoped that the United States could avoid Europe's labor troubles need not have looked for counterevidence further than Pittsburgh, where three years earlier Pattison had called out the state militia to protect Andrew Carnegie's Homestead steelworks after a violent encounter between Carnegie's armed guards and striking workers and their families. It was altogether fitting that the last of the state's orphans were mustered out as the state militia were mustered in to put down the threat of organized labor. Even so, this was an end that Robert Pattison could not have foreseen. And he deserves neither the blame for ending a system that began as an expression of the best impulses of one generation nor sole credit for having exposed the worst blunders of another. Indeed, Pattison set into motion something that had been long in coming. By the late nineteenth century, professional reformers insisted that charitable institutions exacerbated the problem of poverty, and most believed class tension was endemic. In addition, the continued existence of the schools invited apt comparisons between American and European class relations in which the treatment of children figured prominently. Indeed, whereas by the end of the century, middle-class parents increasingly sought to protect children *from* the adult world instead of preparing them *for* it, poor children were neither prepared nor protected. The social context in which poor children grew up had changed considerably since the founding of the orphan schools.

Pennsylvania's Soldiers' Orphan Schools and Antebellum Child Saving

Although perhaps apocryphal, the oft-told story of the origin of the schools became an integral part of Keystone State Republican orthodoxy nonetheless, particularly around election time. On the morning of Thanksgiving, November 26, 1863, two orphaned children "clad in rags, timid, and piteously begging" knocked on the door of the executive mansion in search of food. Governor Andrew Gregg Curtin came to the door to greet the children, learning, according to James Paul's *Pennsylvania's Soldiers' Orphan Schools*, "how their father had been killed in battle, how their mother had since died, and how they had been left utterly friendless and alone." Curtin was so moved by the encounter that later, over dinner, he shared their story with family and friends gathered in the executive dining room. At a speech at the Academy of Music in Philadelphia that winter, Curtin publicly declared his intention to do something to care for children left fatherless by the war, referring to both the children and their widowed mothers as "the children of the State," whose care was a matter not of charity but of "justice." Having secured a donation of $50,000 from the president of the Pennsylvania Railroad to use for the orphans, Curtin appealed to state lawmakers in his annual message to the legislature the following January.[7]

There was little agreement about how to go about caring for the state's military orphans, with some legislators preferring something close to a system of foster care, where the state would subsidize their care in private homes near mothers or siblings, and others insisting that the children should be gathered in institutions for better economy and more efficient supervision. Those who opposed the fostering plan believed that removing the children from their communities was the best way to prevent them from pursuing a life of crime. "By withdrawing them from want," one state lawmaker averred in defense of

Curtin's plan to gather children in institutions, "the State places them beyond the temptation to commit crime to-day [so that] hereafter we may not fill our almshouses and prisons with paupers and criminals." Frustrated by the lack of legislative consensus, in the summer of 1864 Governor Curtin moved forward on a plan, negotiating to place older orphans at boarding schools and younger ones at private orphanages, appointing a superintendent, and devising an admissions process. The legislature eventually approved his plan. But with nine schools up and running, fewer than 100 children had become "children of the state" by December 1864—evidence, perhaps, of widows' reluctance to hand over care of their children to distant institutions. The pace of admissions accelerated rapidly as the war drew to a close—and when the fate of their fathers could no longer be denied—and by the end of 1865, more than 1,000 children had entered institutions. In the next year, the number of orphans in the schools doubled, with a total of 2,681 children enrolled. The superintendent's 1867 annual report expressed concern that with 3,180 orphans, the schools were nearing capacity and that spending would soon exceed state appropriations.[8]

Once established, Pennsylvania's Soldiers' Orphan Schools grew to encompass fifteen schools serving children from ten to sixteen years old and more than twenty schools accepting younger children. Orphan schools were distributed throughout Pennsylvania, with schools for older children located in the west at Mercer, Phillipsburg, and Uniontown; two schools located along Pennsylvania's northern tier at Titusville and Mansfield; and eight clustered near Philadelphia and along the Main Line leading west. The orphan schools were privately owned; many of the schools accepting younger soldiers' orphans predated the war and were religiously affiliated. In a decision that was consistent with care provided by existing private institutions, children of color were cared for in separate institutions. Philadelphia's Girard College began admitting white orphan boys in 1848, setting a racial precedent that would be followed by the soldiers' orphan schools; unlike Girard, though, the orphan schools admitted girls and boys. As at Girard, the children at the orphan schools were technically half-orphans, as their mothers were living but were unable to support them. After 1875, surviving veterans could enroll their children in the orphan schools, if they incurred disabilities related to their service.[9]

The orphan schools quickly became a matter of state pride. The orphans were regularly trotted out for Republican Party rallies and Memorial Day parades, where they sang patriotic songs and displayed the potential of an intensely patriotic curriculum. On July 4, 1866, for instance, children from soldiers' orphan schools throughout the state came to Philadelphia to participate in a grand procession of veterans marking the return of "the colors," the battle flags of Pennsylvania's Civil War regiments. Six hundred fifty orphans joined the parade in front of Independence Hall, falling in behind Governor Curtin. Wearing white, the girls rode in ambulances escorted by colorfully dressed fireman and "delighted the spectators with singing patriotic songs." The boys, wearing military dress and divided into companies, marched alongside the war-worn veterans and their tattered battle flags. Whereas earlier in the day the streets of Philadelphia had swarmed with raucous young boys setting off fireworks and generally running amok, the neatly dressed orphan boys marching with soldierly precision provided a noteworthy contrast, one that the reporter for the *Philadelphia Inquirer* took careful note of as he lavished praise on the latter, whom he called "the Children of the Commonwealth."[10]

With their emphasis on military training for the boys and instruction in domestic work for the girls, the orphan schools reflected a contemporary understanding of childhood as preparation for adulthood. The Civil War created large numbers of orphans, deepened and accentuated class divisions, and sent middle-class and working-class children on divergent paths toward adulthood. During the war, almshouses and city streets filled with the wives and young children of enlisted and drafted men looking for relief and forced northerners to face the grim realities of a long and destructive war. Among families that remained intact, historians have noted significant changes in the experience of childhood, with fathers returning from the war but remaining on the periphery of more intense maternal-child relationships. Middle-class families turned inward in response to wartime disruption, as parents lavished more attention on their children and sought to protect them from— rather than prepare them for—the harsh realities of adult life.[11]

In the meantime, working-class and poor children continued to live on the verge of adulthood, performing key economic functions and filling in for absentee or missing parents. Children's work was as essential to the expansion of industry as it was to working-class family economic survival. Facing declining opportunities to apprentice with a skilled craftsman, children of the working class entered the factories or made their living on the streets. Intent on instructing children in "the greatest variety possible of household and domestic pursuits, and mechanical and agricultural employments," Pennsylvania's Solders' Orphan Schools were an ambitious attempt to rescue children from poverty by providing them with the education and skills their parents could not. Middle-class reformers believed that saving poor children required removing them from the corrupting influences of the streets and often of their parents, resulting in the rapid expansion of private orphanages in the first half of the century.[12]

Full of contradictions, orphanages provided an essential social service but were simultaneously applauded and reviled—often in the same breath. Working-class parents used orphanages as temporary refuge for their children when they could not support them. The popularity of literary orphans such as Dickens's Oliver Twist and Twain's Huckleberry Finn revealed the period's contradictory responses to orphans and the asylums that housed them. Whereas orphans were objects of pity and curiosity, they were also a public nuisance. Orphanages were bleak institutions that bred class resentment, but they also kept orphans off the street and contained their disruptive potential. Considering the growing expense of the schools, Pennsylvania's legislators decided that it was money well spent, particularly when they considered the alternative, estimating that "if only a dozen of these children would be cast out and become vagabonds and useless to society and addicted perhaps to vice and crime, it would be enough of an impulse to continue the schools."[13]

The orphans who came begging at Andrew Curtin's door just a few days after the governor returned from the dedication of the cemetery at Gettysburg were a stark reminder of the toll the Civil War was taking both on and off the battlefield. Collecting the children of men who fell on the battlefield, providing them an education, and training them in a skill was consistent with the work of antebellum reformers intent on saving the unfortunate children of the poor. Schools were a better solution than almshouses that served as shelters of last resort for mothers and the children they could not support but also invalid men and often common criminals. But even as the idea was being hatched by the governor and enthusiastically applauded by middle-class reformers, it represented an ideal of juvenile protection that was out of reach for working class-children and one that the state was ill equipped to provide for them.

A Clash of Expectation and Reality

The mothers' initial reluctance to commit their children to the schools highlights a difference of opinion about the function of the institutions, one that would resurface from time to time for the duration of their existence. Mothers who expected the soldiers' orphans' schools to be responsive to their seasonal need for assistance ran up against the limitations of a state budget that allocated funds in June, leaving the schools pinching pennies and limiting admissions as the colder months approached. An October 1868 article in a Harrisburg newspaper revealed that on a daily basis the state turned away requests "pleading for the admission of children before cold weather sets in" from "mothers sick or out of employment, and unable to supply the actual necessities of themselves and their children." In addition to the limitations of the state budget, parents had to negotiate the schools' academic calendar, which released children for vacations but only those children with letters from family members. Once their children were admitted to the schools, mothers struggled to keep in touch with them, particularly when schools transferred children from overcrowded urban schools to facilities some distance away. Letters to mothers describing abuse periodically found their way into the papers, like one about the Mount Joy School in which a girl described confinement and whippings and begged her mother not to "tell that I wrote this," suggesting that worse punishment would follow. A mother who visited the school in Chester Springs wrote to the paper about her shock at the dirty appearance and "the insolence and impudence" of the students, declaring "that the boys and girls in almshouses and the convicts in the penitentiaries were better off." Through their parents, children revealed that they received good food only when visitors were present. "Here comes Mrs. Hutter, she'll bring some butter," was how the children at one school spread the word. Although the papers periodically offered an alternative to the public's celebration of orphan schools' successes, charges of neglect and corruption at the schools did not lead to public outcry until the 1880s.[14]

School administrators energetically defended the schools from complaints, but the annual reports they filed tell a different story. Finding resistance to and difficulties in placing out children as apprentices, the schools assumed sole responsibility to train them in useful trades, although fulfilling this promise proved difficult. Superintendent George McFarland found a number of deficiencies at the schools in his first annual report, including "grave omissions or abuses in thoroughness and regularity of instruction" and systems of agricultural and industrial training that were "almost total failures." The mostly rural schools were particularly ill equipped to provide anything other than agricultural training, and with the rapid mechanization of agriculture in the postwar era, graduates would likely have found such training to be of little use. Within a decade of opening the schools, administrators began loudly clamoring for them to take up the challenges of providing the children with the skills necessary to perform new specialized industrial jobs. James Wickersham, the superintendent who followed McFarland, believed that what was needed were "schools where boys can be trained in the sciences which are invoked in the every-day business of life," in particular those that would prepare men to work in mines, iron and steel manufacturing, and construction. With schools hamstrung in their ability to provide students with practical skills, administrators struggled to define the purpose of the schools beyond their custodial functions, the provision of rudimentary literacy, and an introduction to military discipline. No one associated with the schools believed that the children were "to be trained up under the impression that they are exempt from the necessity of labor for their bread," as one administrator put it, but critics charged that the schools were doing little to prepare them for the industrial workplace.[15]

Worse, perhaps, than raising the children to have class aspirations were concerns that the schools might foster class resentment. Despite her sanguine assessment of the schools, inspector Elizabeth Hutter expressed concerns similar to Wickersham's and McFarland's. Hutter insisted that the failure of industrial training left graduates of Pennsylvania's Solders' Orphan Schools to compete unfavorably with immigrants, a situation that she found intolerable and potentially dangerous. Forced to accept lower wages and to work for foreigners, local boys, she believed, fell prey to trade unionists and others, forgetting that they had been educated to be "true citizens." Hutter saw her work with the orphans as critically important to combating the twin threats of immigration and labor radicalism. In her 1878 annual report, Hutter congratulated Governor John Hartranft for calling out the National Guard and using federal troops to put down the Great Railroad Strike of 1877, but she warned that "the railroad troubles" had "showed to this people what communism means." "Better pour out the money from the State Treasury to train up the children in the way they should go," she offered, than allow them to "become the prey of rioters." While she celebrated the governor's use of force against striking workers and their families, Hutter entreated the principals of the schools to find alternatives to the use of corporal punishment in the schools. The inspector ran a lonely campaign to combat whipping in the schools, one that she ultimately lost but one that was related to her fears that the schools fostered resentment in young adults—boys, particularly— leaving them vulnerable to the influences of rioters and communists. Rather than warm nests that nurtured their young charges gently to adulthood, Hutter dealt with schools that harshly disciplined children and left them with few useful skills, and that, she believed, had become breeding grounds for the next generation of labor radicals. Despite the hopes expressed in her annual reports, the dramatic newspaper exposé—and the investigation that followed—confirmed Elizabeth Hutter's worst fears.[16]

Hutter's attitude toward immigrants and unions was typical for postwar Americans who resented labor radicalism as un-American and who linked it to the problem of immigration. Immigrants and the incendiary attitudes they brought with them were contributing to a hardening of American class relations, making America look like the Old World. Watching the new arrivals crowding into the streets of postwar Philadelphia, Hutter, like many of her contemporaries, worried about the strange customs they brought with them; these thoughts brought her back to the children at Pennsylvania's Solders' Orphan Schools, where she believed it might still be possible to raise boys and girls to be "true citizens." Shaped by her concerns about assimilation and labor radicalism, Hutter hoped that industrial training in combination with military drill would redeem Pennsylvania's orphan boys, instilling in them the value of hard work and inoculating them against the influences of radicalism. Once trained and drilled, orphans might serve as a source of redemption, securing the nation's industrial future by displacing foreign radicals who dominated the ranks of skilled labor and filling out the ranks of the army. Noting with regret the aging condition of the Civil War veterans who visited the schools, Hutter hoped that the schools might continue to produce "young recruits to fill the ranks." Like the fictional orphan who saves the rich boy from drowning in Horatio Alger's *Ragged Dick* (1867), the children of Pennsylvania's Solders' Orphan Schools might still save postwar America.[17]

Pennsylvania Orphans and the Postwar Politics of Race

In a comparison that revealed the altered social contexts in which the soldiers' orphan schools were operating, *Frank Leslie's* coverage of the controversy spoke of scheming politicians and broken contracts leaving the orphans to fare "somewhat as the Indians." Whereas the *Philadelphia Record's* original exposé sought to attract the public's attention by making marked comparisons to Europe, referring to the schools as Dotheboys Hall and the teachers who would pile their plates high with delicacies as Wackford Squeers, *Leslie's* found a reference closer to home. By the 1880s, the long and costly Indian Wars were nearly complete, and Americans were moved to once again celebrate the U.S. Army's victory over a once intractable enemy. With the 1881 publication of Helen Hunt Jackson's *Century of Dishonor*, public attention had been drawn to the plight of Native Americans forced from their ancestral homes and living in squalid conditions, and the following year, a group of Philadelphia reformers formed the Indian Rights Association intent on "producing such public feeling and Congressional action to bring about the complete civilization of the Indians and their admission to citizenship." Appealing to similar sentiments, *Leslie's* hoped that the orphans would receive justice, "now that the light of public and Legislative attention has been thrown into the dark places"—in this case, Pennsylvania's Soldiers' Orphan Schools.[18]

Referring to orphans as Indians, then, was intended to elicit readers' sympathies: no longer threats, Indians were pitiable, defeated people. On the other hand, Americans now faced pressing questions about what sort of citizenship would be extended to Native Americans and, more significantly, how to assimilate a people to American values who had proved so resistant to them. *Leslie's* images of half-dressed and dirty orphans seemed to confirm the point—rather than turning orphans into citizens, the schools were turning them into Indians. By crowding, neglecting, and misusing them, the orphan schools were producing an environment—similar to those found on Indian reservations and in immigrant neighborhoods and camps of displaced freedmen—in which children grew to reject American values.

These were the same issues Elizabeth Hutter's contemporaries Samuel C. Armstrong and Richard Pratt were attempting to address in building schools for freedmen and American Indians. By 1879, Pratt had begun his assimilation work at Carlisle Indian School, based on an idea he had developed while working with Armstrong, founder of Hampton Institute in Virginia, a school for freedmen and Indians. An appropriate education for morally deficient people of color, Armstrong argued, was one that encompassed "the head, the heart, and the hand." While inspecting the fifteen schools that were part of Pennsylvania's Soldiers' Orphan Schools, Hutter most likely became familiar with Pratt's work; she would have passed through Carlisle traveling between the Mount Joy School in Lancaster and schools farther north and west, such as those at Loysville, Cassville, and McAlisterville. Perhaps she had Carlisle in mind when she called for industrial training for orphans so that "the hand, heart, and head" could be "trained in sweet unison." But whereas Armstrong believed that once civilized by the benign influences of Hampton teachers (head and heart) and having received manual training (hand), freedmen would serve as cultural missionaries to the black community, Pratt insisted civilized Indians must never go back—or, as he liked to put it, "kill the Indian, save the man." So potent was the influence of race on Native Americans, Pratt believed, that assimilation would never be complete.[19]

Comparing orphans to "Indians" indicates how ideas were shared between various reform communities, and the reference reveals how race and class had become conflated. Midcentury reformers believed that education could overcome class and race, educating poor whites, freedmen, and perhaps even Native Americans to citizenship. But even as these ideas came to maturity in institutions created by educators such as Richard Pratt, they came up against strong cultural currents that held separate institutions suspect. Indeed, Pratt identified this tension when he blamed separation for the "suspicions and antagonisms" felt by Indians and whites. At the turn of the century, schools enlisted in the ambitious project of Americanization paid little attention to African Americans or Indians, focusing instead on immigrant workers and the production of industrial peace through assimilation and corporate loyalty.[20]

Pennsylvania's Soldiers' Orphan Schools might have served as models for this new generation of institutions hoping to solve modern problems, but instead the empty schools stood as reminders of a lost opportunity. In the midst of the Civil War, ambitious reformers and lawmakers imagined that, given an education and a trade, the children of poor soldiers might be rescued from poverty—and that the nation, too, might be spared. Having sought to protect their own children from the adult world, they sought to do the same for the children of men who had died on the battlefield. Steeped in the ideology of free labor, Civil War northerners believed that Americans would transcend class divisions, avoiding the bleak future of permanent class conflict they saw unfolding in Europe. The continued need for the schools long after the children who had been orphaned by the war grew up, however, revealed that the war had ushered in two separate paths to adulthood: one traveled by middle-class children and one by the children of the poor. Gone, too, was inspector Elizabeth Hutter, who had believed she might rescue orphans from the industrialists and labor radicals who would exploit them. She was later removed from her position when Governor Pattison discovered that she and others held stock in overcrowded syndicate schools. Hutter's plight reveals how idealism might come to look very much like greed. Without the statewide soldiers' orphan schools, children whose mothers could not support them likely went to work in Pennsylvania's coal mines, lumber yards, oil fields, steel manufacturing, or other industries that relied on the labor of children. Reformers had come to see class like race, as something intractable. By then, the orphan schools had little to offer Americans who, while they continued to entertain the idea that individual children—with all the pluck and resolve of a Ragged Dick, perhaps—could overcome the problem of poverty, there was little hope in an institutional solution.

1. Elizabeth Hutter, "Reports of the Inspectors: Report of Mrs. E. E. Hutter," *Annual Report of the Superintendent of Soldiers' Orphans*, Scotland (PA) School for Veterans' Children, Pennsylvania State Archives, Pennsylvania Humanities and Museum Commission, Record Group 19, 1885, 17.

2. Steven Mintz argues that in the postwar years, the public became more actively concerned with defining and protecting children's welfare, and reformers began to enlist the state for help in solving problems such as child abuse and prostitution and to Americanization efforts, such as Richard Pratt's Indian boarding schools. By the end of the nineteenth century, reformers invoking "the principles of professionalization, scientific expertise, and rational administration" had greatly expanded the role of the state and experts in solving the problems of childhood. The reforms achieved by professional reformers during the Progressive Era are too numerous to name, but they begin with the passage of compulsory school attendance laws and laws restricting child labor, reduction of infant mortality through public health initiatives, and the establishment of the juvenile court system. Steven Mintz, *Huck's Raft: A History of American Childhood* (Cambridge: Harvard University Press, 2004), 167 172, 172–184. For immigrant Americanization, see Selma Berrol, *Immigrants at School* (New York: Arno Press, 1978). And for a damning assessment of the limitations of Progressive era educational reform, see David Macleod, *The Age of the Child: Children in America 1890–1920* (New York: Twayne, 1998).

2. "Soldiers' Orphans, A Syndicate's Traffic Upon Humanity," *Philadelphia Record*, February 22, 1886.

3. "Another Do-the-Boys Hall," *New York Times*, March 17, 1886; "Wright's Letter. A Photograph of the Original Document," *Philadelphia Record*, March 22, 1886; "Orphans' Schools: Overhauling the Clothing Accounts of Do-the-Boys Halls," *Philadelphia Inquirer*, March 30, 1886. *Inquirer* accessed through *America's Historical Newspapers*, ser. 1–5, 1690–1922, December 1, 2009.

4. "The Pennsylvania Soldiers' Orphans' Schools," *Frank Leslie's Illustrated*, March 27, 1886.

5. The complete transcript of Governor Pattison's investigation was entered into public record in the 1887 session of the Pennsylvania legislature. Appendix, *The Legislative Record, Containing the Debates and Proceedings of the Legislature of Pennsylvania, for the Session 1887*, Historical Society of Pennsylvania, nos. 367–399, 2921–3185; testimony of James Ginley, *Legislative Record*, 2951.

6. O. David Gold, "The Soldiers' Orphan Schools of Pennsylvania, 1864–1889" (PhD diss., University of Maryland, 1971), 68–70; "Let Us Have No More Scandals," *Philadelphia Inquirer*, July 31, 1889.

7. James Laughery Paul, *Pennsylvania's Soldiers' Orphan Schools: Giving a Brief Account of the Origin of the Late Civil War, and Rise and Progress of the Orphan System, and Legislative Enactments Relating Thereto* (Harrisburg, PA: Lane S. Hart, 1877), 31; Curtin quotation on p. 33.

8. Paul, *Pennsylvania's Soldiers' Orphan Schools*, 35–43, 58, 52–53, 125–30; George F. McFarland, *Annual Report of the Superintendent*, 1867, 3–4. In 1867 a school for "colored soldiers' orphans" was opened, but few women of color took the state up on its offer, with only 124 children placed by 1868 and only after a committee traveled throughout the state meeting with mothers whom they believed were "entirely ignorant" of state provisions. With no explanation offered, the "Home for Destitute Colored Children" vanished from

McFarland's annual reports in 1869, suggesting that the school was closed after two years or that it no longer received state funding. Unfortunately, no further information has been identified. The following statistics, taken from the first five annual reports, indicate the growth of the system early on: 1866: 2,681 students; 1867, 3,180 (1,306 females); 1868: 3,431 (1,378 females); 1869: 3,631 (1,499 females); 1870: 3,530 (1,468 females). That more than half of all orphans at the schools in any given year were male speaks to contemporary preferences for keeping girls at home, perhaps, and to the expectation that the schools would provide both military and vocational training. Similarly, Richard Pratt had little luck recruiting girls to Hampton, perhaps also a reflection of the former. Donal Lindsey, *Indians at Hampton Institute* (Urbana: University of Illinois Press, 1995), 35.

9. Gold, "The Soldiers' Orphan Schools of Pennsylvania, 1864–1889," 196; Amos H. Mylin, *State Prisons, Hospitals, Soldiers' Homes, and Orphan Schools*, vol. 1 (Harrisburg, PA: Clarence M. Busch, State Printer of Pennsylvania, 1897), 75; Gold, "The Soldiers' Orphan Schools of Pennsylvania, 1864–1889," 4; Russel Weigley, *Philadelphia: A 300-Year History* (New York: Norton, 1982), 293–329; Gold, "The Soldiers' Orphan Schools of Pennsylvania, 1864–1889," 33. Gold lists the following schools for older children operating in 1871, when the system was at its peak, listed with counties: Dayton, Armstrong County; Phillipsburg, Beaver; Mercer, Mercer; Uniontown, Fayette; Titusville, Crawford; Cassville, Huntington; Loysville, Perry; McAlisterville, Juniata; Mansfield, Tioga; Harford, Susquehanna; White Hall, Cumberland; Mt. Joy, Lancaster; Bridgewater, Bucks; Chester Springs, Chester; and Philadelphia. Mylin counted twenty-four schools for younger orphans in 1866, including church orphanages like the Episcopal Church Home in Pittsburgh and the St. James' Orphan Asylum in Lancaster and the Home for Destitute Colored Children in Philadelphia, as well as the Lincoln Institution, which might have also served children of color. Gold, "The Soldiers' Orphan Schools of Pennsylvania, 1864–1889," 196; Mylin, *State Prisons*, 75.

10. "Our Battle Flags: Return of Our War-Worn and Victorious Standards to the State," *Philadelphia Inquirer*, July 5, 1866.

11. Judith Geisberg, *Army at Home: Women and the Civil War on the Northern Home Front* (Chapel Hill: University of North Carolina Press, 2009), 57–63.

12. James Marten, *The Children's Civil War* (Chapel Hill: University of North Carolina Press, 1998), 68–100; Steven Mintz, *Huck's Raft: A History of American Childhood* (Cambridge: Harvard University Press, 2004), 131–32; McFarland, *Annual Report*, 1867, 18.

13. Unnamed Pennsylvania legislator (1883) quoted in Gold, "The Soldiers' Orphan Schools of Pennsylvania, 1864–1889," 63.

14. "Soldiers' Orphans' Department," *Daily Guard* (Harrisburg), October 2, 1868, n.p; "Mothers Complain: Their Children Badly Treated at Chester Springs," *Philadelphia Record*, March 15, 1886; "Ill Treatment of Soldiers' Orphans," *Evening Bulletin* (Harrisburg), December 15, 1869; "Mothers Complain," *Philadelphia Record*, March 15, 1886; Gold, "The Soldiers' Orphan Schools of Pennsylvania, 1864–1889," 127.

15. McFarland, *Annual Report of the Superintendent*, 1867, 16; J. P. Wickersham, "Industrial Education," *Pennsylvania School Journal* 22, no. 2 (August 1873), State Library of Pennsylvania, Harrisburg, Pennsylvania, 51; Superintendent Thomas Burrows (1864), Gold, "The Soldiers' Orphan Schools of Pennsylvania, 1864–1889," 73.

16. Hutter, "Report of Mrs. E. Hutter," *Annual Report*, 1884, no. 6, 20; 1878, no. 9, 31; 1870, 35; 1884, 22.

17. Ibid., 1884, 22; Matthew Frye Jacobson, *Barbarian Virtues: The United States Encounters Foreign Peoples at Home and Abroad* (New York: Hill and Wang, 2000), 88–91; James Marten, *Children for the Union: The War Spirit on the Northern Home Front* (Chicago: Ivan R. Dee, 2004), 161. Hutter shared the apprehensions of educational reformers who lead the charge for immigration restriction. Jacobson, *Barbarian Virtues*, 97–98.

18. "The Pennsylvania Soldiers' Orphans' Schools," *Frank Leslie's Illustrated Newspaper*, March 27, 1886; Herbert Welsh quoted in M. K. Sniffen, "The Record of Thirty Years: A Brief Statement of the Indian Rights Association, Its Objects, Methods, and Achievements," *Indian Rights Association*, no. 87, March 25, 1912, 1, in *The Action of the Interior Department in Forcing the Standing Rock Indians to Lease Their Cattle to Syndicates*, Indian Rights Association, Stanford Library, 55, accessed through Google Books, January 17, 2010.

19. Lindsey, *Indians at Hampton*, 51–53; David Wallace Adams, *Education for Extinction: American Indians and the Boarding School Experience, 1875–1928* (Lawrence: University Press of Kansas, 1995), 45; Marten, *Children for the Union*, 171–72; Hutter, "Report of Mrs. E. Hutter," 1884, no. 6, 20; Adams, *Education for Extinction*, 52.

20. Pratt quoted in Lindsey, *Indians at Hampton,* 27. Indeed, one reason Pratt left Hampton in 1879 was because he believed that the school reproduced a kind of segregation that he believed was harmful to Indians. Lindsey, *Indians at Hampton*, 38–40. For Americanization, see Alan Dawley, *Struggles for Justice: Social Responsibility and the Liberal State* (Cambridge: Harvard University Press, 1993), 114–15.

PART IV

Epilogue

For every Southern boy fourteen years old, not once but whenever he wants it, there is the instant when it's still not yet two
o'clock on that July afternoon in 1863, the brigades are in position behind the rail fence, the guns are laid and ready in the
woods and the furled flags are already loosened to break out.
—William Faulkner, *Intruder in the Dust*[1]

One does not need to be a southerner, or even a boy, to feel chills
when reading the preceding quotation, one of the most famous passages in
midcentury southern literature. The Civil War continues to cast a powerful
shadow over Americans, even if they are not always aware of just how it still
affects their attitudes, their politics, and their race relations. Faulkner's sug-
gestion that it was possible to change the past—to turn back the clock, to
seek an alternative ending to the destruction of the Confederacy, to prevent
the carnage on Cemetery Ridge, so to speak—has long resonated with historians of memory and of the Lost Cause.

But it also seemed to provide a kind of foreshadowing to the "massive
resistance" to the integration of southern schools and public facilities in
the 1950s and 1960s. *Intruder in the Dust* was published a few years before
the *Brown v. Board of Education of Topeka* launched the modern civil rights
movement. But, as J. Vincent Lowery shows in the essay that ends this collection, one of the oldest commemorative associations in the South, the United
Daughters of the Confederacy, seemed to be taking those teenage boys and
other southern youth back to that hot July day in order to mobilize them
against the forces that the defeat at Gettysburg—and at Vicksburg, Peters-
burg, and Mobile Bay, for that matter—had unleashed. Their promotion of
the Children of the Confederacy responded, in fact, not only to the threat of
integration but also to a number of other concerns, including the Cold War,
the supposed postwar increase in juvenile delinquency, and the rise of a dis-

turbing new youth culture. The post–World War II efforts by some southerners to void the changes of the previous century by focusing on their children
were not so different from the efforts by Civil War–era adults to work out
the political, cultural, and racial issues of the sectional conflict through their
children. In the 1950s, as in the 1850s or any other age, Americans sought to
ensure a future that reflected core American values. Some were shared by
many, some by a few, but all were intended to be carried forward by the rising generation.

Despite the fact that the children and youth who appear in this last part
lived nearly a century after the children featured in the first three parts,
it is important to note that, just as slave and free children were viewed as
symbols, as agents of change or of resistance, and as object lessons of great
sectional issues between the 1850s and 1870s, so, too, were youngsters in the
middle of the twentieth century not only implements of adults' strategies but
also actors in their own right. The Children of the Confederacy were, in significant ways, simply mirror images of the black children of Birmingham,
Little Rock, and Greensboro.

Yet the few thousands of children who actually joined the organization—
or, perhaps more accurately, the adults who led them—seem more a product
of the nineteenth than the twentieth century. Like the abolitionists, the publishers and readers of children's magazines, the missionaries and students,
and the orphans of that earlier time, the Children of the Confederacy no
doubt reflected the attitudes of a larger set of children and youth who shared
the same values but not the same commitment to formal display. Their efforts
to hold back change in the 1950s were directly linked to the "Lost Cause"
mentality of the Gilded Age. As a result, although nearly three-quarters of
a century separate the people and events that appear in Lowery's essay from
the men, women, and children in the other dozen pieces, this epilogue provides ample evidence of the lasting legacy of the Civil War in the lives of
American children and in American's thinking about childhood.

NOTES

1. William Faulkner, *Intruder in the Dust* (New York: Random House, 1948; New York:
Vintage, 1972), 194–95.

13

Preparing the Next Generation for Massive Resistance

The Historical Pageantry of the Children of the Confederacy, 1955–1965

J. VINCENT LOWERY

As civil rights activists increased their attack on racial discrimination in the 1950s, many southern white parents feared that "race-mixers" misled white children, inspiring them to question the sanctity of racial segregation. The Citizens' Council, an integral part of southern resistance to the civil rights movement, lamented that the racial and sectional pride of southern white youths appeared to have weakened as a result of "integrationist influences in our schools, colleges and churches." Citing a Purdue University poll of American teenagers' racial views, the Council noted that "even in the South, where presumably we parents seek to instill a sense of race pride and heritage in our children, the poll found surprising deviations," particularly in response to questions about integration and interracial marriage. The Council advised readers to "constantly strive to show our children that we are unswerving in our beliefs, unswayed [] by emotionalism, unshaken by argumentation, undismayed by traitors in our midst."[1] In response to the rising tide of the civil rights movement—not to mention widespread fears of Communist infiltration and juvenile delinquency—many southern white parents rallied to keep their children from falling prey to these influences.

Helping to lead the fight was the United Daughters of the Confederacy (UDC), which believed that southern children would avoid the corruption threatening to destroy southern values if given the proper models to emulate. Formed in 1894 to vindicate the Confederate generation and perpetuate the qualities those men and women presumably embodied, the UDC shared the Citizens' Council's concern about contemporary challenges to the southern way of life. In the mid-twentieth century, this way of life consisted of "a concern for personal and national honor, a suspicion of centralized power and a belief in states' rights, a fundamentalist faith in Protestant Christianity, and a view of history shaped by the region's experiences of slavery, the Civil War, and Reconstruction." Those priorities reached all the way back to the defeat of the Confederacy, nearly a century before, which had forced southern whites to embark on a new but related struggle to preserve a distinctive southern identity. As historian Charles Reagan Wilson observed, "The South's kingdom was to be of culture, not politics." As part of the "Lost Cause" movement, the Daughters strove to transform southern white children into "living monuments" to their Confederate ancestors, assuring the survival of this peculiar way of life by enlisting youths in the ongoing sectional conflict; mid-twentieth-century concerns that at least some southern youth lacked interest in their Confederate heritage inspired the Daughters to renew their commitment to passing Lost Cause values to the rising generation. In the 1950s, when the family was recognized as the foundation of success against threats at home and abroad, the Daughters fulfilled their maternal roles by expanding the functions of the organization's youth auxiliary, the Children of the Confederacy (C of C).[2]

For the Daughters and their auxiliary, the Civil War remained an important part of their identity and their lives; by preserving memories of the war, the Daughters and the C of C contributed to the campaign of massive resistance. The C of C education campaign represented another component of the struggle launched by white southerners in the wake of the Supreme Court's 1954 ruling against segregated schools. Southern white businessmen and politicians mobilized the region to repel yet another challenge to the region's racial order. This response was far from unified; ideology, tactics, and intentions varied. Moreover, as historian George Lewis suggests, the phrase "massive resistance" conceals the complexity of southern attitudes in the mid-twentieth century, in which race was but one element of the tumult. The Daughters' attitudes reflect a widely felt uncertainty about the direction the South appeared to take, prompted not simply by the threat of integration but also by fears of youth culture gone wild, the rapid pace of modernization in the region, and the national security threats posed by the Cold War. Many southern whites feared that these changes would threaten the very existence of a unique southerner and the South. The Daughters looked backward for bulwarks against this turmoil and tried to pass on to their children memories that would presumably stabilize the region. Emphasizing the importance of the work of the C of C, Third Vice President General Lillian Kent Dickens advised her readers, "Right now the spotlight of the world is on the South— we have not asked for such a place of attention, but it has come nevertheless. . . . So boys and girls let us meet this test as our forefathers did and we will emerge in a way that will be pleasing to God and our fellow man." Children who modeled themselves after the Confederate generation of Robert E. Lee, Thomas Jonathan "Stonewall" Jackson, and Jefferson Davis would presumably pass this test.[3]

Many Americans shared the concerns of the Citizens' Council and the UDC that the nation's children were at risk of juvenile delinquency. In the mid-1950s, many middle-class parents believed that mass culture challenged their authority and disrupted the socialization process. Historian James Gilbert argued, "Many of the changes adolescents experienced were disruptions shared equally by adults. . . . But, articulated in rebellious terms and thrust upon the American public by a communications media that emphasized everything new and threatening, the culture of teenagers could easily be mistaken for a new form of juvenile delinquency." Comics and films endured scrutiny for drawing upon working-class standards that middle-class youths consequently emulated. Critics also accused the media of glorifying crime and immorality. Mass culture quickly became the subject of sociological analysis and congressional investigation; reports claimed that these media challenged family values and inspired the rise of juvenile delinquency.[4]

Speaking to the Children of the Confederacy in 1959, sociologist Brooks Thompson dismissed the "criers of doom" who protested that Elvis Presley corrupted southern white youths. Rock and roll popularized black culture among white youths "at the very time that white southerners were emotionally confronting the civil rights movement and trying to preserve segregation." Many white parents feared that the culture of rock and roll "offered a space to negotiate an end to the color line." Thompson proposed that contemporary southern youths, like all generations, practiced "healthy rebellion," and that the UDC and the C of C prevented a "too abrupt and rapid break with the past," predicting that their success would assure that "we would see fewer incidences of young people getting into trouble and of society suffering as a result." He admitted that southern white children were at risk of becoming juvenile delinquents, citing a recent Federal Bureau of Investigation (FBI) report that documented the rising rate of juvenile delinquency, as well as newspaper accounts of rapes and murders that presumably validated the findings of the FBI. Yet Thompson proposed that this crime wave would be quelled by "put[ting] the hero back in the textbooks and in the family." Thompson warned that children who chose the wrong heroes would be lured by "the cult of violence" to live lives of "notoriety and infamy." The most important qualities these organizations could instill were the "ideals of patriotism, brotherhood of man, Christian conduct, and personal integrity." Thompson emphasized that lessons about Lee, Jackson, Davis, and other prominent Confederate heroes would propagate these values and thus assure the future success of the South and the nation. By "living in the minds of others," these men would achieve the immortality that Thompson deemed necessary to assure the character of southern youths.[5]

Parents' fears that cultural transformations threatened their children were not unique to mid-twentieth-century America. After the Civil War, adults became increasingly concerned about the corrupting influences in the lives of children and organized adult-directed children's associations to provide youths with the appropriate guidance. Middle-class men searched for "character-building" activities to protect their sons from the eroding forces of modernity, founding organizations such as the Boy Scouts and the Young Men's Christian Association to achieve this goal. However, American parenting traditions acknowledged the primary role women played in the development of young citizens. Americans understood that political socialization began in childhood and that families were responsible for shaping political culture. The Daughters served the South as "Confederate mothers," resisting the infiltration of Yankee values and honoring the sacrifices of southern men and women during the Civil War. The first chapter of the Children of the Confederacy was formed in 1896—just two years after the founding of the UDC—as an auxiliary of the Mary Custis Lee Chapter of the UDC in Alexandria, Virginia. Three years later, Adelia A. Dunovant, a prominent member of the Texas Division of the UDC, called upon the Daughters to organize a nationwide children's auxiliary. Dunovant imagined the C of C as a means by which to direct the development of southern white children. Mrs. S. E. F. Rose, a prominent Daughter who served the organization as historian-general, advised, "We should ever regard our history as a priceless heritage, cherish and keep green the traditions of the Old South, keep alive its chivalrous spirit, and never tire of telling the story of these lion-hearted men, who made this history for us, and around whose names cluster some of the greatest events of the past." Rose argued that southern children must be immersed in lessons of the southern past in order to be "prepared to fight the battle of life." In order to prepare them for that struggle, the Daughters believed that the principles for which southerners fought the Civil War must not be permitted to fade away but should remain "green" with life. C of C programs, as well as wider UDC educational programs, would permit southern white youths to relive that "green" past, joining their Confederate heroes on the battlefield, and presumably learn the necessary qualities to turn back contemporary threats.[6]

The Daughters devoted considerable energy and resources to care for surviving Confederate veterans during the late nineteenth and early twentieth centuries, but as the number of old soldiers dwindled, the Daughters increasingly turned their attention to the propagation of memories and traditions among the white youth of the South to prepare them to carry on the Lost Cause. Children's chapters formed unevenly in the decades after Dunovant issued her call; the general organization recognized the C of C as its official auxiliary in 1917. The process by which the organization attempted to preserve the memory of the Confederate cause and its soldiers is described by French sociologist Maurice Halbwachs: "To the extent that the dead retreat into the past, this is not because the material measure of time that separates them from us lengthens; it is because nothing remains of the group in which they passed their lives, and which needed to name them, that their names slowly become obliterated. The only ancestors transmitted and retained are those whose memory has become the object of a cult by men who remain at least fictitiously in contact with them." The Daughters propagated memories of the Confederate generation to those with no recollection of the war and little contact with veterans through rituals such as historical catechisms, pageants, and memorial events. The Daughters taught Children about "traditional privileges of race, gender, and class while making them appear to be a natural and inviolable part of history." UDC lessons emphasized the idyllic plantation lifestyle, the bravery of Confederate soldiers and the sacrifice of women on the home front, and the folly of Reconstruction. Memories that cast African Americans as either docile, loyal servants or ignorant criminals made the Children increasingly susceptible to other racist images. These memories also made Children wary of challenges to white upper-class hegemony, particularly by outsiders. Decades later, these memories prevented southern whites from viewing African American demands for civil rights with anything other than contempt.[7]

Immersed in the Lost Cause as a child, Katharine Du Pre Lumpkin illustrated the power of these memories in her 1946 autobiography, *The Making of a Southerner*. Her father, William Wallace Lumpkin, was an active participant in United Confederate Veterans (UCV) events, while her mother and older sister were both members of the UDC, her brothers joined the Sons of Confederate Veterans (SCV) at the appropriate age, and she and her younger siblings took part in the C of C. The Lost Cause was thus an integral part of her childhood. Later in life, Lumpkin became aware of the powerful influence of lessons she received from her family and the broader cult of the Lost Cause of which she was a part through her membership in the

C of C. She realized that she had unconsciously learned important lessons about racial privilege during her childhood, as her "ears were saturated with words and phrases at all times intimately familiar to Southern ears and in those years of harsh excitement carried a special urgency: 'white supremacy,' 'Negro domination,' 'intermarriage,' 'social equality,' 'impudence,' 'inferiority,' 'uppitiness,' 'good darkey,' 'bad darkey,' 'keep them in their place.'" "As time passed," Lumpkin recalled, "I myself would learn to speak these words, perhaps with special emphasis, given the times and the tones of others' voices saying them, even before I had the understanding to grasp all they stood for." The teachings of the Lost Cause held a powerful grip on the minds of southern youths; Lumpkin was a rare child of the Lost Cause who escaped its grasp. From a distance, she realized the extent to which this cult shaped her thoughts about race before she even understood the concept, conferring to future generations an unquestioning commitment to the southern racial order. Historian Jennifer Ritterhouse contends that southern white children, like their African American counterparts, learned about the meaning of race at an early age. Collectively, southern white children learned to interact with African Americans, "performing" as racial superiors. Ritterhouse argues that the preservation of the racial structure in the South required constant vigilance by parents who taught each generation to follow the racial script and perpetuate Jim Crow. In the mid-twentieth century, the UDC remained willing to defend the South from challenges to regional traditions, even as other dangers emerged alongside the recurring threats to racial segregation.[8]

In order to counter these threats in the mid-twentieth century, the Daughters did not dramatically alter their historical perspective. They employed new media to counter destabilizing influences in the lives of southern youths. UDC programs appeared on local television and radio stations. Perhaps most important, the Daughters understood that youths would be attracted to the C of C by relevant histories, brought to life by comparisons with contemporary struggles. Although the Daughters generally avoided political discussions, the pages of the *UDC Magazine* reveal efforts to teach Children their responsibilities as southerners and the qualities necessary to fulfill their responsibility to uphold the legacy of the Confederate generation in an era of such profound change, preserving their peculiar southern way of life "by keeping it alive in our own way of living, the best of the Past that it might have its place in our Present and Future."[9]

In 1953, the Daughters began to meet the challenges presented by the modern attitudes and behaviors by planning the reorganization of the C of C, granting the auxiliary a degree of independence in its operations while preparing southern youths for the threats the region faced. The Daughters registered their children and grandchildren as early as possible to begin their Confederate educations. Babies who were registered in the C of C at birth were cherished as expressions of reverence for Confederate ancestors and proof of the survival of southern ideals. They boasted an expanding membership from 3,474 in 1921 to 45,190 in 1953 that suggested southern white youths were prepared to fulfill the legacy of the Confederate generation in such troubling times. The only evidence of dissent centered on the name of the children's auxiliary, which some C of C members believed should be changed to "Youth of the Confederacy." Bob Hess, president of the Florida Division of the C of C, argued that the new name would help the C of C lure new members otherwise confused by the similarities between the names of the Children of the Confederacy and the Chamber of Commerce and turned off by the C of C's age-specific name. Moreover, Hess argued that the Children's increasing responsibilities within the auxiliary justified the more age-appropriate name that reflected members' commitment to the preservation of southern ideals. His proposal thus rested in part on the claim that the Children accepted their responsibilities as white southerners and Confederate descendants in a time of such great turmoil. However, in an era in which parents feared losing their children to corrupting influences, the Daughters resisted relinquishing too much independence to the Children, even in name. Equally important, the voices of the Children were typically quiet in the pages of the *UDC Magazine*, with the Daughters most often speaking for the members of the auxiliary. Editor Mrs. John L. Woodbury dismissed the proposal, citing an argument "that youth is an indefinite period, whereas the relationship of parent and child is all inclusive and lasting."[10]

In 1955, the first annual general convention of the Children of the Confederacy gathered in Atlanta, Georgia. The convention was charged with excitement; one Daughter noted that "you could hear everything from the Rebel Yell to the building of better Citizens and Americans, with Christ as the foundation of the home." From the Daughters' perspective, the Children appeared poised to assume their ordained roles in the region, the nation, and the world.[11]

The Daughters believed that the C of C offered members "friendship, interesting historical programs, social activities and the perpetuation of the memories of those who have gone before us," but the parent group also understood that other forces contended for the attention of southern white youths. The Daughters believed that lessons on the Confederate past would protect the Child from "his weaknesses, his lack of experience and information. His mind an [*sic*] heart are in a fresh pure state, and ready to receive impressions, which will guide his life. A child is precious, not for what he is now, but for what he will become." In 1954, Mrs. Belmont Dennis expressed concern about the lagging participation in the C of C. She feared that southern white youths might turn to the cinema for entertainment, a source of concern for parents across the country. Miss Emma McPheeters, second-vice-president general, identified the threats that southerners, particularly "precious" youths, faced: "juvenile delinquency, yes, and adult delinquency, the teaching of Communism, the low moral standards so prevalent."[12]

Daughters directed C of C activities at the national, division, and chapter levels, but Children served the auxiliary as officers. One national director cited the "inspiration, challenge, and renewed faith" she received from the Children with whom she worked. In particular, these Children displayed a "profound honor and respect for their heritage and face the challenge of participating in today's history with vigor and a fine sense of Christianity and patriotism for America and a deep respect and feeling of responsibility for this world in which they live." Fearful that southern white youths had forgotten their Confederate ancestors and identified a less honorable group of contemporary "heroes," the Daughters could take solace in the Children's interest in their heritage during such troubling times.[13]

Children typically gathered once a month under the supervision of the local UDC chapter to study the history of the South and to display pride in their Confederate heritage. One C of C historian general recommended that each monthly meeting open with a Pledge of Allegiance and salutes to the Confederate and state flags, followed by the Lord's Prayer and various southern songs, all suggestive of the Children's unique identities as both Americans and southerners. Child Sharon Lee Dennis, chaplain general of the C of C, offered a prayer to open each meeting suggestive of this unique distinctiveness: "Our Father, we thank thee for our beautiful Southland. Make us willing to give our strength to the weak, and sympathy to the sorrowing. Help us live as devoted children of Thine." History programs guided by national outlines formed the central component of each meeting. Topics included prominent Confederate generals, politicians, and literary figures, the Confederate navy, the historical origins of the principle of states' rights, and life on the home front. The Daughters perceived that they inherited the legacy of service bequeathed to them by the generation of Confederate women. The Daughters honored the women who fed and clothed Confederate soldiers, gave up comforts and niceties, staffed hospitals, endured Yankee insults and assaults, and even served the Confederacy themselves during the war. C of C historical programs emphasized the same pantheon of heroes that the UDC honored from its inception and Thompson predicted would provide younger generations with the proper direction in their lives. Stories of Jefferson Davis, Robert E. Lee, and Thomas Jonathan "Stonewall" Jackson emphasized the character traits the Children should learn from their studies of these men. In Lee and Jackson, one *UDC Magazine* contributor detected "their nobility of character, their loyalty to their people, their undeviating adherence to principle, their generosity to a worthy foe, their greatness in victory, and their nobility in defeat." The Daughters echoed these observations while also stressing the Christian faith of Confederate heroes such as Lee and Jackson. American religious leaders cast the Cold War as a struggle between believers and the godless, conferring to Christianity immense political importance during the Cold War. However, segregationists also claimed divine sanction, arguing that the physical separation of the races and the preservation of racial purity merely obeyed God's will. As Wilson argued, from the beginning the Lost Cause was heavily invested with Christian principles that explained defeat and provided an antidote to the forces of modernism, preserving the culture of the Confederacy even after its defeat.[14]

In order to assure the success of their education, Children played an active role in the functions of their chapters as officers, providing the organization with their own historical, political, and religious voices. Children were encouraged to participate in essay contests and attend division and national conventions, when the organization distributed a variety of awards to honor evidence of chapters' and individuals' commitment to preserving the Confederate past. In addition, C of C chapters sometimes produced historical pageants and hosted costume balls, providing the Children with the opportunity to momentarily live the past they sought to preserve, making the Civil War contemporary in ways that were essential to pass on those memories to those with no contact with the sectional conflict. Children who served the auxiliary as officers encouraged members to actively participate in these C of C events and to spread the truth about the Confederacy by introducing elements of C of C activities in their schools, thus expanding the influence of the Confederate heritage movement. In addition to these programs, the Daughters expected Children to collect money for various UDC programs and participate in commemorative events, assuring the perpetuation of Confederate ideals through scholarships, relief aid, and memorials. As Lumpkin herself observed, this type of immersion in the cult of the Lost Cause could easily shape the minds of participants, as the past became the lens through which the present was seen. As C of C president general John Baxter Flowers asserted, "The Children of the Confederacy is a proud organization. Our heritage is a great one which still lives. It is not a thing of the past as many would have us believe. The principles for which it stands hold good today. The Children of the Confederacy helps mold the minds of many young people who will one day take the reins of government. Study history and know the past. A knowledge of the truths of history sheds light on the problems of today."[15]

Most of the Daughters' work responded to the contemporary crises in implicit ways, avoiding overt commentaries on the most contentious issues, notably segregation. The Daughters and the Children rarely spoke openly about politics, even criticizing those who seized upon Confederate symbols for their own political purposes. In 1948, southern college students introduced the Confederate battle flag as an unofficial symbol of the states' rights movement associated with Strom Thurmond's presidential campaign. The Confederate battle flag continued to be potent symbol of protest in the 1950s and 1960s, suggestive of the parallel southerners drew between the "War between the States" and the defense of states' rights in the mid-twentieth century. The Daughters resisted the political applications of their cherished flag, but they welcomed politicians like Thurmond who drew rhetorical comparisons between Civil War–era and mid-twentieth-century conflicts. As the most visible participants in the massive resistance movement, they were uniquely positioned to educate the Daughters and Children about the troubles that their homeland faced. Speaking to the Daughters at the annual convention in 1962, Senator Sam Ervin Jr. of North Carolina declared, "Let us preserve for ourselves and our prosperity our goodly heritage—economic liberty, political liberty, and religious liberty. This is our obligation. We must perform it. As Americans, we cannot do otherwise." Senator John Stennis of Mississippi appraised the legacy of Jefferson Davis for the Daughters, suggesting that Davis had always served American principles of states' rights, leaving an obligation to defend the same principles to his descendants. In 1957, Thurmond spoke to the South Carolina Division of the UDC, admonishing violence but advising his audience, "We are going to fight as long as we have breath, for the rights of the States and for the rights of our people under the Constitution of the United States." Thurmond drew direct parallels between the contemporary struggle and the ordeal of the South during Reconstruction, claiming that outsiders once again disrupted otherwise peaceful race relations. Seven years later, Thurmond attended the annual convention of the South Carolina Division of the C of C, advising the Children that another proposed civil rights bill would again usurp states' rights. His appearance came during a period in the civil rights movement in which

African American youths joined their parents in the streets to demand equality. Thurmond's observations suggested that, similarly, southern white parents' struggle was their children's as well, a point the Daughters stressed through their historical lessons.[16]

Historian Robert J. Cook has suggested that this campaign of massive resistance against integration ultimately found little use for comparisons between the Confederacy and the segregationists' own struggle, especially during the Civil War Centennial commemoration beginning in 1961. The architects of the Centennial believed that the commemorative events would solidify the nation by eliminating sectional tensions and presenting a united front to the world, thus strengthening the American struggle against Communism. As the Centennial unfolded, professionally trained historians wrested control away from those officers who appealed to southern sentiments; under new leadership, events became more inclusive of African Americans. Cook concludes that white southerners displayed little interest in the Centennial. However, the Daughters perceived that the Civil War Centennial would provide an unparalleled opportunity to honor the Confederate generation. At the beginning of the Centennial, the president general encouraged the Daughters to invite the public, particularly young southerners, to attend and participate in commemorative events. She predicted, "When you eulogize our Confederate heroes, when you place a wreath at a Confederate monument, when you place flowers on the graves of the Confederate soldiers, you are actually living history, keeping memory alive in the most beautiful, enduring way." The Daughters recognized the power of commemorative events and seized the opportunity to bring the history of the South to life for those who lacked any contact with the War between the States. For example, the C of C successfully petitioned the mayor of Athens, Georgia, to declare April 26, one of several Confederate memorial days observed across the South, a citywide holiday. Confederate heritage organizations planned these events to convey the proper reverence for Confederate bravery and sacrifice in defense of sacred American principles once again being threatened.[17]

After the close of the Centennial celebrations, C of C director Jewell F. Renfroe called upon all UDC divisions to renew their commitment to the Children. At the same time, however, she acknowledged that the auxiliary had failed to meet the expectations of the Daughters. Renfroe attributed the dwindling interest of southern white youths to the failure of the Daughters to "stand behind her [the division director] and the children," implying that the white children of the South were eager to celebrate their Confederate heritage but merely lacked the appropriate guidance. This harkened back to earlier concerns about the role models that these children might choose to follow and fears of juvenile delinquency if those choices were not properly directed. Indeed, the pages of the *UDC Magazine* reveal a consistent desire to increase C of C membership rolls and frustrations that these objectives were elusive while the Children themselves remained relatively silent, subsumed beneath the parent organization. The Daughters of the 1950s and 1960s, most of whom had been members of the C of C, discovered that fewer and fewer southern white youths wished to live in the Confederate past. The failure of the Daughters' Centennial campaign was, perhaps, inevitable, given the changes wrought by the civil rights movement and the ongoing urbanization and industrialization that had moderated the South's distinct regional identity and undermined the Daughters' mission. As C. Vann Woodward observed in 1958, these forces of change threatened to erode southern uniqueness, compelling some to assume a final stand in defense of that distinction against the trend toward consolidation within the national landscape. Woodward asked, "Has the Southern heritage become an old hunting jacket that one slips on comfortably while at home but discards when he ventures abroad in favor of some more conventional or modish garb? Or is it perhaps an attic full of ancestral robes useful only in connection with costume balls and play acting—staged primarily in Washington, DC?" The Children, like those in Athens, Georgia, displayed the necessary commitment to perpetuating the memories of the Confederacy by living in that past; the Daughters only regretted that too many southern white youths apparently answered Woodward's questions affirmatively, embracing the national present over the sectional past.[18]

NOTES

1. "Need for Teen Training," *Citizens' Council*, May 1958, 3. Studies of the Citizens' Council include Neil R. McMillen, *The Citizens' Council: Organized Resistance to the Second Reconstruction, 1954–1965* (Urbana: University of Illinois Press, 1971); Numan Bartley, *The Rise of Massive Resistance: Race and Politics in the South during the 1950s* (Baton Rouge: Louisiana State University Press, 1969), esp. chap. 6; and Joseph Crespino, *In Search of Another Country: Mississippi and the Southern Counterrevolution* (Princeton: Princeton University Press, 2007), esp. chaps. 1 and 2.

2. Jeff Woods, *Black Struggle, Red Scare: Segregation and Anti-Communism in the South, 1948–1968* (Baton Rouge: Louisiana State University Press, 2004), 2; Charles Reagan Wilson, *Baptized in Blood: The Religion of the Lost Cause, 1865–1920* (Athens: University of Georgia Press, 1980), 1; C. Vann Woodward, *The Burden of Southern History* (1960; Baton Rouge: Louisiana State University Press, 1993), 3–25; Elizabeth Gillespie McRae, "To Save a Home: Nell Battle Lewis and the Rise of Southern Conservatism, 1941–1956," *North Carolina Historical Review* 81 (July 2004): 261–87.

3. George Lewis, *Massive Resistance: The White Response to the Civil Rights Movement* (London: Hodder Arnold, 2006), 13; Lillian Kent Dickens, "News from the Children of the Confederacy," *UDC Magazine*, May 1956, 3. Examples of studies of the politics of postwar domesticity and motherhood include Elaine Tyler May, *Homeward Bound: American Families in the Cold War Era* (New York: Basic Books, 1988); Joanne Meyerwitz, ed., *Not June Cleaver: Women and Gender in Postwar America, 1945–1980* (Philadelphia: Temple University Press, 1994).

4. James Gilbert's *A Cycle of Outrage: America's Reaction to the Juvenile Delinquent in the 1950s* (New York: Oxford University Press, 1988), 18.

5. Ibid., 18; Pete Daniel, *Lost Revolutions: The South in the 1950s* (Chapel Hill: University of North Carolina Press, 2000), 165. See also Michael T. Bertrand, *Race, Rock, and Elvis* (Urbana: University of Illinois Press, 2000), 187–88; Brooks Thompson, "Identification and Heroes," *UDC Magazine*, February 1961, 21–22.

6. David I. Macleod, *Building Character in the American Boy: The Boy Scouts, YMCA, and Their Forerunners, 1870–1920* (Madison: University of Wisconsin Press, 1983), xi–xviii; Linda K. Kerber, *Women of the Republic: Intellect and Ideology in Revolutionary America* (Chapel Hill: University of North Carolina Press, 1980), chap. 9; Karen L. Cox, *Dixie's Daughters: The United Daughters of the Confederacy and the Preservation of Confederate Culture* (Gainesville: University Press of Florida, 2003), chap. 7; Adelia A. Dunovant, *Report of the Historian of the Texas Division to the Fourth Annual Convention, Austin, Texas, November 29–30, 1899* (n.p., n.d.), Adelia A. Dunovant File, United Daughters of the Confederacy Collection, Eleanor S. Brockenbrough Library and Archives, the Museum of the Confederacy, Richmond, Virginia; *Minutes of the Eighth Annual Meeting, United Daughters of the Confederacy, Wilmington, North Carolina, November 13–16, 1901* (Nashville: Foster and Webb, n.d.), 128; Mary B. Poppenheim et al., *The History of the United Daughters of the Confederacy*, vol. 1, *1894–1929* (Raleigh, NC: Edwards and Broughton Company, 1956), 181–87; Mrs. S. E. F. Rose, *The Ku Klux Klan or Invisible Empire* (New Orleans: L. Graham Co., 1914), 75–76; Mrs. S. E. F. Rose, "The UDC, Its Object and Mission," *Our Heritage*, June 1910, 1–2. For a discussion of the early history of the C of C, see Cox, *Dixie's Daughters*, 134–39; J. Vincent Lowery, "Reconstructing the Reign of Terror: Popular Memories of the Ku Klux Klan, 1877–1921" (Ph.D. diss., University of Mississippi, 2008), chap. 4 (esp. 132–36, 151–52).

7. Maurice Halbwachs, *On Collective Memory*, ed., trans., and introduction Lewis A. Conser (Chicago: University of Chicago Press, 1992), 73; Cox, *Dixie's Daughters*, chap. 7; Cleta Seward McDowell, "Of Blessed Memory," *UDC Magazine*, January 1955, 31; quotation from W. Fitzhugh Brundage, "White Women and the Politics of Historical Memory in the New South, 1880–1920," in *Jumpin' Jim Crow: Southern Politics from Civil War to Civil Rights*, ed. Jane Dailey, Glenda Elizabeth Gilmore, and Bryant Simon (Princeton: Princeton University Press, 2000), 117. On the functions and structure of the C of C Catechism, see Amy Lynn Heyse, "The Rhetoric of Memory-Making: Lessons from the UDC's Catechisms for Children," *Rhetoric Society Quarterly* 38 (October 2008): 408–32. Historians Karen Cox and Francesca Morgan both attribute resistance to integration to historically conservative lessons taught by the UDC. See Cox, *Dixie's Daughters*, 162; Francesca Morgan, *Women and Patriotism in Jim Crow America* (Chapel Hill: University of North Carolina Press, 2005), 162.

8. Katharine Du Pre Lumpkin, *The Making of a Southerner* (1946; Athens: University of Georgia Press, 1991), 130; Jacquelyn Dowd Hall, "'You Must Remember This': Autobiography as Social Critique," *Journal of American History* 85 (September 1998): 439–65; Ritterhouse, *Growing Up Jim Crow*, 55; Lowery, "Reconstructing the Reign of Terror," 151–52.

9. See, e.g., "News from the Children of the Confederacy," *UDC Magazine*, March 1956, 5, 8; Libbie Cameron Wade, "Third Vice President," ibid., February 1962, 6.

10. "Children of the Confederacy News," ibid., January 1961, 27; "Youngest C of C Is Registered," ibid., July 1961, 43; "Children of the Confederacy News," ibid., June 1962, 13; "Youngest Member of Bertie Thompson C of C," ibid., April 1954, 40; "Youth of the Confederacy vs. Children of the Confederacy," ibid., June 1954, 34; Mrs. John L. Woodbury, "Children of the Confederacy," ibid., September 1954, 25, 27, quotation on 27.

11. "Children of the Confederacy General Convention Held in Atlanta, Georgia," ibid., September 1955, 20, 30.

12. Mrs. John L. Woodbury, "Children of the Confederacy," ibid., September 1954, 25; Mrs. Belmont Dennis, "Message from the President-General," ibid., January 1954, 2–3; Emma McPheeters, "Message of the Second Vice President General," ibid., January 1955, 5; Mrs. Guy Hudson Parr, "Message from the Patriotic Service Chairman," ibid., October 1956, 22.

13. Mrs. Fred E. Rogers, "Children of the Confederacy News," *UDC Magazine*, December 1958, 6; Libbie Wade Cameron, "Third Vice President General," ibid., September 1962, 9. Although the media frequently interpreted any opposition to integration expressed by southern white youths as simply mimicry of their parents' racial views, C of C activities reveal a more deliberate aspect of the campaign of massive resistance. For a discussion of southern white youths and massive resistance, see Rebecca de Schweinitz, *If We Could Change the World: Young People and America's Long Struggle for Racial Equality* (Chapel Hill: University of North Carolina Press, 2009), 113–20.

14. Mrs. William F. Dickens, "News from the Children of the Confederacy," *UDC Magazine*, May 1956, 3; Joseph Hayes Jackson, "Our Double Heritage," ibid., March 1956, 41; "Children of the Confederacy News," ibid., August 1961, 19; Stephen J. Whitfield, *The Culture of the Cold War* (1991; Baltimore: Johns Hopkins University Press, 1996), chap. 4; Jane Dailey, "Sex, Segregation, and the Sacred after Brown," *Journal of American History* 91 (June 2004): 119–44; Wilson, *Baptized in Blood*; Alice Whitley Jones, "Contributions of the Southern Women to the Cause of the Confederacy," *UDC Magazine*, October 1963, 13, 39, 41, 43; Alice Whitley Jones, "Contributions of the Southern Women to the Cause of the Confederacy," ibid., November 1963, 14, 37–38.

15. Mrs. J. S. Goldsmith, "News from the Children of the Confederacy," ibid., July 1954, 9; Mrs. Fred E. Rogers, "Children of the Confederacy News," ibid., July 1958, 7; "Children of the Confederacy News," ibid., April 1960, 14; LaVerne H. Watson, "Third Vice President General," ibid., December 1962, 5; "Children of the Confederacy News," ibid., October 1962, 20.

16. "Children of the Confederacy News," ibid., February 1958, 10; John M. Coski, *The Confederate Battle Flag: America's Most Embattled Emblem* (Cambridge: Belknap Press of Harvard University Press, 2005), chaps. 5–8; Sam J. Ervin Jr., "Our Heritage: A Blessing and an Obligation," *UDC Magazine*, December 1962, 14; John Stennis, "A Reappraisal of the Life of Jefferson Davis," ibid., June 1956, 26; Strom Thurmond, "South Faces Second 'Tragic Era,'" ibid., January 1958, 15; "Children of the Confederacy News," ibid., July 1964, 35.

17. Robert J. Cook, *Troubled Commemoration: The American Civil War Centennial, 1961–1965* (Baton Rouge: Louisiana State University Press, 2007); "Message of the President General," *UDC Magazine*, May 1961, 3; "Children of the Confederacy News," ibid., August 1962, 18.

18. Jewell F. Renfroe, "Third Vice President General," *UDC Magazine*, May 1965, 5; Woodward, *Burden of Southern History*, 3.

—— DOCUMENTS ——

Through the Eyes of
Civil War Children

Just as the Civil War inspired untold thousands of American adults to record their thoughts and experiences, their fears and inspirations, it encouraged children and youth to write down their perceptions of the war and its aftermath. Although many of the preceding essays did draw on sources produced by children—or by adults recalling their childhoods—the documents in this part all provide specific points of view of young participants in the Civil War. They range from a southern girl besieged by Yankee troops to a young northern woman besieged by wartime responsibilities and hardships, from northern schoolboys experimenting with political rhetoric and patriotism to southern boys trying out the principle of states' rights as it applied to their own concerns, and from a brief oral history of a slave's wartime life and a poignant description of the moment of freedom on a small plantation to a memoir of the equally complex emotions sparked by the return of a soldier-father. Several are reminiscences written years after the war, but one is a famous—and rare—child's diary, and two others are articles from an even rarer high school newspaper. Together they show that children and youth of the Civil War era were not simply victims or passive bystanders, but active participants with their own particular experiences and insights.

"I Hope by My Next Birthday We Will Have Peace in Our Land": Carrie Berry Endures the Fall of Atlanta

Carrie Berry was not so much politicized by the war as she was worn down by it. During the fighting around Atlanta in August 1864 and for nearly a year afterward, the ten-year-old kept a terse diary that is one of the only first-person accounts of the war by a young child as she actually lived it. Virtually every moment of Carrie's life was dominated by the war, even after the battle was over and most of her friends and neighbors had evacuated the city. The Berry family moved to supposedly safer quarters on more than one occasion, and they often spent hours or entire nights in a bomb shelter. Carrie frequently wished that she could return to school and to church, and quietly reported on her tenth birthday that "I did not have a cake times were too hard." A good day was a day with little or no shelling or a treat like the bunch of "nice grapes" her aunt somehow scrounged. When the siege ended with the evacuation of the city by the Confederates, she was happy to have a chance to play with a friend for the first time in six weeks. The excerpts offer a cross section of the experiences of southern children who came in harm's way during the war. It is worth noting that Carrie survived the war and married a young veteran named William Macon Crumley. Together they raised four children; she died in Atlanta in 1921.[1]

Aug. 1. Monday. It was raining this morning and we thought we would not have any shelling today so I nurst Sister while Mama would do a little work, but before night we had to run to the cellar.

Aug. 2. Tuesday. We have not been shelled much today, but the muskets have been going all day. I have done but little today but nurse Sister. She has not been well today.

Aug. 3. Wednesday. This was my birthday. I was ten years old, But I did not have a cake times were too hard so I celebrated with ironing. I hope by my next birthday we will have peace in our land so that I can have a nice dinner.

Carrie Berry Diary Typescript, Atlanta History Center, Atlanta, Georgia

Aug. 4. Thurs. The shells have ben flying all day and we have stayed in the cellar. Mama put me on some stockings this morning and I will try to finish them before school commences.

Aug. 5. Friday. I knit all the morning. In the evening we had to run to Auntie's and get in the cellar. We did not feel safe in our cellar, they fell so thick and fast.

• • •

Aug. 7. Sun. We have had a quiet day it all most seems like Sunday of old. Papa and I went to Trinity Church. Mr. Haygood preached. It is the first time I have been to Church in a month.

• • •

Aug. 9. Tues. We have had to stay in the cellar all day the shells have ben falling so thick around the house. Two have fallen in the garden, but none of us were hurt. Cousin Henry Beatty came in and wanted us to move, he thought that we were in danger, but we will try it a little longer.

Aug. 10. Wed. We have had but few shells to day. It has ben raining nearly all day and we had to stay in the house very close.

• • •

Aug. 14. Sun. Sure enough we had shells in abundance last night. We averaged one every moment during the night. We expected every one would come through and hurt some of us but to our joy nothing on the lot was hurt. They have ben throwing them at us all day to day but they have not ben dangerous. Papa has ben at work all day making the cellar safe. Now we feel like we could stay at home in safety. I dislike to stay in the cellar so close but our soldiers have to stay in ditches.

Aug. 15. Mon. We had no shells this morning when we got up and we thought that we would not have any to day (but, my, when will they stop) but soon after breakfast Zuie and I were standing on the platform between the house and the dining room. It made a very large hole in the garden and threw the dirt all over the yard. I never was so frightened in my life. Zuie was as pale as a corpse and I expect I was too. It did not take us long to fly to the cellar. We stayed out till night though we had them all day but they did not come so near us again.

• • •

Aug. 21. Sun. This was a dark rainy morning and we thought we would have a quiet Sunday but we were disappointed. Papa says that we will have to move down town some where. Our cellar is not safe.

Aug 22. Mon. I got up this morning and helped Mama pact up to move. We were glad to get out of our small cellar. We have a nice large cellar here where we can run as much as we please and enjoy it. Mama says that we make so much noise that she can't here the shells.

Aug. 23. Tues. We feel very comfortable since we have moved but Mama is fretted to death all the time for fear of fire. There is a fire in town nearly every day. I get so tired of being housed up all the time. The shells get worse and worse every day. O that something would stop them.

• • •

Aug. 26. Fri. Cousin Henry came in this morning and told us we need not fear the shells any more. The Yankees left there brest works and he hoped they were on the way back to Tennessee. We have had such a delightful day. We all wanted to move to day but we will wait til to morrow and see if the Yankees have gone.

Aug. 27. Sat. We moved home this morning and we have ben busy trying to get things regulated. I feel so glad to get home and have no shells around us.

Aug. 28. Sun. Everything seemed so quiet this morning. I wish the people would come back so we could have Church and Sunday School. Mr._____ came in this morning and brought some shells which Cousin Henry sent us. He got them from the Yankees. Cousin Eddy came in this morning to tell us goodbye. We feel sorry he was going to move so far. We all ways love to see him and Cousin Henry.

• • •

Sept. 1. Thurs. We did not get home untill twelve o'clock. We had a very pleasant time and every thing seemed quiet. Directly after dinner Cousin Emma came down and told us that Atlanta would be evacuated this evening and we might look for the federals in the morning. It was not long till the hole town found it out and such excitement there was. We have ben looking for them all the evening but they have not come yet. Mr. _____ came in to tell us that dear Cousin Henry was wounded and he thought he would not get well. We are so sory to here it. We loved him so much. I finished my stockings to day.

Sept. 2. Fri. We all woke up this morning without sleeping much last night. The Confederates had four engenes and a long train of box cars filled with amunition and set it on fire last night which caused a grate explosion which kept us all awake. It reminded us of the shells—of all the days of excitement we have had it to day. Every one has been trying to get all they could before the Federals come in the morning. They have ben running with saques of meal, salt and tobacco. They did act rediculous breaking open stores and robbing them. About twelve o'clock there were a few federals came in. They were all frightened. We were afraid they were going to treat us badly. It was not long till the Infantry came in. They were orderly and behaved very well. I think I shall like the Yankees very well.

Sept. 3. Sat. 1864. The soldiers have ben coming in all day. I went up to Aunties this morning and she said that she had a yankee officer to spend the night with her. We have not seen much of them. Only two of them have ben here to beg some thing to eat. We have had a rainy day and we all feel gloomy.

Sun. Sept 4. Another long and lonesome Sunday. How I wish we could have Church and Sunday School. We have ben looking at the soldiers all day. They have come in by the thousand. They were playing bands and they seemed to be rejoiced. It has not seemed like Sunday.

• • •

Wed. Sept. 14. I helpt to wash till dinner time and then I got dinner by myself. It made me very warm and tired but I supose I will have to learn to wirk. I have ben resting all the evening and I think I will sleep right sound to night if the musquitoes dont bite me too much.

• • •

Fri. Sept. 16. I ironed till dinner and got through and I had a hollowday the rest of the evening. We have had a nice time playing and I think I will sleep sound to night.

• • •

Sat. Oct. 1. It is very warm for the first day of October but we will look out for a frost before long. I have been making my doll a frock for Sunday.

Sun. Oct. 2. This has ben a very pretty day. I went around to Mrs. Lesters. Ella and I took a walk to see how the soldiers had torn down the fine houses. It is a shame to see the fine houses torn down.

• • •

Sun. Oct 23. This has ben a beautiful day since the sun has come out. Mama and Papa took a walk this evening and they say that they never saw a place torn up like Atlanta is. Half of the houses are torn down.

Mon. Oct. 24. I went to see Ellen Flemming this evening, one of my old school mates. I had a nice time. She is a very nice little girl.

Tues. Oct. 25. Zuie and I went around to spend the evening and we had a very nice time playing with our dolls. That is all I have to interest me. Ella has had my doll a week or two and Ella made her so many nice clothes that she was dressed up so fine.

• • •

Sun. Oct. 30. I have ben over to Julia Lowry this evening. They are all ready to move and it looks like every body is going to leave here from the way the soldiers are moving about. Our sargent left us this morning. We all were sorry to part with him. He has ben a very good friend to us.

• • •

Mon Nov. 7. Every boddie seems to be in confusion. The black wimmen are running around trying to get up north for fear that the Rebels will come in and take them.

Tues. Nov. 8. This is Zuie's birthday and she has been very smart. We lost our last hog this morning early. Soldiers took him out of the pen. Me and Buddie went around to hunt for him and every where that we inquired they would say that they saw two soldiers driving off to kill him. We will have to live on bread.

• • •

Sat. Nov. 12. We were fritened almost to death last night. Some mean soldiers set several houses on fire in different parts of the town. I could not go to sleep for fear that they would set our house on fire. We all dred the next few days to come for they said that they would set the last house on fire if they had to leave this place.

Sun. Nov. 13. The federal soldiers have ben coming to day and burning houses and I have ben looking at them come in nearly all day.

Mon. Nov. 14. They came burning Atlanta to day. We all dread it because they say that they will burn the last house before they stop. We will dread it.

Tues. Nov. 15. This has ben a dreadful day. Things have ben burning all around us. We dread to night because we do not know what moment that they will set our house on fire. We have had a gard a little while after dinner and we feel a little more protected.

Wed. Nov. 16. Oh what a night we had. . . . it looked like the whole town was on fire. We all set up all night. If we had not set up our house would have ben burnt up for the fire was very near and the soldiers were going around setting houses on fire where they were not watched. They behaved very badly. They all left the town about one o'clock this evening and we were glad when they left for no body know what we have suffered since they came in

• • •

Fri. Nov. 18. We children have ben plundering about to day seeing what we could find. Mama has been trying to straiten up for the house was torn up so bad.

• • •

Tues. Nov. 22. It is just a week to day since the federals were burning. Papa and Mama say that they feel very poor. We have not got anything but our little house. It is still very cold.

• • •

Mon. Nov. 28. We have all ben picking up nails to day and we are all about tired down.

Tues. Nov. 29. We have ben picking up nails again to day and it has made me sore.

Wed. Nov. 30. We have ben resting to day. The cittizens are still coming in and it wont be very long untill they get the railroad fixed up from here to Macon and then I hope I can see Grandma.

• • •

Wed. Dec. 7. This has ben a election day for Mayor and council men but the election was broken up. I had a little sister this morning at eight o'clock and Mama gave her to me. I think its very pretty. I had to cook breakfast and dinner and supper.

Thurs. Dec. 8. I have ben cooking and cleaning house and waiting on Mama and little sister Maggy. I have learnt to make nice egg bread and how to cook very nice.

Fri. Dec. 9. I made up some buiskets last night and Mama says that they were nice. Every moment I can get I am making things to do on the [Christmas] tree. Ella and I are going to have one together. This has ben a cold sleaty day.

• • •

Tues. Dec. 20. I have ben buisy making presents all day. I went down to Mrs. Lesters to make Mamas. Miss Matt helped me. I think it is so pretty. I fear we will not get through with our presents Christmas is getting so near.

• • •

Thurs. Dec. 22. We went to get our Christmas tree this evening. It was very cold but we did not feel it we were so excited about it.

Fri. Dec. 23. I went down to Mrs. Lesters and Ella and me planted the tree and finished making the last presents. I came home and strained some pumpkins to make some pies for Christmas.

Sat. Dec. 24. I have been buisy to day making cakes to trim the tree and Ella and I have it all ready trimed and we are all going to night to see it. I think it looks very pretty. We will be sorry when it is all over.

Sun. Dec. 25, 1864. We all went down last night to see the tree and how pretty it looked. The room was full of ladies and children and Cap. gave us music on the pianno and tried to do all he could to make us enjoy our selves and we did have a merry time. All came home perfectly satisfied. This has ben a cold dark day but we all went down to see how the tree looked in the day time but it was not as pretty as at night.

• • •

Sunday. Jan. 1. 1865. This is New Year day. I woke up this morning . . . but did not get anything the times is too hard. I stayed at home untill evening and then I went down to Mrs. Lesters . . . . [W]e played around there and then we came around home and we sat down and wrote a little letter and then Ella and Anna went home.

Mon. Jan. 2. We all started to school this morning to Miss Mattie. Ella, me and Buddie are studying arithmetic, spelling, reading and geography. We are all trying to see which will learn the most.

Tues. Jan. 3. I had a hard geography lesson and Ella came home with me and we studied the geography untill we knowed it perfect. We have to study very hard and we dont get time to do much of anything but we have ben playing long enough to spend our time on our books.

* * *

Tues. Feb. 14. This has ben a bad day it would rain a little while and then it would freeze and the ground was so slick that we could scarcely walk. We went to school and Miss Mary told us to go back home and she sayd that it was so cold that we could not study. This has been valentine day. I got a valentine. I think it came from Eddy Adamson.

"A Strenuous and Tragic Affair":
Life on the Northern Home Front

Unlike Carrie Berry, Anna Howard never had to worry about enemy fire or occupation. But Anna, who as an adult would become a pioneering Methodist minister, doctor, and advocate for women's suffrage, represents the ways that many girls and boys in the North were affected by the absence of fathers and older brothers. Born in England in 1847, Anna was raised in New England, where her father provided for his growing family as a laborer and craftsmen but also took part in many liberal causes, including abolitionism. Their lives changed forever when he moved them to the Michigan wilderness with a group of other Englishmen. Anna was twelve when they moved to their new farm a hundred miles from the railroad. Mr. Howard deposited his family on the frontier and promptly returned to New England, where he continued working for two years. He finally joined the family just about the time the war was starting, but within a year had joined the Union army with his two oldest sons. At the age of fifteen, Shaw was the main breadwinner for her family, and life had become "a strenuous and tragic affair." The family somehow survived, and all of the men came back from the war, but before long Anna left home to begin her life as a pioneering feminist—perhaps inspired by the trials and freedoms she had experienced during the war.

In the meantime war had been declared. When the news came that Fort Sumter had been fired on, and that Lincoln had called for troops, our men were threshing. There was only one threshing-machine in the region at that time, and it went from place to place, the farmers doing their threshing whenever they could get the machine. I remember seeing a man ride up on horseback, shouting out Lincoln's demand for troops and explaining that a regiment was being formed at Big Rapids. Before he had finished speaking the men on the machine had leaped to the ground and rushed off to enlist, my brother Jack, who had recently joined us, among them. In ten minutes not one man was

---

Anna Howard Shaw, *The Story of a Pioneer* (New York: Harper and Brothers, 1915), 51–54

left in the field. A few months later my brother Tom enlisted as a bugler—he was a mere boy at the time—and not long after that my father followed the example of his sons and served until the war was ended. He had entered on the twenty-ninth of August, 1862, as an army steward; he came back to us with the rank of lieutenant and assistant surgeon of the field and staff.

Between those years I was the principal support of our family, and life became a strenuous and tragic affair. For months at a time we had no news from the front. The work in our community, if it was done at all, was done by despairing women whose hearts were with their men. When care had become our constant guest, Death entered our home as well. My sister Eleanor had married, and died in childbirth, leaving her baby to me; and the blackest hours of those black years were the hours that saw her passing. . . . Her baby slipped into her vacant place and almost filled our heavy hearts, but only for a short time; for within a few months after his mother's death his father married again and took him from me, and it seemed that with his going we had lost all that made life worth while.

The problem of living grew harder with every day. We eked out our little income in every way we could, taking as boarders the workers in the logging-camps, making quilts, which we sold, and losing no chance to earn a penny in any legitimate manner. Again my mother did such outside sewing as she could secure, yet with every month of our effort the gulf between our income and our expenses grew wider, and the price of the bare necessities of existence climbed up and up. The largest amount I could earn at teaching was six dollars a week, and our school year included only two terms of thirteen weeks each. It was an incessant struggle to keep our land, to pay our taxes, and to live. Calico was selling at fifty cents a yard. Coffee was one dollar a pound. There were no men left to grind our corn, to get in our crops, or to care for our live stock; and all around us we saw our struggle reflected in the lives of our neighbors.

At long intervals word came to us of battles in which my father's regiment—the Tenth Michigan Cavalry Volunteers—or those of my brothers were engaged, and then longer intervals followed in which we heard no news. After Eleanor's death my brother Tom was wounded, and for months we lived in terror of worse tidings, but he finally recovered. I was walking seven and eight miles a day, and doing extra work before and after school hours, and my health began to fail. Those were years I do not like to look back upon—years in which life had degenerated into a treadmill whose monotony was broken only by the grim messages from the front. My sister Mary married and went to Big Rapids to live. I had no time to dream my dream, but the star of my one purpose still glowed in my dark horizon. It seemed that nothing short of a miracle could lift my feet from their plodding way and set them on the wider path toward which my eyes were turned, but I never lost faith that in some manner the miracle would come to pass. As certainly as I have ever known anything, I knew that I was going to college!

The end of the Civil War brought freedom to me, too. When peace was declared my father and brothers returned to the claim in the wilderness which we women of the family had labored so desperately to hold while they were gone.

"The Threshold of a New Year":
High School Journalists Weigh In on the Civil War

When it opened in 1855, Newark High School was one of the first high schools in the country. Although its 370 students were about evenly split between girls and boys, during the Civil War, a few of its leading male students decided to publish a school newspaper called the Athenaeum. The handwritten monthly featured stories, poems, and essays that seem to have been written originally as class assignments. They ranged from a two-part narrative of a classmate's hair-raising escape from the 1863 sack of Lawrence, Kansas, to an editorial arguing that the moral courage of patriots had to match their physical courage, and to the humorous story "Uncle Zeke at the Fair," where a cranky old man battled crowds and high prices at the local Sanitary Fair. The following two selections both appeared in the January 1864 edition; in looking back at the year just ended and forward at the year to come, both mimicked the style and predictions of grown-up editorialists. If they proved to have been a little too optimistic—the war did not, of course, end in 1864—they nevertheless reflected the way that young northerners were politicized by the war.[2]

E. P. Holloway, "The Old and New Year"

Again in the course of events another year has rolled away and 1863 is no more and now upon the threshold of a new year let us pause and look back over the history of the past year. The first of January 1863 will long be remembered throughout the world, as the day on which the famous emancipation proclamation took effect. This proclamation though of little apparent importance yet is slowly but surely undermining the whole system of slavery. The bravery of our soldiers has been shown on many a hard fought battlefield, twice did they march on Fredricksburg into the very jaws of death and as often were they were compelled to retreat. Not

---

Newark High School *Athenaeum*, January 1864, from the Collections of the New Jersey Historical Society, Newark, New Jersey

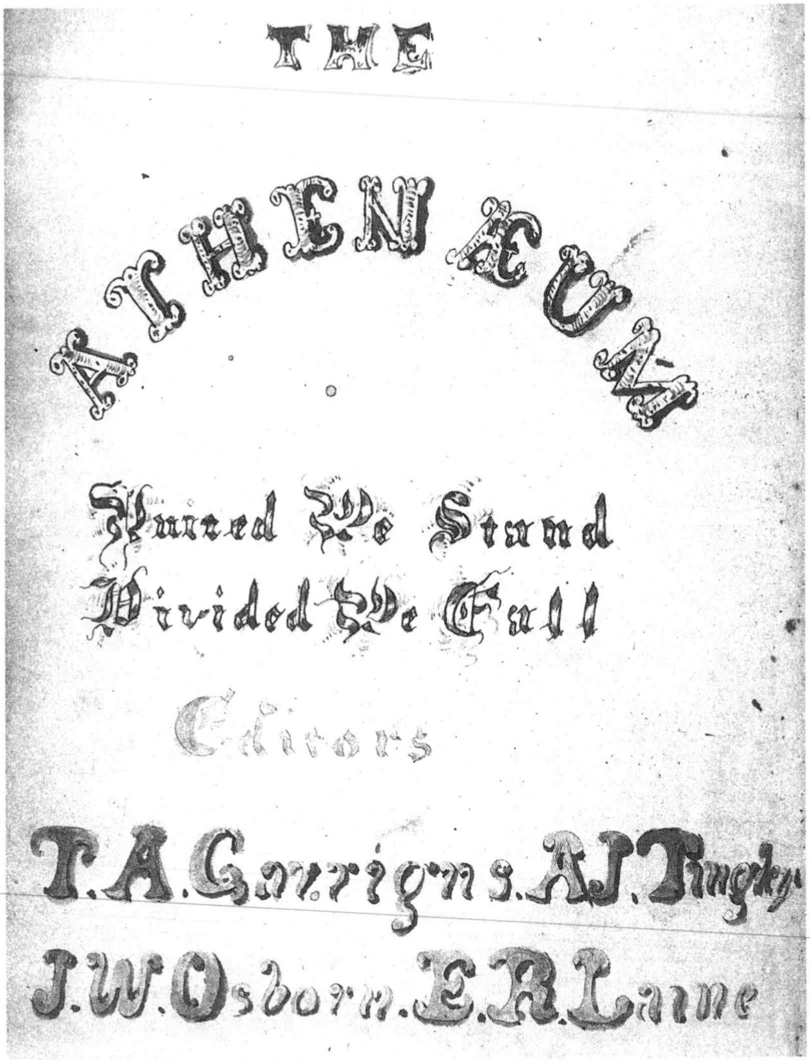

Figure 13.1. Title page, Newark High School *Athenaeum*, October 1863, New Jersey Historical Society.

so however at Gettysburgh where the very existence of the nation seemed trembling in the balance, then did they nobly meet and battle with the foes of liberty. With what feelings can we now look back upon the few days which immediately preceded the 4th of July 1863, for we felt and saw that upon the issue of that battle depended the safety and happiness of our own firesides and there with what feelings of joy did we hail the tidings of victory as they were flashed over the wires on the anniversary of the nation's birth. Joy which was only to be heightened in a few days by the news of the surrender of Vicksburg and Port Hudson. These glorious victories were followed by a long term of comparative quiet during which all was quiet "along the lines." But at length a shout of victory was heard in the south west, and Chattanooga was the scene of another triumph of the Union army. General Grant had granted us another glorious victory. But these victories have not been secured without great loss of life, and while we rejoice over our victories, let us not forget the many homes that have been made desolate during the past years by the ravages of war. And let us ever cherish the memory of those who laid down their lives in the defense of Liberty. And now we have entered upon the year 1864 a happy year may it be to each of us and if it be the evil of Providence may it be a happy year to our beloved land. And may the close of this year witness the close of this struggle, and the return of unity and peace to our now divided and distracted country.

T. A. Garrigus, "The Speedy Restoration of the Union"

Glorious news! Cheering the hearts of anxiously waiting millions wafting sweet balm to the sorrowing mothers, and weary wives, because of the long absence of her son, or, her husband. But if some never return— If husbands forever stay away—If the breaking hearts of mothers are never healed—If the weary wife never smiles on the husband again—If all this desolation and down heartedness come upon us may it be our earnest desire that this war shall not end until this rebellion is entirely crushed, until every traitor in arms shall have thrown them down, and every traitor in heart shall have acknowledged his country's government or shall have had his breath stopped. Then and not until then, may war end in our land. But appearances are now that very soon the banner we love, will not have one opposing enemy. The leading men of the rebel armies are getting discouraged and the privates of their armies are almost persuaded to lay down their arms. The principal papers that have done their best to sustain Rebellion are about giving up the Phantom Ship. They report that their armies are badly in want of provisions. They are starving on short rations. They are freezing because of their nakedness. They are aware that if they give up and will fight no more that Uncle Sam has enough and to spare. While they are feeding on Husks hardly fit for swine. Yes! The war evidently will soon end even now the "Rebs" are deserting in large numbers and surrendering to the Yankees. Then let us hope that [on] our fourth of July 1864 there may be a double celebration including our independence and the surrendering of the traitorous hordes—and that anon may be fired in honor of a pure and spotless Flag—not a star faded from its field of blue—that then "The star spangled Banner in triumph shall wave ov'r the land of the South and Jeff Davis's Grave."

"Sports in the Days of the Sixties": War and Play

The war inserted itself into the lives of children throughout the Union and the Confederacy in unfortunate and tragic ways. But virtually all children sought to engage the war meaningfully, and for many, that meant incorporating it into their play. One of the most frequently mentioned forms of play in diaries and memoirs was, not surprisingly, "playing army." Boys—and a few girls—created their own companies, practiced the manual of arms, and staged battles. Sometimes the "boys' companies" got out of hand; in Richmond, they became little better than gangs that went about robbing other boys and breaking windows. Six decades after the war, the Georgian D. F. Morrow published a long reminiscence of the Civil War era in his little hometown of Burnt Chimneys that included a long passage about the most elaborate expedition mounted by a boys' company: a raid on the watermelon patch. The owner had broken a community custom of allowing boys to take melons whenever they wanted to, prompting the boys, under the command of the redoubtable Phip Flaxon, to duplicate the actions of their fathers and brothers and defend their "watermelon rights." This and the countless other memoirs that mention various kinds of war play indicate the extent to which the war made an impact on children at the most basic level.

Now, those melons were not at that time grown for the market as they are now in many parts of Georgia and other places, but simply for the use of the farmer, his friends and neighbors. They were considered kinder free to all who might be passing and see them when ripe, if he was thirsty or hungry and wanted a melon. Even a stranger would dismount and help himself, for such was the custom in those days.

This now would be larceny; at that time, nothing more than a trespass, if that. But once in a while there would be some neighbor who did not like for the boys of the community to make a raid on his patch. And such was old

D. F. Morrow, *Then and Now: Reminiscences and Historical Romance, 1856–1865* (Macon, GA: J. W. Burke, 1926), 65–73

Sam Canahan of our good settlement, in and around Burnt Chimneys, now Forest City. Old Sam had not lived very long in our section, but he was a very knowing kind of a man, and was much heard from in all the gatherings, at church, or gatherings of any kind. Sam could be counted on to do the most of the talking and most of his talk was about himself and his son, Tad, for that was his boy's name. Sam knew everything or at least he thought he did, and what he did not know, Tad did. But such people make mistakes once in a while as well as other folks. Old Sam made his mistake one day at Church in July, 1863, when he was telling a big crowd about his watermelon patch. He said that he had the finest one in the county and he and Tad had decided to watch it and see that the boys did not go there at night or any other time without permission, for he and Tad both had guns and were prepared to protect them, that is the watermelons. Now, at this meeting and hearing was Phip Flaxen, and a number of his pals who composed the boys' brigade of Watermelon Rights and Community Entertainments, in Cool Springs Township and Burnt Chimneys Muster Ground. These boys were well organized, Phip Flaxen was the captain, and he was on the job all the time. He studied the condition of things in the community at all times, even on Sundays and when he heard old Sam Canahan talking at the church about his watermelon patch, there and then the captain decided that the Watermelon Rights of the Boys' Brigade of the Burnt Chimneys Township or Muster Ground were being assailed and questioned by old Sam Canahan and his son, Tad. This was something new, for up until this time the right to watermelons had been in Phip's bailiwick, a kind of community right. That is, every boy, man or woman in the community had a right, by custom, to any watermelon patch in the community and had no questions asked. Phip Flaxen was the captain, and had the right to call out the brigade at any time. Phip just called them his boys, and they were, for they would do anything he said. Phip was about twelve years old, large for his age, had "kinder" white hair, not gray, but thin on the top of his head, very fair skin, red face, and was as brave as boys could be at his age. Now, as you know, this was in time of the war. Phip had heard much of States' Rights among the men and neighbors and was taught to believe that the men had the right to defend States' Rights and if they did why should not boys defend and protect their right to the watermelon patch? Phip said they did and told the boys so.

That very day, and while the services were going on in the church, Phip called some of his boys together and they went out behind the church, under a big tree, and there held a council of war and it was decided that if Sam Canahan and Tad were going to shoot any boy found in their watermelon patch, that they should have a chance to do so on Tuesday night and he, then and there, issued orders for all the brigade to meet at Hill's Cross Roads promptly at nine o'clock. It was only a mile down the river from this place to Canahan's watermelon patch. Phip instructed all the boys to procure light shot guns and have them loaded with powder and peas. These guns, so loaded, would not kill, Phip said, but would scare as well as if they were loaded with buck shot. Now, Tom was acting sergeant under Phip but was instructed not to bring his dog, Dixie, for he might bark at the wrong time. This was an act of the brigade a little out of the ordinary, for heretofore it had only been chicken fights and camp suppers, but here was a case entirely different. The boys' Watermelon Rights had been assailed by Canahan and his son, in public, in fact, right at the meeting house, and in the presence of lots of the meeting house folks in the presence of Phip, the Captain, and something must be done. The Captain being a cautious officer, in his council of war, had decided that all must be kept a secret, and for this reason had issued orders and sent them out to all the boys not present at the meeting, that whatever information might be delivered to them about the meeting at the cross roads, should be kept a secret. Now, this order was delivered to the sergeant, who was instructed by the Captain to tell all the boys to keep quiet and come prepared for a great time "feast and fishing party." This was a hoax order, of course, but it served its purpose. Tom was busy all Monday and Tuesday, notifying the boys. The order was not only to bring the guns loaded with powder and peas, but for some one to bring a hen, and another to bring a corn "dodger" or two, and some one else to bring salt and match (which in this day was scarce), another a pot and still another to see that each had his fishing pole, line and hook, and all to meet promptly at Hill's Cross Roads at nine o'clock, sharp, on Tuesday night, July 30, 1863. Signed Phip Flaxen, Capt. Executed by Tom W., Sergeant.

Just at 5:30 p. m., July 30, 1863, the sergeant, Tom, made his report to Captain Phip, at his headquarters, at 'Squire Flaxen's place, that all the orders had been executed and that all the boys with the equipment would be on hand at Hill's Cross Roads. Tom had told Uncle Johnny and Aunt Julia that he was going over to 'Squire Flaxen's to spend the night with cousin Phip. For this is what Tom called the captain, except when on duty. So Tom remained with Captain Phip for supper and then both Phip and Tom told the 'Squire that they were going fishing along with the boys and might not get back till late.

Just at nine at the Hill, or Hill-Morrow Cross Roads Captain Phip's brigade or company assembled. The roll was called by the Sergeant, Tom, and every one answered present and also reported that all equipment asked for in the order was on hand. After a short parley, it was decided to march quietly to the river at the mouth of Chinquapin Creek and there to confiscate Annie Lightfoot's fishing canoe or boat and make their way down the river to Canahan's farm and watermelon patch; which was right on the bank of the river. Soon they were at the boat. Now, the order was to load all guns, stores, bag and baggage, onto the boat and then all boys on top and row on down the river. There are some things hard to do in life and one of those was for the boys to keep quiet while on their sail down the river. You know it is hard for a woman to keep a secret or quit talking, and just as hard for a boy, or harder, to keep his mouth shut, especially when out sailing a boat or on a fishing party. But these boys knew the order and kept it. The order by the captain to halt was given in low tone. The boat was soon anchored to a willow tree by a rope right up to the bank and in front of old Sam Canahan's watermelon patch. Order again, "Boys all out! Baggage all to remain in the boat, except the guns." In a short time all the boys with guns, ten in number, were posted along the river banks, standing down at the water's edge. The banks at this place were about four feet high and each boy was ordered to level his gun out on the bank toward the melon patch and the Canahan home. This being done in good order they were instructed by the Captain and Sergeant to remain in that position, and to listen for, and obey any order that might be given. There were some boys who did not have guns and these were detailed by the Captain to mount over the bank and into the watermelon patch, in double quick time and they did and the orders were to get five of the best watermelons in the patch. This order was executed in silence. In a short time the detail reported with the melons, and they were put on the boat with the other baggage and supplies of the company.

As these rolled into their places on the other junk in the boat a kind of "Rebel yell" went up from all the boys and it was sanctioned by the captain, for he joined in. This was a signal for Canahan that his patch was being raided and if he and Tad wanted to come out and shoot, "let um cum," the boys said for every one now was safe behind the bank and down near the water and the boat. The captain gave an order to the boys at the guns, loaded with peas and leveled upon the banks, to cock their guns and be ready to fire at the command, but not to fire till the command was given, and in this order: At first command, two first standing next to the officer, to fire, and at the second command all the other eight to fire as near at one time as they could. Just at this time the boys heard Canahan's dog bark and running in the direction of the watermelon patch. Captain Phip raised up just a little, looked over the bank and said, "Quiet men," for that is what he called the boys, "Canahan and Tad are coming and they have their guns." At this each gunman dropped to his knees but held their guns over the bank and pointing right in the direction of old Sam, Tad and the dog. Now there was quiet on our line for those who did not have guns, had fallen flat on the sand behind the gunmen and the bank. Tom, the Sergeant, was brave as a lion, for he said he was, but just at this moment, he dropped on the sand so hard Capt. Phip laughed and some of the other boys, too. But Tom was not laughing; he was making some kind of a queer noise and shaking like he was laughing, but he was not. The old dog came nearer the bank and was barking like he had treed a coon or something.

Captain Phip again raised himself up just a little and started to look over the bank, but before he could get straight up, old Sam's gun went off and it sounded like a cannon to us. Capt. Phip fell flat on his back on the sand and shouted the command: "Fire! One and all." And poor Tom said, "Lord, he is killed." But our boys with the guns began to fire and they were not as loud as Sam's but the pop, pop was fierce and as the sound of the firing died away, we heard Sam's old dog yelling and running back toward the house. By this time all the boys rose to their feet and looking over the bank could see Tad, old Sam, and the dog going up the hill toward the house. Tad in front, dog next and old Sam bringing up the rear, but both had dropped their guns. The battle was over. The dog had been hit with peas and Sam and Tad scared out of their wits.

Such was some of the sports in the days of the sixties and the customs of the country in the South at that time.

"De drums wus beatin'":
Caroline Richardson Meets the Yankees

One of the richest—if problematic—sources for the experiences of African Americans during the Civil War are the famous "slave narratives," oral histories taken down by Work Projects Administration interviewers in the late 1930s. Eventually more than 2,300 former slaves were interviewed; all but forgotten in state and federal archives for decades, the transcripts of the interviews appeared in print for the first time in the forty-one-volume The American Slave: A Composite Autobiography (Westport, CT: Greenwood Press, 1972–79), edited by George P. Rawick. Although the mostly white interviewers cluttered the transcripts with misspellings in an effort to capture "negro dialect," and although many were less word-for-word transcriptions than they were sometimes creative retellings of conversations, the slave narratives provide the most important set of documents offering the points of view of men and women who had been slaves more than seven decades earlier.

Caroline Richardson's oral history briefly recalls her childhood on a plantation in central North Carolina. She remembers her master as a relatively kind man and, like many slaves living far from the actual fighting, indicates that the war was not a major factor in her life—until both Confederate and Yankee troops passed by during the final months of the conflict. The excitement of meeting the men in blue—apparently members of General William T. Sherman's army, who had turned north from Savannah after their "March to the Sea" and forged through South and North Carolina—dominates her account.

I reckin dat I is somers 'bout sixty year old. Anyhow I wus ten or twelve when de Yankees come ter Marse Ransome bridgers' place near Clayton. Dat's whar I wus borned an' my pappy, my mammy an' we 'leben chilluns 'longed ter Marse Ransome an' Mis' Adeline. Dar wus also young Marse George an' young Miss Betsy who I 'longed to. . . .

George P. Rawick, ed., The American Slave: A Composite Autobiography, 41 vols. (Westport, CT: Greenwood Press, 1972–79), vol. 11, pt. 2, 199–200

We ain't heard much 'bout de war, nothin' lak we heard 'bout de world war [the First World War]. I knows dat nobody from our plantation ain't gone ter dat war case Marse Ransome wus too old an' Marse George wus a patteroller [a member of a slave patrol], or maybe he wus just too young. Dar wus a little bit of talk but most of it we ain't heard. I tended to de slave babies, but my mammy what cooked in de big house heard some of de war talk an' I heard her a-talkin' to pappy about it. When she seed me a-listenin' she said dat she'd cut my years off iffen I told it. I had seen some of de slaves wid clipped years an' I wanted to keep mine, so I ain't said nothin'.

One day Mis' Betsy come out ter de yard an' she sez ter we chilluns, "You has got de habit of runnin' ter de gate to see who can say howdy first to our company, well de Yankees will be here today or tomorrow an' dey ain't our company. In fact iffen yo' runs ter de gate ter meet dem dey will shoot you dead."

Ober late dat evenin' I heard music an' I runs ter de gate ter see whar it am. Comin' down de road as fast as dey can I sees a bunch of men wid gray suits on a-ridin' like de debil. Dey don't stop at our house at all but later I heard dat dey wus [Confederate general Joseph] Wheeler's cavalry, de very meanest of de Rebs, though 'tis said dat dey wus brave in battle.

About a hour atter Wheeler's men come by de Yankees hove into sight. De drums wus beatin', de flags wavin' an' de hosses prancin' high. We niggers has been teached dat de Yankees will kill us, men women an' chilluns. De whole hundret or so of us runs an' hides.

Yes mam, I 'members de blue uniforms an' de brass buttons, an' I 'members how dey said as dey come in de gate dat dey has a good as won de war, an' dat dey ort ter hang de southern men what won't go ter war.

I reckin dat dey talk puty rough ter Marse Ransome. Anyhow, mammy tells de Yankee Captain dat he ort ter be 'shamed of talkin' ter a old man like dat. Furder more, she tells dem dat he died en dat's de way dey're gwine ter git her freedom, she don't want it at all. Wid dat mammy takes Mis' Betsy upstairs whar de Yankees won't be a-starin' at her.

One of de Yankees fin's me an' axes me how many pairs of shoes I gits a year. I tells him dat I gits one pair. Den he axes me what I wears in de summertime. When I tells him dat I ain't wear nothin' but a shirt, an' dat I goes barefooted in de summer, he cusses awful an' he damns my marster.

Mammy said dat dey tol' her an' pappy dat dey'd git some land an' a mule iffen dey wus freed. You see dey tried to turn de slaves agin dere marsters.

At de surrender most of de niggers left, but me an' my family stayed fer wages. We ain't really had as good as we done before the war, an' 'cides dat we has ter worry about how we're goin' ter live....

"A Momentous and Eventful Day":
Freedom Comes to Booker T. Washington

Although most of us naturally assume that all slaves rejoiced with the end of slavery and the beginning of their new lives as free people, as the oral history from Caroline Richardson showed, the reality was more complicated. The first few pages of one of the only memoirs by a former slave child suggests why the transition from slavery to freedom was difficult. Booker T. Washington was still a little boy when the war ended, but many years later, when he was a famous educator and spokesperson for his race, he wrote of the last day of slavery on the farm on which he grew up with insight and sympathy—and with a particular point of view. His postwar life was rather hand-to-mouth for Booker, his siblings, his ailing mother, and his luckless stepfather. He worked for a time in a West Virginia salt mine and learned to read and write at night school. A much better situation emerged when he took a job as houseboy for a wealthy white family, where he learned notions of thrift, cleanliness, and hard work from his transplanted Yankee employer. He eventually graduated from Hampton Institute in Norfolk, Virginia, founded Tuskegee Institute in Alabama, and became world famous. His reflections on the instant that slavery ended were shaped by his boyhood on a backwoods dirt farm and in the dreary salt mines afterward. They taught him that emancipation had given his people nothing more than the freedom to work hard and that they could expect little more from whites than the opportunity to perform the hardest jobs available. Although not all freedmen, women, and children would have described their feelings in quite the same way as he did, the first chapter or two of Washington's Up from Slavery *provides an important impression of the first moments of freedom for the children of slavery.*

So far as I can now recall, the first knowledge that I got of the fact that we were slaves, and that freedom of the slaves was being discussed, was early one morning before day, when I was awakened by my mother kneeling over her children

---

Booker T. Washington, *Up from Slavery: An Autobiography* (Garden City, NY: Doubleday, Page, 1901), 6–10, 19–22.

and fervently praying that Lincoln and his armies might be successful, and that one day she and her children might be free. In this connection I have never been able to understand how the slaves throughout the South, completely ignorant as were the masses so far as books or newspapers were concerned, were able to keep themselves so accurately and completely informed about the great National questions that were agitating the country. From the time that Garrison, Lovejoy, and others began to agitate for freedom, the slaves throughout the South kept in close touch with the progress of the movement. Though I was a mere child during the preparation for the Civil War and during the war itself, I now recall the many late-at-night whispered discussions that I heard my mother and the other slaves on the plantation indulge in. These discussions showed that they understood the situation, and that they kept themselves informed of events by what was termed the "grape-vine" telegraph.

During the campaign when Lincoln was first a candidate for the Presidency, the slaves on our far-off plantation, miles from any railroad or large city or daily newspaper, knew what the issues involved were. When war was begun between the North and the South, every slave on our plantation felt and knew that, though other issues were discussed, the primal one was that of slavery. Even the most ignorant members of my race on the remote plantations felt in their hearts, with a certainty that admitted of no doubt, that the freedom of the slaves would be the one great result of the war, if the Northern armies conquered. Every success of the Federal armies and every defeat of the Confederate forces was watched with the keenest and most intense interest. Often the slaves got knowledge of the results of great battles before the white people received it. This news was usually gotten from the coloured man who was sent to the post-office for the mail. In our case the post-office was about three miles from the plantation and the mail came once or twice a week. The man who was sent to the office would linger about the place long enough to get the drift of the conversation from the group of white people who naturally congregated there, after receiving their mail, to discuss the latest news. The mail-carrier on his way back to our master's house would as naturally retail the news that he had secured among the slaves, and in this way they often heard of important events before the white people at the "big house," as the master's house was called.

· · ·

Of course as the war was prolonged the white people, in many cases, often found it difficult to secure food for themselves. I think the slaves felt the deprivation less than the whites, because the usual diet for the slaves was corn bread and pork, and these could be raised on the plantation; but coffee, tea, sugar, and other articles which the whites had been accustomed to use could not be raised on the plantation, and the conditions brought about by the war frequently made it impossible to secure these things. The whites were often in great straits. Parched corn was used for coffee, and a kind of black molasses was used instead of sugar. Many times nothing was used to sweeten the so-called tea and coffee.

• • •

Finally the war closed, and the day of freedom came. It was a momentous and eventful day to all upon our plantation. We had been expecting it. Freedom was in the air, and had been for months. Deserting soldiers returning to their homes were to be seen every day. Others who had been discharged, or whose regiments had been paroled, were constantly passing near our place. The "grape-vine telegraph" was kept busy night and day. The news and mutterings of great events were swiftly carried from one plantation to another. In the fear of "Yankee" invasions, the silverware and other valuables were taken from the "big house," buried in the woods, and guarded by trusted slaves. Woe be to any one who would have attempted to disturb the buried treasure. The slaves would give the Yankee soldiers food, drink, clothing—anything but that which had been specifically intrusted to their care and honour. As the great day drew nearer, there was more singing in the slave quarters than usual. It was bolder, had more ring, and lasted later into the night. Most of the verses of the plantation songs had some reference to freedom. True, they had sung those same verses before, but they had been careful to explain that the "freedom" in these songs referred to the next world, and had no connection with life in this world. Now they gradually threw off the mask, and were not afraid to let it be known that the "freedom" in their songs meant freedom of the body in this world. The night before the eventful day, word was sent to the slave quarters to the effect that something unusual was going to take place at the "big house" the next morning. There was little, if any, sleep that night. All was excitement and expectancy. Early the next morning word was sent to all the slaves, old and young, to gather at the house. In company with my mother, brother, and sister, and a large number of other slaves, I went to the master's house. All of our master's family were either standing or seated on the veranda of the house, where they could see what was to take place and hear what was said. There was a feeling of deep interest, or perhaps sadness, on their faces, but not bitterness. As I now recall the impression they made upon me, they did not at the moment seem to be sad because of the loss of property, but rather because of parting with those whom they had reared and who were in many ways very close to them. The most distinct thing that I now recall in connection with the scene was that some man who seemed to be a stranger (a United States officer, I presume) made a little speech and then read a rather long paper—the Emancipation Proclamation, I think. After the reading we were told that we were all free, and could go when and where we pleased. My mother, who was standing by my side, leaned over and kissed her children, while tears of joy ran down her cheeks. She explained to us what it all meant, that this was the day for which she had been so long praying, but fearing that she would never live to see.

For some minutes there was great rejoicing, and thanksgiving, and wild scenes of ecstasy. But there was no feeling of bitterness. In fact, there was pity among the slaves for our former owners. The wild rejoicing on the part of the emancipated coloured people lasted but for a brief period, for I noticed that by the time they returned to their cabins there was a change in their feelings. The great responsibility of being free, of having charge of themselves, of having to think and plan for themselves and their children, seemed to take possession of them. It was very much like suddenly turning a youth of ten or twelve years out into the world to provide for himself. In a few hours the great questions with which the Anglo-Saxon race had been grappling for centuries had been thrown upon these people to be solved. These were the questions of a home, a living, the rearing of children, education, citizenship, and the establishment and support of churches. Was it any wonder that within a few hours the wild rejoicing ceased and a feeling of deep gloom seemed to pervade the slave quarters? To some it seemed that, now that they were in actual possession of it, freedom was a more serious thing than they had expected to find it. Some of the slaves were seventy or eighty years old; their best days were gone. They had no strength with which to earn a living in a strange place and among strange people, even if they had been sure where to find a new place of abode. To this class the problem seemed especially hard. Besides, deep down in their hearts there was a strange and peculiar attachment to "old Marster" and "old Missus," and to their children, which they found it hard to think of breaking off. With these they had spent in some cases nearly a half-century, and it was no light thing to think of parting. Gradually, one by one, stealthily at first, the older slaves began to wander from the slave quarters back to the "big house" to have a whispered conversation with their former owners as to the future.

"Born in the First Smoke of the Great Conflict":
Hamlin Garland's Father Comes Home

The Gilded Age author Hamlin Garland grew up on a tiny farm near La Crosse in western Wisconsin. When he was very young, his father volunteered for the Union and for the next two years fought in Mississippi, Tennessee, Georgia, and the Carolinas. Garland spent the first few pages of his autobiography describing his father's return from the army, when neither Garland nor his younger brother recognized their long-gone father. Garland also wrote of his father's homecoming in a short story called "The Return of a Private," published two decades earlier. This excerpt from the autobiography suggests some of the strains that the absence of fathers in the army—and their return from war— put on hundreds of thousands of families.

My father who had bought his farm "on time," just before the war, could not enlist among the first volunteers, though he was deeply moved to do so, till his land was paid for—but at last in 1863 on the very day that he made the last payment on the mortgage, he put his name down on the roll and went back to his wife, a soldier.[3]

I have heard my mother say that this was one of the darkest moments of her life and if you think about it you will understand the reason why. My sister was only five years old, I was three and Frank was a babe in the cradle. Broken hearted at the thought of the long separation, and scared by visions of battle my mother begged the soldier not to go; but he was of the stern stuff which makes patriots—and besides his name was already on the roll, therefore he went away to join Grant's army at Vicksburg. What sacrifice—what folly! Like thousands of others he deserted his wife and children for an abstraction, a mere sentiment. For a striped silken rag—he put his life in peril. For thirteen dollars per month he marched and fought, while his plow rusted in the shed and his harvest called to him in vain.

Hamlin Garland, *A Son of the Middle Border* (New York: Macmillan, 1917), 6–8, 11

My conscious memory holds nothing of my mother's agony of waiting, nothing of the dark days when the baby was ill and the doctor far away—but into my sub-conscious ear her voice sank, and the words Grant, Lincoln, Sherman, "furlough," "mustered out," ring like bells, deep-toned and vibrant. I shared dimly in every emotional utterance of the neighbors who came to call and a large part of what I am is due to the impressions of these deeply passionate and poetic years.

Dim pictures come to me. I see my mother at the spinning wheel, I help her fill the candle molds. I hold in my hands the queer carding combs with their crinkly teeth, but my first definite connected recollection is the scene of my father's return at the close of the war.

I was not quite five years old, and the events of that day are so commingled with later impressions,—experiences which came long after—that I cannot be quite sure which are true and which imagined, but the picture as a whole is very vivid and very complete.

Thus it happened that my first impressions of life were martial, and my training military, for my father brought back from his two years' campaigning under Sherman and Thomas the temper and the habit of a soldier.

He became naturally the dominant figure in my horizon, and his scheme of discipline impressed itself almost at once upon his children.

I suspect that we had fallen into rather free and easy habits under mother's government, for she was too jolly, too tender-hearted, to engender fear in us even when she threatened us with a switch or a shingle. We soon learned, however, that the soldier's promise of punishment was swift and precise in its fulfillment. We seldom presumed a second time on his forgetfulness or tolerance. We knew he loved us, for he often took us to his knees of an evening and told us stories of marches and battles, or chanted war-songs for us, but the moments of his tenderness were few and his fondling did not prevent him from almost instant use of the rod if he thought either of us needed it. . . .

As I was born in the first smoke of the great conflict, so all of my early memories of Green's coulee are permeated with the haze of the passing war-cloud. My soldier dad taught me the manual of arms, and for a year Harriet and I carried broom-sticks, flourished lath sabers, and hammered on dish-pans in imitation of officers and drummers. Canteens made excellent water-bottles for the men in the harvest fields, and the long blue overcoats which the soldiers brought back with them from the south lent many a vivid spot of color to that far-off landscape.

NOTES

1. Lucian Lamar Knight, *A Standard History of Georgia and Georgians*, vol. 4 (Chicago: Lewis Publishing, 1917), 1930.

2. "Chronological History of the Newark Schools," http://www.nps.k12.nj.us/history.html (accessed January 9, 2010).

3. Hamlin Garland, "The Return of a Private," in *Main-Traveled Roads* (New York: Harper and Bros., 1891), 167–94.

Questions for Consideration

1. How did the wartime experiences of children differ from the wartime experiences of adults? How did children *perceive* that their experiences differed from those of adults?
2. What does it mean to argue that children and youth were *actors* in the historical events of the Civil War era rather than simply *victims* or *observers*?
3. What lessons or meanings did young Americans—North and South, black and white—take away from their experiences during the war?
4. Northern and southern children were obviously affected differently by the sectional conflict and Civil War, especially in terms of the material effects of the war. But how did the war affect the ways that northern and southern youngsters thought about themselves? Their families? Their nation?
5. Children naturally try to fit unusual or even frightening experiences into their lives. They like to maintain routines and believe that familiar assumptions remain in force. How did children during the Civil War era integrate the war into the "normal" facets of their lives?
6. Americans have tended to see the results of the Civil War as a clear-cut ending to slavery. How do the experiences of former slave children challenge that straightforward interpretation of history?
7. In what ways did children and youth experience the war differently? Of course, to answer this, one needs to define those terms. During the Civil War era, where did Americans draw the line between childhood and youth (which might be called adolescence today)?
8. How might the war have changed the ways that adults thought about their roles as parents? How might the war have changed the ways that Americans thought about what a "normal" childhood should be?
9. Studying the points of view of children and youth is supposed to expand our traditional understanding of historical events. How is that true for the Civil War era?
10. What elements of the lives of children and youth remained unchanged by the war?

Suggested Readings

Adams, David Wallace. *Education for Extinction: American Indians and the Boarding School Experience, 1875–1928*. Lawrence: University Press of Kansas, 1995.

Bardaglio, Peter. "The Children of Jubilee: African American Childhood in Wartime." In *Divided Houses: Gender and the Civil War*, edited by Catherine Clinton and Nina Silber. New York: Oxford University Press, 1992, 213–29.

———. *Reconstructing the Household: Families, Sex, and the Law in the Nineteenth-Century South*. Chapel Hill: University of North Carolina Press, 1995.

Berry, Stephen W. *All That Makes a Man: Love and Ambition in the Civil War South*. New York: Oxford University Press, 2003.

Blair, William A. *Cities of the Dead: Contesting the Memory of the Civil War in the South, 1865–1914*. Chapel Hill: University of North Carolina Press, 2004.

Carmichael, Peter S. *The Last Generation: Young Virginians in Peace, War, and Reunion*. Chapel Hill: University of North Carolina Press, 2005.

Cashin, Joan E., ed. *The War Was You and Me: Civilians in the American Civil War*. Princeton: Princeton University Press, 2002.

Censer, Jane Turner. *The Reconstruction of White Southern Womanhood, 1865–1895*. Baton Rouge: Louisiana State University Press, 2003.

Clement, Priscilla Ferguson. *Growing Pains: Children in the Industrial Age, 1850–1890*. New York: Twayne, 1997.

Clinton, Catherine. *Southern Families at War: Loyalty and Conflict in the Civil War South*. New York: Oxford University Press, 2000.

Cohen, William. *At Freedom's Edge: Black Mobility and the Southern White Quest for Racial Control, 1861–1915*. Baton Rouge: Louisiana State University Press, 1991.

Cox, Karen. *Dixie's Daughters: The United Daughters of the Confederacy and the Preservation of Confederate Culture*. Gainesville: University Press of Florida, 2003.

Crenson, Matthew A. *Building the Invisible Orphanage: A Prehistory of the American Welfare System*. Cambridge: Harvard University Press, 1998.

Degler, Carl. *At Odds: Women and the Family in America from the Revolution to the Present*. New York: Oxford University Press, 1981.

de Schweinitz, Rebecca. *If We Could Change the World: Young People and America's Long Struggle for Racial Equality*. Chapel Hill: University of North Carolina Press, 2009.

Drago, Edmund L. *Confederate Phoenix: Rebel Children and Their Families in South Carolina*. New York: Fordham University Press, 2008.

Fahs, Alice. *The Imagined Civil War: Popular Literature of the North and South, 1861–1865*. Chapel Hill: University of North Carolina Press, 2001.

Faust, Drew Gilpin. *Mothers of Invention: Women of the Slaveholding South in the American Civil War*. Chapel Hill: University of North Carolina Press, 1996.

Fellman, Michael. *Inside War: The Guerrilla Conflict in Missouri during the American Civil War*. New York: Oxford University Press, 1989.

Frank, Lisa Tendrich. "'To 'Cure Her of Her Pride and Boasting': The Gendered Implications of Sherman's March." Ph.D. diss., University of Florida, 2001.

Frankel, Noralee. *Freedom's Women: Black Woman and Families in Civil War Era Mississippi*. Bloomington: Indiana University Press, 1999.

Gardner, Sarah. *Blood and Irony: Southern White Women's Narratives of the Civil War, 1861–1937*. Chapel Hill: University of North Carolina Press, 2004.

Geisberg, Judith. *Army at Home: Women and the Civil War on the Northern Home Front*. Chapel Hill: University of North Carolina Press, 2009.

Gilbert, James. *A Cycle of Outrage: America's Reaction to the Juvenile Delinquent in the 1950s*. New York: Oxford University Press, 1988.

Green, Elna C., ed. *Before the New Deal: Social Welfare in the South, 1830–1930*. Athens: University of Georgia Press, 1999.

———. *This Business of Relief: Confronting Poverty in a Southern City, 1740– 1940*. Athens: University of Georgia Press, 2003.

Grimsley, Mark. *The Hard Hand of War: Union Military Policy toward Southern Civilians, 1861–1865*. New York: Cambridge University Press, 1995.

Grossberg, Michael. *Governing the Hearth: Law and the Family in Nineteenth-Century America*. Chapel Hill: University of North Carolina Press, 1985.

Hawes, Joseph M. *The Children's Rights Movement: A History of Advocacy and Protection*. Boston: Twayne, 1991.

Horowitz, Helen Lefkowitz. *Campus Life: Undergraduate Cultures from the End of the Eighteenth Century to the Present*. Chicago: University of Chicago Press, 1987.

Jabour, Anya. *Marriage in the Early Republic: Elizabeth and William Wirt and the Companionate Ideal*. Baltimore: Johns Hopkins University Press, 1998.

———. *Scarlett's Sisters: Young Women in the Old South*. Chapel Hill: University of North Carolina Press, 2007.

———. *Topsy-Turvy: How the Civil War Turned the World Upside Down for Southern Children*. Chicago: Ivan R. Dee, 2010.

Janney, Caroline E. *Burying the Dead but Not the Past: Ladies' Memorial Associations and the Lost Cause*. Chapel Hill: University of North Carolina Press, 2008.

Jones, Jacqueline. *Labor of Love, Labor of Sorrow: Black Women, Work, and the Family from Slavery to the Present*. New York: Basic Books, 1985.

Kaestle, Carl. *Pillars of the Republic: Common Schools and American Society, 1780–1860*. New York: Hill and Wang, 1983.

Kickler, Troy L. "Black Children and Northern Missionaries, Freedmen's Bureau Agents and Southern Whites in Reconstruction Tennessee, 1865–1869." Ph.D. diss., University of Tennessee, Knoxville, 2005.

King, Wilma. *Stolen Childhood: Slave Youth in Nineteenth-Century America*. Bloomington: Indiana University Press, 1995.

Lewis, George. *Massive Resistance: The White Response to the Civil Rights Movement*. London: Hodder Arnold, 2006.

Lockley, Timothy James. *Welfare and Charity in the Antebellum South.* Gainesville: University Press of Florida, 2007.

Macleod, David I. *Building Character in the American Boy: The Boy Scouts, YMCA, and Their Forerunners, 1870–1920.* Madison: University of Wisconsin Press, 1983.

Marten, James. *The Children's Civil War.* Chapel Hill: University of North Carolina Press, 1998.

Mason, Mary Ann. *From Father's Property to Children's Rights: The History of Child Custody in the United States.* New York: Columbia University Press, 1994.

May, Elaine Tyler. *Homeward Bound: American Families in the Cold War Era.* New York: Basic Books, 1988.

McCurry, Stephanie. *Masters of Small Worlds: Yeoman Households, Gender Relations, and the Political Culture of the Antebellum South Carolina Low Country.* New York: Oxford University Press, 1995.

Mintz, Steven. *Huck's Raft: A History of American Childhood.* Cambridge: Belknap Press of Harvard University Press, 2004.

Mintz, Steven, and Susan Kellogg. *Domestic Revolutions: A Social History of American Family Life.* New York: Free Press, 1988.

Morris, Robert C. *Reading 'Riting, and Reconstruction: The Education of Freedmen in the South, 1861–1870.* Chicago: University of Chicago Press, 1982.

Murray, Gail Schmunk. *American Children's Literature and the Construction of Childhood.* New York: Twayne, 1998.

Ott, Victoria E. *Confederate Daughters: Coming of Age during the Civil War.* Carbondale: Southern Illinois University Press, 2008.

Pace, Robert F. *Halls of Honor: College Men in the Old South.* Baton Rouge: Louisiana State University Press, 2004.

Paludan, Phillip Shaw. *A People's Contest: The Union and Civil War, 1861–1865.* 1988. Lawrence: University Press of Kansas, 1996.

Ritterhouse, Jennifer. *Growing Up Jim Crow: How Black and White Southern Children Learned Race.* Chapel Hill: University of North Carolina Press, 2006.

Roth, Sarah. "The Mind of the Child: Images of African Americans in Early Juvenile Fiction." *Journal of the Early Republic* 25 (2005): 79–109.

Rubin, Ann Sarah. *A Shattered Nation: The Rise and Fall of the Confederacy.* Chapel Hill: University of North Carolina Press, 2005.

Schwartz, Marie Jenkins. *Born in Bondage: Growing Up Enslaved in the Antebellum South.* Cambridge: Harvard University Press, 2000.

Stanley, Amy Dru. *From Bondage to Contract: Wage Labor, Marriage, and the Market in the Age of Slave Emancipation.* Cambridge: Cambridge University Press, 1998.

Swint, Henry L. *The Northern Teacher in the South, 1862–1870.* Nashville: Vanderbilt University Press, 1941.

Taylor, Amy Murrell. *The Divided Family in Civil War America.* Chapel Hill: University of North Carolina Press, 2005.

Werner, Emmy E. *Reluctant Witnesses: Children's Voices from the Civil War.* Boulder, CO: Westview Press, 1998.

Whites, LeeAnn. *The Civil War as a Crisis in Gender, Augusta, Georgia, 1860–1890.* Athens: University of Georgia Press, 1995.

Whites, LeeAnn, and Alecia P. Long, eds. *Occupied Women: Gender, Military Occupation, and the American Civil War*. Baton Rouge: Louisiana State University Press, 2009.

Wishy, Bernard. *The Child and the Republic: The Dawn of Modern American Child Nurture*. Philadelphia: University of Pennsylvania Press, 1967.

Wood, Marcus. *Blind Memory: Visual Representations of Slavery in England and America*. Manchester: Manchester University Press, 2000.

Zipf, Karin L. *Labor of Innocents: Forced Apprenticeship in North Carolina, 1715–1919*. Baton Rouge: Louisiana State University Press, 2005.

About the Contributors

THOMAS F. CURRAN received his PhD from the University of Notre Dame and teaches at Cor Jesu Academy in St. Louis. He has taught at Saint Louis University, was managing editor of the *Journal of Policy History*, and was an assistant editor on the Andrew Johnson Papers Project. In addition to a number of scholarly articles, he is author of *Soldiers of Peace: Civil War Pacifism and the Postwar Radical Peace Movement* (New York: Fordham University Press, 2003). He is currently writing a book on Confederate women and military justice in St. Louis.

REBECCA DE SCHWEINITZ, who received her PhD from the University of Virginia, is assistant professor of history at Brigham Young University and the author of *If We Could Change the World: Young People and America's Long Struggle for Racial Equality* (Chapel Hill: University of North Carolina Press, 2009). She would like to thank the Gilder Lehrman Center for the Study of Slavery, Resistance, and Abolition, and BYU's Family Studies Center for supporting her (ongoing) research on childhood and slavery.

LISA TENDRICH FRANK is an independent scholar who received her PhD from the University of Florida in 2001. She is currently completing a book on the gendered implications of Sherman's march for Louisiana State University Press. She is editor of *Women in the American Civil War* (Santa Barbara, CA: ABC-CLIO, 2007); *Women in American Military History* (Santa Barbara, CA: ABC-CLIO, forthcoming); and *The Civil War: People and Perspectives*, a book of original essays in the Perspectives in American Social History Series (Santa Barbara, CA: ABC-CLIO, 2009). She is also coeditor of *Honoring a Master: Essays in Honor of Bertram Wyatt-Brown*, which is forthcoming from the University Press of Florida.

JUDITH GEISBERG is author of *"Army at Home": Women and the Civil War on the Northern Home Front* (Chapel Hill: University of North Carolina Press, 2009) and *Civil War Sisterhood: The United States Sanitary Com-*

mission and Women's Politics in Transition (Boston: Northeastern University Press, 2000). She received her PhD from Boston College in 1997 and is associate professor of History at Villanova University.

CATHERINE A. JONES received her PhD from Johns Hopkins University in 2006 and is currently assistant professor of history at the University of California, Santa Cruz. She was the Watson-Brown Foundation Post-Doctoral Fellow at the Institute for Southern Studies, University of South Carolina in 2006–7. She is at work on a book manuscript entitled *Intimate Reconstructions: Children in Postemancipation Virginia* and is an editor of H-Childhood.

TROY L. KICKLER earned his PhD at the University of Tennessee in 2005. He is director of the North Carolina History Project and is currently revising his dissertation, "Black Children, Northern Missionaries, the Freedmen's Bureau, and Southern Whites in Reconstruction Tennessee, 1865–1870," and editing *Nathaniel Macon: Collected Letters and Speeches.*

ELIZABETH KUEBLER-WOLF received her PhD in art history and American studies at Indiana University in 2005, where her dissertation was titled "'The Perfect Shadow of His Master': Proslavery Thought in American Visual Culture, 1780–1920." She was a research fellow at the Institute of Southern Studies, University of South Carolina, in 2001–2, and is currently an assistant professor of art history at the University of Saint Francis in Fort Wayne, Indiana. She has delivered papers at the Organization of American Historians, the Southern Historical Association, and the American Studies Association and is the author of several essays, book reviews, and exhibit catalog entries.

J. VINCENT LOWERY received his PhD from the University of Mississippi in 2008 and currently teaches at the University of Wisconsin at Green Bay. His dissertation was "Reconstructing the Reign of Terror: Popular Memories of the Ku Klux Klan, 1877–1915." In addition to delivering papers at meetings of the Southern Historical Association and the Southern Association of Women Historians, he was associate editor of *Southern Historian* in 2006–7 and a researcher for the Wilmington Race Riot Commission at the North Carolina Department of Archives and History. He has published several encyclopedia entries and "*Dr. Strangelove*: or How I Learned to Stop Worrying and Teach the Film in the Classroom," in the Organization of American History's *Magazine of History.*

JAMES MARTEN is professor of history at Marquette University. He is the author or editor of more than a dozen books, including *The Children's Civil War* and two previous anthologies published by NYU Press: *Children in Colonial America* and *Children and Youth in a New Nation*. He is vice president/president-elect of the Society for the History of Children and Youth and president of the Society of Civil War Historians.

STEVEN MINTZ is currently director of the Graduate School of Arts and Sciences Teaching Center at Columbia University, after serving as John and Rebecca Moores Professor of History at the University of Houston for a number of years. He has received nearly $6 million in grants from the NEH and other agencies for teacher education and other programs. He is a past president of both H-Net: Humanities and Social Sciences Online and of the Society for the History of Children and Youth. Among his books are *A Prison of Expectations: The Family in Victorian Culture* (New York: NYU Press, 1983); *Domestic Revolutions: A Social History of American Family Life* (New York: Free Press, 1988—co-author); *Moralists and Modernizers: America's Pre–Civil War Reformers* (Baltimore: Johns Hopkins University Press, 1995); *The Boisterous Sea of Liberty: A Documentary History of America from Colonization through the Civil War* (New York: Oxford University Press, 1998—coeditor); and *Huck's Raft: A History of American Childhood* (Cambridge: Belknap Press of Harvard University Press, 2004), which, among other awards, won the OAH Merle Curti Award for Best Book in American Social History.

MARY NIALL MITCHELL is associate professor at the University of New Orleans and the author of *Raising Freedom's Child: Black Children and Visions of the Future after Slavery* (New York: NYU Press, 2008), as well as articles and reviews on race and emancipation in the U.S. South and the Americas. She has received fellowships and awards from the American Council of Learned Societies, the Harry Frank Guggenheim Foundation, and the Gilder Lehrman Institute of American History. She is currently researching race and the Fugitive Slave Act in the 1850s.

VICTORIA E. OTT received her PhD from the University of Tennessee and is currently assistant professor of history at Birmingham-Southern College. In addition to many book reviews, encyclopedia entries, and essays, she is the author of *Confederate Daughters: Coming of Age during the Civil War* (Carbondale: University of Southern Illinois Press, 2008).

PAUL B. RINGEL received his PhD at Brandeis University in 2005 and is an assistant professor of history at High Point University. He has published essays, book reviews, and encyclopedia articles on childhood, print culture, and consumer culture and has delivered papers at meetings of the American Historical Association, the American Antiquarian Society, the Society for the History of Children and Youth, and the Popular Culture Association. He is currently revising his dissertation, "Commercializing Childhood: The Children's Magazine Industry and American Gentility, 1823–1918."

SEAN A. SCOTT received his PhD from Purdue University in 2008 and is currently an assistant editor with the Papers of Abraham Lincoln. He is the author of *A Visitation of God: Northern Civilians Interpret the Civil War* (New York: Oxford University Press, 2010).

KANISORN WONGSRICHANALAI received his PhD from the University of Virginia and is assistant professor at Angelo State University. He has published several articles and book reviews and delivered papers at conferences, including the Society of Civil War Historians and the Society of Historians of the Early American Republic.

Index